THE ORIKI OF A GRASSHOPPER
AND OTHER PLAYS

THE **ORIKI** OF A **GRASSHOPPER** AND OTHER PLAYS

FEMI OSOFISAN

With an Introduction by
Abiola Irele

HOWARD UNIVERSITY PRESS
Washington, D.C.
1995

The Oriki of a Grasshopper and *Esu and the Vagabond Minstrels* were originally published by New Horn Press, Nigeria. *Morountodun* was originally published by Longman, Nigeria. *Birthdays Are Not for Dying* was originally published by Malthouse Press, Nigeria.

Digitally printed in Canada on acid-free paper by WEBCOM Ltd. Production management and project consultation provided by Abram Hall Alternatives, Inc.

Library of Congress Cataloging-in-Publication Data

Osofisan, Femi.
    The oriki of a grasshopper, and other plays / Femi Osofisan ; with an introduction by Abiola Irele.

        p.   cm.
    ISBN 0-88258-181-3
    1. Nigeria—Drama.   I. Title.
PR9387.9.O85O75   1995
822—dc20   95-6636
                                                     CIP

This is for you,
Ọyinlola Ádenikẹ—
the woman whom I called Princess,
and who, one unforgettable morning,
agreed to be my wife—
one little keepsake, a lifetime
of tender moments:
memories are made of these . . .

CONTENTS

INTRODUCTION
Abiola Irele

Of the various art forms that have flourished in the especially fertile atmosphere in which cultural production has proceeded in Nigeria, drama has been, and remains, the most vibrant. More than any other form, drama, both in its literary/textual embodiments and as it manifests itself or inheres in other performance modes in the country, has exhibited most distinctly the dynamic interplay between the various factors that animate the manifold texture of life in contemporary Nigeria. The theatrical elements in the traditional performance modes—festivals, ceremonials, masquerades, rituals, and enactments of mythic narratives that constitute an integral part of social processes, cultural expression, and communal awareness of the various ethnic groups brought together within the framework of the modern nation-state and that have been carried over into its defining context of collective existence and awareness—these elements provide the background, indeed, a massive reference, for the more recent forms of dramatic expression that have been elaborated in this context.

For the playwrights and theatre practitioners involved in the two principal areas of this contemporary expression—the popular drama of the traveling theatres,[1] and the literary drama in English and, increasingly, in the vernacular languages—the precolonial tradition defines a cultural and aesthetic resource that is vital to their creative endeavors. This implies not so much a question of reclaiming a heritage that has been obscured—of "going back to roots," as it were—as a natural extension and reformulation of the traditional forms in vigorous existence, in a continuous development that seeks to sustain the living principles of these forms under the changed circumstances of a new sociopolitical order and the conditions of a problematic modernity. The primary interest of these more recent elaborations of theatrical practice and dramatic art in Nigeria thus derives from their bearing the impress, in terms of their themes and expressive modes, of the extensive transformations provoked by the impact of British colonialism and its concomitant pressures of social and cultural change.

It is a commonplace of critical observation that modern African literature in the European languages has been distinguished largely by its engagement with the theme of transition, and no area of the corpus has illustrated this feature more than Nigerian literature. The theme determines the local inflection writers have sought to give to their expression, arising from the need to reflect as fully as possible their immediate environment in its unique quality. This need is all the more imperative in drama, which must incorporate an immediate sense of locale and cultural atmosphere to carry any conviction with the audience to which it is addressed in the first place. Nigerian dramatists writing in English have been especially responsive to this imperative, which has resulted in their producing perhaps the most substantial body of work for the theatre on the continent. This they have achieved largely through what one might call a process of osmosis, manifested at the level of form by their conscious infusion of the literary modes of Western drama along with the European language they employ, with the principles and mechanisms of the performance modes prevalent within their own environment. This convergence of thematic preoccupations and formal adaptation of medium has imprinted a distinctive character on English-language and university-based drama, pioneered in the late fifties and early sixties by Wole Soyinka, John Pepper Clark-Bekederemo, and Ola Rotimi.

To appreciate the significance of Femi Osofisan's plays, a selection of which is presented in this volume, they must be placed in this general perspective of the development of Nigerian drama in English. They confirm the dynamism of an evolving modern literary and theatrical tradition, while at the same time seeking to reverse its dominant trends and to redefine its areas of emphasis. Two related factors, one sociopolitical, and the other literary, account for this purposive reorientation of Nigerian drama, which has been the fundamental impulse behind Osofisan's work. The first has to do with the aftereffects of the Nigerian civil war, which has been, without question, the decisive event in the evolution of Nigerian history. Indeed, the war may be said to have marked the true beginning of this history, if by this is meant the taking up by Nigerians themselves, for good or ill, of the initiative for their own collective destiny. Osofisan belongs to the generation of writers and intellectuals that emerged in the aftermath of the war, and whose responses to its social implications have given a new direction and imparted a new temper to the artistic, cultural, and intellectual life of the country.

The second factor arises from this observation, which relates to the vigor with which these younger writers have sought to revitalize the established literature that preceded their own productions, a literature associated essentially with the coming into being of the national community. They had before them an antecedent body of works that had become more or less institutionalized, and while they acknowledged the achievement of their predecessors as a valuable national resource, it was obvious to them that they had to open up new perspectives in their own work, more in keeping with the changed circumstances that the trauma of the civil war and the subsequent emergence of new social forces had imposed as a compelling reference of imaginative expression, as indeed of intellectual reflection.

These younger writers, who began to emerge during the era of the so-called oil boom, which lasted through the early seventies into the mid-eighties, produced their work in a social atmosphere that had been radically transformed by a major national crisis, followed by the establishment of what they saw as an authoritarian and prebendary state. They wrote from their perception of a condition of systemic dysfunction into which the country was being locked by the policies of successive regimes. The primacy they have accorded to social and political themes stems directly from an initial focus on the civil war itself as a salient event of the national history and consciousness; this focus became expanded in the critical literature directed against the pattern of economic and social arrangements that were rapidly put in place in the immediate aftermath of the war. For these writers, a socially responsible literature seemed the only adequate response to what they saw as comprehensive, gross distortions in the national life, and to the range of human issues this situation presented to their minds and their imaginative sensibilities.

Although poetry and fiction have served as important means of expression for these writers in their effort to establish what the poet Funso Aiyejina has called an "alter/native" tradition, drama has, for obvious reasons, taken pride of place in their output. The determining consideration has been that drama provided the most direct artistic medium not only for articulating public concerns but also for communicating in a cultural milieu that continues to place a premium on the oral mode, more so where this is channeled through the gestural and specular protocols of theatre. Femi Osofisan is not only one of the most prominent members of this new generation of Nigerian writers but also, in the general estimation, the most accomplished among the dramatists.[2]

Born in 1946 in Iloto, among the Ijebu, one of the major subgroups of the Yoruba, Osofisan grew up in an environment in which the traditional beliefs and practices were still normative factors of communal life. His father died when he was very young, so he never got to know him and instead was reared by his uncle under extremely trying conditions. This biographical detail, to which he makes a significant reference in his play *No More the Wasted Breed*, has an immediate interest for any appraisal of his work. For one thing, his early circumstances fostered in him a recognition of the humane potential of the communal ethos, as exemplified in his case by the bonds of the extended family, the basis of the structure of solidarities that have functioned as the only means of social security in contemporary Africa. Moreover, the hardships he endured as a child may be considered to have predisposed him for the sharp social consciousness that underlies his plays, the deep concern for and understanding of the underprivileged that stands as the affective core of all his dramatic output. These two factors account for the fact that, although a disenchantment with the traditional worldview pervades his work, its essential inspiration flows from a grounded faith in the common people.

Osofisan went on as a scholarship student to Government College, Ibadan, an elite school located at the other end of the same city as Nigeria's premier university, which Wole Soyinka had also attended. He credits his early interest in drama to the fact that theatrical productions were the most important extracurricular activity at the school, largely because of the enthusiasm of the English headmaster, Derek Bullock. This interest was reinforced by the proximity of Ibadan University's Arts Theatre, a modest but well-equipped facility that had been built in the late fifties and had come fully into its own in the early sixties as a lively center of cultural activity, not only for those directly connected with the academic, cultural, and intellectual life of the campus but also for the social elite of the city. Osofisan has recalled the profound impression made on him by one of the early productions to which his class had been taken, at the university's Arts Theatre, of Soyinka's *Kongi's Harvest*, an experience that proved to be an early intimation of the enduring, albeit ambiguous, relationship he later developed with the older writer.

Osofisan entered the University of Ibadan in October 1966 as a French Honors student. The civil war broke out less than a year later, and although the university was safely removed from the theatre of hostilities, the war cast its long shadow over the institution. A general sense of insecurity was a natural consequence of a national emergency, the outcome of which was for long uncertain. In addition, the arrest and imprisonment in 1967 for antifederal activities of Soyinka, who was director of the School of Drama, created disarray at the university, with pronounced effects at the school, where it nearly proved crippling for its academic and theatre program. Osofisan himself had just made the personal acquaintance of Soyinka and had begun to collaborate with him. Although at first disoriented by these developments, Osofisan soon became an active member of the acting company Soyinka had formed as part of his professional commitments at the school. During this period Osofisan wrote his first play, later published under the title *Red is the Freedom Road*, for a student production.

On his graduation in June 1970, some six months after the end of the civil war, Osofisan remained at the university to begin work on a doctoral dissertation in drama. As part of his research program, he was sent to Paris, where he spent the academic years 1971–73. His encounter with French theatrical life during his Paris sojourn not only extended his earlier awareness of the French classical theatrical tradition, gained through his studies at the University of Ibadan, but also enlarged his view of drama considerably, bringing him in touch, notably, with the dramatic literature and theoretical texts of such leading figures of modern French drama as Jean-Paul Sartre, Antonin Artaud, Arthur Adamov, Jean Genet, and Samuel Beckett. As we shall see, the influence of these figures on his work, in terms both of world outlook and of dramatic style, is palpable in many of his plays. Moreover, through the agency of Soyinka, in exile in Europe at the time, he was inducted into the group around Jean-Marie Serreau, the innovative producer who had introduced Brecht to the French public and who, after staging the plays of the Martinican poet Aimé Césaire and the Algerian novelist Kateb Yacine, was actively promoting Third World drama in the French capital. Osofisan's observation at first hand of Serreau's production techniques influenced his dramaturgy.[3]

After his return to Ibadan in 1973 to write and defend his doctoral dissertation on "The Origins of Drama in West Africa," Osofisan was appointed to the faculty and awarded a university grant for a research journey. This took him for three months across West Africa in 1974, with the objective of collecting additional material for the expansion and revision of his dissertation, with a view to its publication. The journey enabled him to establish contact with theatre movements in Ghana, the Ivory Coast, and Senegal and may well have confirmed his resolve to become a playwright in his own right and thus to make a personal contribution to the development he had studied in his dissertation. However, his first published work was not a play but a satirical novel, *Kolera Kolej*, from which an extract appeared in the first edition of New Horn, a campus journal started in 1975.[4]

The years that followed may be considered the decisive ones in Osofisan's development as a dramatist and a man of theatre. Although his official position was lecturer (assistant professor) in French in the Department of Modern Languages, his real interests inevitably drew him to the Department of Theatre Arts (the new designation of the School of Drama), with which he became increasingly associated, a fact that was later acknowledged by his formal transfer to this department. The Arts Theatre, with its core of student actors, complemented by a handful of professionals (notably Jimi Solanke), provided him with a ready testing ground for his early plays in which he began to experiment with new techniques of dramatic writing and production. Alongside his activities as university teacher and his work in the theatre during this early period, Osofisan became engaged in important intellectual work. Although his dissertation was never published, he drew on it for some of the critical essays[5] in which he began to elaborate his ideas on literature and drama, and on society in general. The failure of the established conventions of academic scholarship to engage the relationship between these areas actively was the theme of his controversial Faculty of Arts lecture at the University of Ibadan, "Do the Humanities Humanise?" delivered in 1981.

It is indicative of his position that he became at this time closely identified with an eclectic group of radical university teachers and intellectuals that came to be known as the Ibadan-Ife axis. What distinguished the group was less the strict doctrinal affiliations of its members than their common disaffection for the power structure in Nigeria and their passion for a profound reordering of their society along socialist and egalitarian lines. The intellectual activity of this group was centered on the journal Positive Review, founded in an effort to initiate critical reflection on the many problems of the country, and run under the responsibility of an "Editorial Collective" that included Osofisan himself. The centrality of literature for any understanding of social mechanisms became a cardinal principle of their critical outlook, and their literary preferences predictably inclined toward works that promoted an assertive conscious-ness in the general society, as a countervailing force to what they saw as the overbearing hegemony of the political class.[6]

The group's adversarial posture toward the ruling class may be considered their way of resisting co-optation into this class, to which they were bound by many ties, notably those of a common Western education and sometimes even of economic interests. This became for them the source of a dilemma that Osofisan examines in his play *The Oriki of a Grasshopper*. Whether this dilemma was more a matter of psychology than of ideology is perhaps beside the point; what is clear is that the intellectuals associated with *Positive Review* illustrate in a striking way a phenomenon that has become characteristic of most African states—a cleavage between the intellectual elite and the political class on the continent in the postindepen-dence period.

That this cleavage was no mere theoretical matter was brought home to Osofisan himself by the difficulties he en-countered shortly after his appointment in 1983 as professor of drama at the University of Benin, where he soon came into conflict with the traditional authorities who objected to what they regarded as the irreverent tenor of his plays. Abandoning the hope that had attracted him to Benin of helping to develop a Performing Arts Department there, he moved in 1985 to the University of Ife (now Obafemi Awolowo University) to take up the chair of drama recently vacated by Soyinka. His tenure at Ife proved especially productive and has been made memorable by the impact of his two plays *Morountodun* and *Esu and the Vagabond Minstrels*, both written for and produced at official university ceremonies. He moved back to Ibadan in 1987, where he has since held the position of professor of drama and head of the Department of Theatre Arts.

An extremely productive writer, Osofisan has written some forty plays, many of them still to be published. Consciously pitched from play to play at various levels and registers,[7] his work has touched nearly all facets of life in contemporary Nigeria and has earned him a wide audience in the country, where his columns in the leading national newspapers have also contributed to his national reputation as a leading voice of

progressive social consciousness in Nigeria. His consistent expression of this consciousness and the technical sophistication
of his dramatic writing have established for him this reputation, which now extends beyond the borders of his country.
The plays in this volume, which can be considered among the
most significant of his dramatic output to date, reflect the
spectrum of his achievement.

The seriousness of purpose with which Osofisan engages
the realities of his society in his work becomes apparent from a
consideration of the introspective quality of the one-act play
The Oriki of a Grasshopper. The dramatic presentment of the
practical dilemmas that confront the radical intellectual in the
specific sociohistorical context of a developing Third World
country, such as Nigeria, affords the occasion for a probing of
the radical consciousness itself, of its turns and ambiguities in
its grappling with the actualities of social existence. The play's
mode is essentially one of self-scrutiny and reflects the inter-
rogative stance in relation to which the human interest in
Osofisan's plays takes its moral bearings.

The circumstances in which the play was written and produced account for its discursive tenor. Written on the occasion
of one of the annual African literature conferences organized by
the University of Ibadan's Department of English and staged on
the floor of the university's conference center, the play's primary intention seems to confront a select audience of the
intellectual elite with issues of life beyond the "ivory tower."
But it is instructive of its approach that it does not make an
ideological point as such, developing its theme rather as a
reflection on the moral basis and practical implications of the
ideological options of the radical intellectual. What gives the
play its primary interest is the uncompromising nature of this
reflection, which raises the possibility of a divergence between
the rhetoric of ideology and the objective conditions for the
implementation of the revolutionary project.

The play's economy of means, limited as these are to a triad
of characters and involving minimal stage business, throws
into relief the conflict of ideas and interests at the heart of the

playwright's exploration of the social issues evoked in the play. The radical Imaro, modeled on a type of individual Osofisan was acquainted with in his own circles, is flanked on one side by the debonair capitalist Claudius, and on the other by Moni, the impatient student idealist. His vacillations at the center of this conflict, which, we are to understand, permeates the larger society as represented by the characters, provide the substance of the play's strategy. This consists in showing Imaro pulled by opposite impulses, as the very ground of his ideological options is contested on both sides. The flesh and blood humanity of the character, caught in the bind of his contradictions, leads him to a lucid appraisal of his objective situation: "Maybe I made the wrong choice, gave my life to a cause I could only end up by betraying. Maybe I'm just too much on the other side."

The apparent irresolution Imaro displays here reflects his awareness of the practical impossibility, for the petty bourgeois intellectual that he is, of commiting "class suicide" at the personal level, if the gesture is unrelated to a wider mobilization of revolutionary energies in the society. In another passage, Imaro indicates the formidable nature of the pressures that militate against such an eventuality and against his own resolve:

> What have I achieved? I have talked and talked. Like all the others. I've tried to teach my students that we can build a new world. That a brave new world is within our grasp. But to what purpose? Our society has marked us out as eccentrics. Worse, as felons! And I am tired. I can't live my whole life as a fugitive.

The reference here is not only to the repressive organs of the State but also to the unresponsiveness of the populace, even of its advanced wing represented by the students, on whose behalf Imaro commits himself to social struggle. Thus, while mirroring in the play a real dilemma with an obvious personal significance for himself, Osofisan refuses the simple antinomy between an inflexible commitment on one hand, and on the other, the easy compromises individuals often make to negotiate the course of their lives in the social sphere. Although Imaro is not exactly cast as a prophet crying in the wilderness, it is equally apparent that the ideal he enunciates here, despite its ambiguous context, is central to the play's meaning.

Following the nuanced rehearsing of the problems the play deals with, Imaro's total recovery of revolutionary zeal at the end of the play may give the impression of a too simple resolution of his dilemma. However, the emphasis in the play is not so much on the characters themselves as on the ideas and values they embody. The stress throughout is on the necessity for moral courage and intellectual lucidity as preconditions for effective action in the social sphere. It is this point, essential to what may be considered the didactic intent of the play, that gives credibility to its idealistic conclusion, which might otherwise seem too contrived.

The pared-down form that frames the reflection in the play helps to focus interest on the discourse it develops. That Beckett's *Waiting for Godot* is evoked as its "pre-text" indicates Osofisan's debt for this form to a certain convention of modern "absurdist" drama in French, though the texture of Osofisan's play recalls more strongly Sartre's *Huis Clos*, whose rhetoric, focused as it is on a moral dilemma, is rooted in the tradition of French classical drama. Osofisan's play, however, is too particularized to be considered simply derivative of these French sources. It may even be thought that his closest affinity in this play is with Athol Fugard, whose method of employing scenic contraction as a figure for the embattled consciousness of his characters reinforces their apprehension of a hostile outer world.[8]

These literary and dramatic references suggest another thematic direction, which is not overtly indicated in the play, but toward which what I've called its "texture," points our responses, namely, the issue of the effective value of committed literature implicated in its argument. The play poses the question of the relation between the ideas and the moral demands projected in socially responsible literature on one hand, and on the other, the actualities of existence that stand beyond the text. It broaches, in other words, the problem inherent in the tension between the aesthetic dimension of literature and the larger context of collective life it seeks to represent.

This question, which is central to any overall appraisal of Osofisan's work, is raised more directly by another short play, *No More the Wasted Breed*. This work articulates a conception of individual and collective fate founded on the affirmative

potential of a forceful human awareness, in which a tragic
conception of life, presented as the effect of a disabling fatalism
generated by an ignorant mysticism, can have no operative
place. In working out in this play the rejection of metaphysics
and the supernatural as relevant considerations in human affairs, Osofisan has deliberately chosen the character of the
scapegoat/carrier figure in traditional society, to position himself firmly against the spiritualist premise on which Soyinka's
The Strong Breed is based, and in which this figure is endowed
with heroic stature. Osofisan's play subverts the notion that
the lone hero who assumes the community's burden and ac-
cepts ritual sacrifice for its sake embodies a transcendent value.
The play dramatizes the futility of such sacrifice; the ritual of
the carrier is seen to correspond to nothing beyond the horizons
of the social realm in which human action has meaning. Its
demonstration goes further in its insistence on the ideological
uses to which myth and ritual lend themselves, even in the
self-contained world of traditional life where they could be
deemed to have a measure of functional validity. This polemi-
cal contestation of the social role of myth and ritual is put
across in simple but strong terms by Saluga, who embodies
revolutionary consciousness in the play. His perception—that
the metaphysical realm is inhabited merely by the projections
of the fears of the common people, and is manipulated by the
corrupt repositories of the traditional order—provides the key-
note of the play: "I see you, god and goddess. Just as I've always
imagined you to be. Fat and cruel."

The dissident note of Saluga's statement is rung on a com-
plementary key that modulates the action, one related to the
idea of the inhibiting effect of the anachronisms that have
persisted in contemporary African societies. It is Togun, the
self-interested priest of the god Olokun, who, in a moment of
ironic prescience, intimates this purport of the play:

> The times changed and so did our people. . . . Lots of strangers have
> come to settle among us, bringing new habits, new systems of
> thought. The old customs have crumbled. The old gods have fled
> into retreat.

Within the movement of the play, the passage stands out, it

seems to me, rather awkwardly, as a self-conscious striving after rhetorical effect. It has its place, nonetheless, as an uncluttered statement of the point the playwright is obviously at pains to make: the supersession by a modern awareness of large areas of the traditional scheme of values. We might observe, then, that the progressive viewpoint advanced in the play derives from the radical skepticism such an awareness promotes, with regard especially to the conceptual system that regulates collective life in traditional society.

This gives special interest, from the point of view of dramaturgy, to the deliberate invocation in the play of key elements of this conceptual system as the organizing principle of its thematic development, thereby setting up a calculated dissonance between its background of mythic references and its pronounced ideological message. The device achieves particular effect in the scene in which Saluga is struck down by the goddess Elusu and then magically resuscitated by the god Olokun, a device that draws directly on the theatrical conventions of Yoruba popular theatre, in which the recourse to mysticism has been a staple procedure for creating the other-worldly atmosphere of its plots.[9] Saluga's unrepentant stance and defiant mood on his coming back to life serve precisely to counteract the insidious appeal of this popular convention, and thus to highlight the character's position as a vindication of the emancipatory will, which finally compels the demission of the gods. Thus Olokun, echoing his priest, gives us what is intended to be the last word in the play: "Beloved, time is no longer on our side. See, men have changed. They have eaten the salt of freedom and moved beyond our simple caprices."

The textual resonances of Olokun's words are, of course, unmistakable. They reach beyond Soyinka's The Strong Breed, which, as we have observed, is its immediate "counterreference"; to Shakespeare's King Lear, with its central character's tragic conception of himself as "sport for the gods"; and further back, to Greek tragedy, in particular Sophocles's Oedipus Rex, which has been given an appealing Yoruba adaptation by Ola Rotimi in The Gods Are Not to Blame. Moreover, the striking parallel between the dramatic treatment of the issues of human fate raised in the play and in Sartre's *Les Mouches* suggests that Osofisan has deliberately transposed the French writer's existentialist ethics to the African context. Like Jupiter in Sartre's play, Olokun is faced with the affirmative gesture of an exemplary character and is obliged, through him, to concede existential freedom to humanity. Against this background, Osofisan's play takes on an obvious significance as an exercise in transhistorical and transcultural demystification. It dramatizes in its very movement the repudiation of tragedy as an inevitable component of the human condition, and in its formal/dramatic representation, as an aesthetic that corresponds to an enduring feature of the human condition. It seeks in particular to penetrate the nature of myth in its ideological implications, not merely as a form of "false consciousness," but as a significant component of domination and of the perennial language of hegemony.

No More the Wasted Breed contrasts sharply with *Oriki* in its unabashed partisanship. The simple outline of the action, coupled with the direct tone of address that propels its rhetoric, is calculated to give the greatest clarity to its ideological message. It is open to question, however, whether, in its particular context, the playwright's effort can work effectively through the form of the play as he has conceived it. It is indeed to be feared that the dramatic device on which the play relies for its impact may undermine rather than enforce the import of its contradictory discourse. It may be too keyed to the traditional belief system of its audience to convey the full charge of its intended message.

Once Upon Four Robbers charts a different course in its articulation of Osofisan's social vision. This play is notable for its shock value, a function both of its urgent focus on a disturbing social issue, as regards its theme, and its demonstration, in its structure and mechanisms, of the playwright's conception of theatre as a communicative medium. Both aspects of the play have made it perhaps his most controversial work. The play stands as a sardonic comment on the public anxiety about the spate of armed robbery that erupted in Nigeria after the civil war, and as the playwright's personal intervention, through the expressive medium of drama, in the national debate about the effectiveness of a severe measure—the public execution, by a firing squad, of armed robbers convicted by a special tribunal—which had been decreed by the military regime in its desperate effort to combat what was described as a national scourge. This contextual background situates the play, as regards both its theme and its unusual form, in its moral perspective, for its is nothing less than a comprehensive indictment of contemporary Nigerian society. This direction of the play is developed through the allegorical foundation of its plot, and highlighted by its ambivalent ending, in which the playwright leaves the judgment of the robbers to the audience, a move that is in the nature of an invitation addressed to this audience, generally composed of the middle class, to cast the biblical first stone.

In its explicit theme, the play moves between an examination of armed robbery in Nigeria as a symptom of social crisis—of a generalized state of "anomy"—and a critique of the apparatus of repression in the State. The idea of the immediate correlation between social inequities and crime, which the play develops as the conceptual support of this theme, is of course not an original one. What lends interest to Osofisan's demonstration is the thematic and dramatic complication he give to this idea in the specific context of his play that saves it from being a tedious presentation of a sociological platitude. The stark realism of its depictions is perfectly in tune with the violent environment reflected in the play's theme and setting. At the same time, the allegorical mode of its ground plan serves as counterpoint to the surface action, in a dialectic, very much in the manner of the traditional folk tale, of social reference and moral fable. Central to the scheme of the play is the character Aafa, who, in his multiple roles as narrator, directing presence, and incarnation of the trickster god Esu, sets the action into motion and assumes the burden of the fable.

The dominant mode of the play remains, however, its realism. It takes us out of the confined space of *Oriki* and the limited horizons of *Wasted Breed*, into the larger world at which they hint, that of the gross modernity of contemporary Nigeria, with corruption at every level of public life and misdirection of purpose as its inevitable consequences. The confusion of values that reigns everywhere receives an intense focus in the peculiar combination of robust ebullience and crude dispositions in the psychology of the robbers. This confusion is given full expression in their behavior and is presented as simply a reflection of the entire society. The undifferentiated thrust of the playwright's indictment assumes its pertinence from this Hobbesian image of a Nigerian society in which self-interest has become the rule of conduct.

From this point of view, the play's theme opens out to a wider sociological perspective: that of the pathology of development. Osofisan proposes a historical and "materialist" interpretation of this pathology, whose source he locates in the cult of commodity culture and the frenetic consumerism that characterized postindependence Nigeria, a carryover and distortion of the economic impact of the cash nexus introduced by colonialism. This interpretation is summed up in the marketwomen's song:

> The lure of profit
> has conquered our souls
> and changed us into cannibals
> oh praise the selfless British
>
> . . . .
>
> The lust for profit
> keeps us in this world
> this life that is a market
> refuse to join and perish
> rebel, and quench!

The crassness of the song is obviously an effect of the playwright's sarcasm projected onto the characters themselves and presented as their self-image. It ought to be noted, however, that the song does no more than reflect the spirit of much of Yoruba juju music, whose lyrics often celebrate the material success of prominent members of the dominant class. It is thus intended to translate the degraded ethos that has blunted the moral sensibilities of both the privileged in society and the rest of the populace that takes its cue from them. The travesty of art made vulgar by its diversion to the service of a harsh and insensitive system of social inequalities is thus represented in and through the song. The relation of the aesthetic to the ideological that this association entails gives to Osofisan's play another meaning implicit in its elaboration. There is a sense in which the playwright undertakes in this play to restore dignity to art by restating for it a higher purpose—its commitment to the cause of truth and justice. We take it as axiomatic for him that the social dimension of art most properly brings out this moral requirement of art, and *Once Upon Four Robbers* can be considered a demonstration of this conviction on which its inspiration is founded.

The open-ended design of the play has already been commented on in its moral significance. We might add that the ploy, which consists in leaving the decision about the fate of the robbers to the audience, represents a formalization of the well-attested phenomenon of audience participation, which often takes on a lively character in theatre performances in most of Africa. To reinforce the moral of his fable of modern Nigeria, the playwright calls into play, through this formal device, what we might call a conditioned response, to emphasize the continuity between the drama enacted on stage and that which takes place in the wider world.

This observation points to what seems to me the deep significance of the play, beyond its reference to the Nigerian situation. The conception of theatre as the displaced arena of social drama has become a commonplace of both dramatic and sociological theory. Nowhere perhaps does this theory find a more concrete validation than in the open atmosphere of the African marketplace, whose function as both economic sphere and social space has made it a prominent reference of the African imagination.[10] Osofisan's choice of the marketplace as the main setting for the action in *Once Upon Four Robbers* represents in this light an appropriate cultural expression of the dynamics of social conflict. Because the African marketplace, particularly the Yoruba marketplace, is characteristically infused with the energies of social life, it features in the play as the symbolic site of all forms of social transactions, of which the violence and the counterviolence of social struggles are often the inevitable component, manifestations of the fissures by which societies are everywhere differentiated. Osofisan presents in this play a localized image, rendered in contemporary terms, of the universal play of social forces. His challenge of the coercive power of the State, invariably placed at the disposal of the dominant classes, derives its point from his incisive deployment of the image.

This challenge is extended back in time and prompts a reconsideration of history, from the point of view of the oppressed, in *The Chattering and the Song* and *Morountodun*. Both plays are closely related, insofar as they recall two important moments of social struggle in the Yoruba experience, both involving a peasant revolt, one in the relatively distant past, the other within recent memory. The involved structure in both plays conveys the complex interaction of past and present, the vicissitudes of historical memory and the modes of its reproduction as discourse and as a means of social control. They seek to give coherence to historical experience by projecting a view, ultimately Marxist, in which the struggle for social justice represents the fundamental principle of the historical process and the criterion for its intelligibility. The two plays represent exemplifications of this view in the specific case of the Yoruba experience.

The extended scale of the dramaturgy in *The Chattering and the Song* contributes to a sense of time in its social dimensions, involving the interconnection between the objective lives and subjective states of individuals who make up its compact aspect. The central reference for this enactment of social time is presented in the play within the play, in which, as in Soyinka's *A Dance of the Forests*, characters drop their roles in the present and assume historical roles related to their contemporary situation. This enables Osofisan to revisit Yoruba history, and to offer, in particular, a radical revision of official accounts concerning the reign of Abiodun, an eighteenth-century king of Oyo, and of the rebellion against him by Latoye. This event, which has received scant attention in the historical accounts of this period, becomes the focus of Osofisan's play, which repudiates the pious image, perpetuated by official history, of Abiodun as a benevolent ruler. Osofisan's reconstitution highlights Latoye's rebellion and proposes a contrary view of Abiodun's reign. The long view of history in which the play's reconstitution of Yoruba history is inscribed emerges from Latoye's remonstrance to King Abiodun:

> For centuries you have shielded yourself with the gods. Slowly, you have painted them in your colour, dressed them in your own cloak of terror, injustice and bloodlust. . . . In your reign, Abiodun, the elephant eats, and nothing remains for the antelope. The buffalo drinks, and there is drought in the land.

The passage gives epochal resonance to the lives and actions of the characters in their present situation, and amplifies the play's historical and social message.

Osofisan's revisionism is nowhere more in evidence than in *Morountodun*, in which he stages a confrontation with history in its aspect as celebratory narrative. The legend of Moremi, who occupies a special place in Yoruba collective memory, provides him with the pretext, in both senses of the word, for the unraveling of the dominant discourse, a move all the more calculated to unsettle in that the play was written for an official ceremony at the University of Ife, at which, it ought to be noted, the women's hall of residence is named after Moremi. This was a form of modern consecration of the heroism attributed to her in the Yoruba oral tradition. In an annual festival at Ife, Moremi was celebrated for putting her femininity to use in penetrating the ranks of the Igbo, in order to discover the secret of their power in their predatory raids on the city and thus to deliver her people from a historical menace.

As can be seen, Moremi as a figure of legend belongs to a cluster of exceptional women, such as Esther in the Old Testament and Lady Godiva and Joan of Arc in Western European historical narratives, who have either turned their femininity to advantage or overcome its limitations in exemplary action on behalf of their people. They function as agents of a providential history and as archetypes of historical consciousness, and as such have been incorporated into national mythologies. The consecration of Moremi by the University of Ife, an institution

associated with the Yoruba middle class, appears in this light as
an instance of a process of mythmaking by which a class seeks
to legitimize its present dominant position by appropriating
tradition. Osofisan's play represents a contestation of this process at the very seat of Moremi's official consecration in modern
times.

In *Morountodun*, history is not so much revisited as employed as a sounding board for an assessment of the community's present and its prospects for the future. The immediate
reference of the play is the substantial revolt of Yoruba farmers
during the Nigerian civil war, which forced the federal government to divert its energies toward its suppression, in the midst
of its prosecution of the larger war against secessionist Biafra.
The justified nature of the farmers' grievances, succinctly
stated in the name they gave their movement, "Agbekoya,"
meaning "The farmers refuse suffering," was ultimately acknowledged as genuine by the government, which finally had
to negotiate a settlement with them. This justification is the
basis for the conversion to the farmers' cause that Osofisan
makes his character Titubi undergo, after her infiltration of
their ranks, in the manner of the legendary Moremi.

The parallel of Titubi's conversion with the celebrated case
of the American Patty Hearst is apparent in the play, and is
emphasized by Titubi's privileged social position at the beginning of the play and her renunciation of it in the course of her
activism. The parallel is developed toward the proper logical
conclusion that this other case, which serves as the obvious
subsidiary reference of the play, did not in the event attain.
Thus, Titubi declares:

I went, and returned, triumphant.
But I am not the same as I went away.
A lot has happened.

The play dramatizes the events that fill in the interval between
her going and her return, the process of transformation that
results in her triumph over her class conditioning and enables
her to come to a new understanding of history and its social
implications:

I am not Moremi! Moremi served the state, was the state, was the spirit of the ruling class. But it is not true that the state is always right. . . . Let a new life begin.

Commenting on the ideological emphasis of Osofisan's revision of the Moremi legend, Soyinka has objected to it in the following terms:

The patriotism and heroism of the historic Moremi is thus summarily dismissed. . . . It is in fact a valid thesis—but only on the surface. And only if one is prepared to join—in a different vein—in the game of traducing one's history for ideological gains.[11]

The short answer to Soyinka's objection is that the point at issue here is precisely that of the limitations of an unreflective patriotism. The point is all the more pertinent to the play's meaning and purpose in that the Moremi legend has been enlisted, along with those of other ethnic groups—such as those connected with the Bini queen Idia and the Hausa princess Amina—in the fabrication of a modern national mythology for Nigeria. The iconoclastic spirit that informs Osofisan's play thus has a wider aim than its specific Yoruba reference; it extends to the overt manipulation of history demonstrated in the endeavor to provide Nigerians with national heroes. The patently factitious character of the endeavor belies the assumption that underlies Soyinka's comment, that of an objective history, decontextualized, transcending all interests, which can thus be "traduced." Osofisan rejects this reification of history, offering in its place a relativized conception in the critical light of the contemporary situation. This new conception of history finds symbolic expression in the confrontation of Titubi and Moremi that closes the play.

Coming after *The Chattering and the Song, Morountodun* confirms Osofisan's determined retextualization of received history, what one might call, after Paolo Freire, "a pedagogy of the oppressed." More than Titubi, it is the character Marshall who brings out most forcefully this aspect of the play. As a freedom fighter, he represents the active force of revolutionary pressures disseminated throughout the Third World. The name *Morountodun,* meaning "I have found a sweetness," which he gives Titubi and which provides the play's title, indicates both the affective basis of his dedication to the revolutionary cause and, once again, the intimate relation of aesthetics to morality that governs Osofisan's conception of dramatic art. The evocative terms of Marshall's renaming of Titubi thus become significant:

> Now I call on this earth I am standing on. . . . I call on you trees and animals which people our forests and are our kinsmen. I summon the seeing eyes of our ancestors. And you, my very dear friends, standing in this charged embrace of sunlight and wind, bear witness. . . . I name her MOROUNTODUN!

This is a paean by Marshall, both to Titubi, his companion in struggle, and to the natural world that shelters the combatants during their struggle and nourishes their spirit. We might say, then, going by this passage, that Osofisan's play is, ultimately, a celebration of the Revolution as Muse.

Two other plays carry forward Osofisan's concerns in a largely symbolic register. Both are reworkings of antecedent texts, one of which is by himself and the other by an older writer. In *Esu and the Vagabond Minstrels*, Osofisan returns to the structural scheme of *Once Upon Four Robbers*, in order to give its theme a more pronounced emphasis as a parable, whereas in *Another Raft*, a rereading of John Pepper Clark-Bekederemo's play *The Raft*, Osofisan provides a more complex treatment of the carrier theme than in *No More the Wasted Breed*.

The new dimension in these plays is indicated in *Esu and the Vagabond Minstrels* by the reappearance of the character Aafa in his real identity as Esu, the divinity who, in the Yoruba world concept, mediates between the gods and humanity. His reversion to his original form determines the transfer, from one play to the other, of the setting from the marketplace to the crossroads, the metaphysical space that is the proper realm for the manifestation of Esu's powers.[12] Esu's link with the human world through the Ifa divination system supplies the thematic foundation of the play, which revolves around a question of moral choice.[13] Omele, who is the embodiment of conscience in the play, supplies its dramatic climax by offering a moving demonstration of this principle of individual choice through his willing embrace of the leper-stricken couple, a gesture that, in the circumstances, assumes a properly religious significance.

The linear structure of the parable that frames the action and its more intense ritual tonality set in relief the overt didacticism of the play. The virtue of compassion on which this is centered is shown to have both an individual redemptive value and a liberating social significance, for the lesson that the play seeks to enforce is that the only acceptable form of social arrangement is one that is predicated on humane values. Once again, the human world is set against the supernatural realm, a note that is struck at the very outset of the play by the minstrels' declared intention, born out of desperation, to desecrate this realm. Thus, the notion of sacrifice is desacralized at the very outset and recentered on human needs. This note is amplified in the final song that seeks to dispel the illusion of Esu's determining role in the play and affirms his irrelevance to its moral. In its Nietzschean overtones, the song proclaims the death of the gods.

If *Esu* is a development on the playwright's earlier work, *Another Raft* is intended as an inversion of the terms of Clark-Bekederemo's *The Raft*, which it "signifies" upon. This inversion is signaled by the fact that the roles of the three Yemossa, normally female in the Yoruba tradition, are played by male actors. As the play unfolds, we also learn that the carrier destined for sacrifice, whom the other characters imagine to be a woman, is in fact a man, an armed soldier at that, whose holdup of the bewildered occupants of the raft on the high seas constitutes a turning point in the drama. Osofisan's play thus presents itself as an updating of the topical references in what has generally been taken to be Clark-Bekederemo's representation, in *his* play, of the troubled situation of Nigeria in the period before the Nigerian civil war, and as a refocusing of what Osofisan himself may well have considered its abstract depiction of the human condition. In his version of a raft adrift at sea, Osofisan adopts a contradictory posture by placing his emphasis on the social determinations and motivations of the characters. The occupants of the raft are no longer archetypes of humanity in the grip of impersonal or supernatural forces over which they have no control, but social types, standing in for the various specialisms, notably that of the military, which have come to specify the socioeconomic environment in Nigeria, with the political consequences this has entailed.

It is perhaps not too simple a reading of the play to see Agunrin's role in this perspective, as both pivotal to the drama it enacts and central to its symbolic meaning: the military, which carried the burden of the country's problems during the civil war and its aftermath, is transformed into a dominant and menacing force as a result of its control of the means of violence. This political interpretation of the play becomes all the more plausible when we consider the ironic mode of the world vision the play projects outward from the immediate Nigerian situation from which it draws its specific elements. This vision embraces the black world in its relation to the West and finds expression in the words given to the character Gbebe:

> The sea . . . the sea is never thirsty, it has enough water of its own. It is never hungry, in its belly are numerous kinds of meat. It carries salt, it carries sharks, it carries other fishes. The sea is history.

The image of the sea here situates the stakes involved in the unfolding drama of Nigeria, the focus hitherto of Osofisan's concerns, in the wider perspective of the contemporary world order. It registers an expansion of the ideological and moral space of his dramatic work. To judge from this play, we might conjecture that his work will henceforth take a new direction and assume a new dimension.

Femi Osofisan's singular contribution to Nigerian drama in English has been to consolidate its development and practice as a viable form of cultural production in the modern context of a plural society. What I have called earlier the process of osmosis by which this drama has been constituted is in full evidence in his plays, in which heterogeneous elements from various sources are held in balance and marshaled to give dramatic effect to his thematic concerns and dramatic purpose. Such is the quality of their interanimation that it is often difficult to identify the precise provenance of a particular element in many of his plays. They collaborate to define an aesthetic of theatre that is both original and appropriate to their time and place.

The preoccupation with technique in these plays results in a virtuosity that occasionally verges on a mannered theatrical style. But the self-consciousness this implies bears witness to the self-reflexivity that is an essential function of drama.[14] Osofisan's objective seems to be to remind us of the origins of drama in ritual, as an extension of the processes of communal life. This implies a process of *stylization*, centered on the need to reformulate experience in symbolic terms. Thus, his dramatic style emphasizes the reciprocity between drama and life, so well expressed in the phrase from Shakespeare's *As You Like It* ("All the world's a stage") with which every Nigerian schoolchild is familiar. As Osofisan himself has declared in an interview, Nigeria is "an intensely dramatic society." Theatre serves him, then, as a mode for the reenactment in significant form of the tensions at work in this society, of the predicaments with which it is beset.

It is in this respect that myth and ritual intervene as expressive resources for Osofisan's dramatic practice. It ought to be clear by now that the view sometimes expressed of his work as "mythopoeic" is mistaken. Myth functions in Osofisan's work primarily as an anchor in the communal sensibility for the thematic unfolding of the action and symbolic schemes of the plays rather than as substantive reference. In this sense, Osofisan's approach provides an instance of what I have called elsewhere an "aesthetic traditionalism" that is a means by which modern African literature has sought validation.[15] This is borne out by Osofisan's constant striving to mark an intellectual and emotional distance to the belief system in which the mythical discourse itself is grounded. Thus, despite the frequent evocation of the supernatural, the constant reference of his plays is to the human world.

We have commented on the risk involved in this studied detachment from the appeal of myth and ritual in his work. Apart from this risk, it presents a problem that Soyinka has pointed out in this observation: "Fascinated with myth and history, clearly, is Osofisan. . . . But an ideological conviction and the aesthetic of theatre which he attaches to it places him, in company with a number of a new generation of writers, in a confused, ambivalent creative existence towards the past."[16]

There is, it seems to me, a misapprehension involved in Soyinka's observation, which ignores the fact that the discourse of myth and of ritual (as well as of history, as we have seen) derives not from a concrete grasp of "essences" but is related to the fabric of existence. For Soyinka, as for those who have contributed to its systematization in the African context, myth is often presented as substantial, with ritual as its signifying text. In so doing, they disregard the mobility of myth as reference, and of ritual as a form of social practice, a condition of the intentionality with which they are invariably charged and which therefore constitutes them into social forces.

It needs to be stressed in this respect that within Yoruba, as indeed within other African cultures, myth and ritual have not always had the stable meanings assigned to them in their systematic ordering by academics and intellectuals. They are not the autonomous systems of apprehension and of signification they are made out to be. Ritual, in particular, although rooted in the deeply affective narrative of myth, is ultimately no more than a strategy of negotiation: between humans and gods and between social actors. Both myth and ritual involve a constant symbolic reshuffling of the cards, so to speak, according to the needs of the moment and of circumstance, and thus present themselves as forms of discourse that serve to position the motives and interests of collectivities, as a function of their modes of insertion in the scheme of things. They are thus, we might say, "relational" by definition and function.[17]

This understanding of the critical, "deconstructive" function of myth and ritual informs Osofisan's dramatic practice. His conception of drama as a mode of communication extends to myth, one of the means by which it is regularly codified in the traditional culture, and to ritual, its performative mode. The arbitrary nature of this code enables the playwright to mobilize its suggestive potential in the expressive strategy of his plays, as a comprehensive metaphor of human existence within which dramatic form itself has its operative life. But far from precluding a challenge of the belief system to which it is bound, this "second order" status of myth within the framework of drama calls attention to its contingency, to its lack of necessity, thus leaving open the possibility of its dissociation from any structure of belief. This sheds light on what Soyinka describes as "ambivalence" in Osofisan's deployment of myth and ritual: it assumes a *tropological* character as regards formal function and a *transgressive* one as regards ideological intent.

The more serious problem that arises from the plays is their constant didactic orientation, which is inseparable from their ideological inspiration. In the Preface to *Aringindin and the Nightwatchmen*, his latest published play (not included in this volume), Osofisan has restated the social purpose of his work, which brings this conjunction into direct view:

> This play is a mirror of what we do, and fail to do—deliberately magnified of course, but only in order to increase the shock, the awareness of the peril we continue to run, all of us, by preventable choice.

The problem here is one that haunts all forms of partisan literature (as distinct from what Barbara Harlow has called "resistance literature"), which cannot but openly manifest "its palpable design" on our responses. Too often, this leads to a rhetorical utopianism that disturbs the formal coherence of the work, as in the final scene of *The Chattering and the Song*. Here, as elsewhere in the work, the platform manner of Osofisan's insistence on his ideological message betrays him into a stridency out of tune with the artistic demands of his medium. But if Osofisan does not always avoid these pitfalls of committed literature, his plays are redeemed in the end by the overall sense of form and the fine artistic sensibility they display.

This observation prompts a final question concerning the relation between content and form in the plays. That Osofisan himself is conscious of the implications of this question is made clear in the following declaration by a character in another of his plays, *Farewell to a Cannibal Rage*:

> Revolutionaries come with every season
> The words of fire flare and fade to ashes
> Only the songs of the artist remain

Yes! Only the works of beauty
Are not quenched in the floods of time.

Osofisan seems to insist here on the primacy of the aesthetic
dimension, even in committed art, and to discount the effectiv-
ity of such art as a practical proposition. Yet the whole tenor of
his work demonstrates his rejection of art as merely a self-re-
warding activity and his belief in its relevance to immediate
social and moral concerns. This suggests that his work hovers
between the imperatives of ideology and the appeal of the
aesthetic. Sandra Richards has commented on this aspect of
Osofisan's work: "The distancing or alienating devices . . . may
work effectively, thereby stimulating audiences to reflect upon
the explicit social critique. But there exists the alternate possibility that sensual delight in the ingeniousness of the theatrical
spectacle overtakes a critical sensibility."[18]

Yet, to pose these questions at all is to recognize the significance of Osofisan's work as a powerful statement of the social
and existential dilemmas of his time and place, a preoccupation
the new literature in Nigeria, and especially drama, has elected
as its province. His best work illuminates with an especial
intelligence and force of feeling his exploration of these dilemmas, and by taking this exploration to its furthest limits of
moral interrogation, Osofisan's plays compel attention and
achieve distinction.

Columbus, Ohio
June 1993

NOTES AND REFERENCES

1. The term *traveling theatre* was introduced by Biodun Jeyifo in
his seminal study of this dramatic form in the Yoruba-speaking areas
that extend beyond Nigeria, into the Benin Republic and Togo. (See
The Yoruba Popular Traveling Theatre, Lagos: Nigeria Magazine,
1984.) Jeyifo's term, a free translation of the Yoruba word *alarinjo*, has
now replaced the earlier term *folk opera* that used to be attached to
this form of modern popular theatre derived from traditional performance modes, of which the leading practitioners have been Hubert
Ogunde, Duro Ladipo, Kola Ogunmola, and Moses Olaiya (more

widely known as "Baba Sala," the character he plays in his popular television series).

2. For an excellent review of the new drama in Nigeria, see Sandra Richards, "Nigerian Independence Onstage: Responses from 'Second Generation' Playwrights," *Theatre Journal* 39,2 (May 1987): 215–27. Chris Dunton's study, *Make Man Talk True: Nigerian Drama in English Since 1970* (Oxford: Hans Zell Publishers, 1992), contains an informed critical account of the subject.

3. Osofisan's sense of obligation to Jean-Marie Serreau is reflected in the moving obituary he wrote on the death of the French director, which was published in *The Benin Review*, 1,1 (June 1974).

4. The full text of the novel was published in book form later that same year by New Horn Press. It is of some interest to note that the publishing house itself was started specifically to publish Osofisan's novel, which has also been adapted for the stage and was produced with great success at the University of Ibadan Arts Theatre in 1978.

5. Notably the essay "Tiger on Stage," in *Drama in Africa*, ed. Oyin Ogunba and Abiola Irele (Ibadan: Ibadan University Press, 1978).

6. A representative selection of critical essays by the group has been published; see Georg M. Gugelberger, *Marxism and African Literature* (New Jersey: African World Press, 1985).

7. The variety of approaches in Osofisan's work is demonstrated by his satirical comedy, *Who's Afraid of Solarin?*, his adaptations of Gogol's *The Government Inspector*, a Yoruba version of which has been produced, the burlesque, *Midnight Hotel*, based on Feydeau's *Paradise Hotel*, and *Birthdays Are Not for Dying*.

8. See Biodun Jeyifo, "The Reductive 'Two Hander' Dramaturgy of Athol Fugard: Aspects of the Art and Society Dialectic," in *The Truthful Lie: Essays in the Sociology of African Drama* (London: New Beacon Books, 1985), 98–104.

9. The carryover of this convention from theatre into the cinema industry that is emerging from the Yoruba popular theatre is especially noticeable in Hubert Ogunde's film *Aiye*.

10. The marketplace features, along with the forest, as one of the two principal settings for the action in folktales. For an appreciation of its deep conditioning of the Yoruba imagination, consider the significance of the marketplace and of the character Iyaloja ("Mother of the Market") in Soyinka's *Death and the King's Horseman*.

11. Wole Soyinka, "The External Encounter," in *Art, Dialogue and Outrage* (Ibadan: New Horn Press, 1988), 241.

12. The fact that the crossroads (*orita*) opens out in several directions at once explains its association with Esu, the god of indeterminacy in Yoruba religious belief. This association persists in African-derived religions in Cuba, Haiti, and Brazil, and is one of the most striking African retentions in the New World. The association may also underlie the mystical significance attached to crossroads in black folk belief in the southern United States, especially in Missis-

sippi, where it is not expressly linked to religious practice but carries the notion of danger, of a place where one may encounter the Devil.

13. It has been statistically demonstrated that Ifa's prescriptions are in reality far from constraining and that the outcome of the divination process depends more often than not on the supplicants, who are actively involved in the divination process concerning them and who are left to act on the diviner's interpretation according to their individual circumstances.

14. For a discussion of the self-reflexive function of drama, see Victor Turner, *From Ritual to Theatre: The Human Seriousness of Play* (New York: PAJ Publications, 1982).

15. Abiola Irele, "African Letters: The Making of a Tradition," *The Yale Journal of Criticism*, 5,1 (Fall 1991).

16. See *Art, Dialogue and Outrage*, 241.

17. For a fuller discussion of this character of myth and ritual in Yoruba society and culture see Andrew Apter, *Black Critics and Kings: The Hermeneutics of Power in Yoruba Society* (Chicago: Chicago University Press, 1992).

18. Sandra Richards, "Brecht in Nigeria: A Consideration of Plays by Wole Soyinka and Femi Osofisan," in *On Stage: Proceedings of the Fifth International Janheinz Jahn Symposium on Theatre in Africa*, ed. Ulla Schild (Göttingen: Editions RE, 1992). In the preface to his book *The Playful Revolution: Theatre and Liberation in Asia* (Bloomington: Indiana University Press, 1992), Eugène van Erven has suggested that the highbrow appeal, stemming from a concern for artistic integrity—of the sort displayed by Osofisan—has severely limited the audience of avant-garde theatre in the West and has also been responsible for its failure to achieve a sense of social relevance. This he finds in full evidence in what he calls "the theatre of liberation" in Asia, notably in the Philippines.

THE **ORIKI** OF A **GRASSHOPPER** AND OTHER PLAYS

THE ORIKI
OF A GRASSHOPPER

A One-Act Play

CHARACTERS

Claudius, a wealthy businessman
Imaro, a university lecturer and socialist
Moni, Imaro's girlfriend and fellow socialist

Office: symbolic furnishing—an empty bookcase, a few cartons, conspicuous; a table—on top, a copy of Beckett's Waiting for Godot, a couple of glasses, unwashed; half-used toilet roll; a few chairs . . .
In the dark, sound of guitar or mouth organ, increasing as lights gradually rise.
Leaning against a table, in simple cotton buba and jeans, probably wearing a pair of glasses, is Imaro, playing to the tune of "Where Have All the Flowers Gone?"
Claudius appears at the door, casually but expensively dressed; even at a glance, he must convey an immediate, strong impression of his wealth, self-confidence, and assurance. Under his arm, a leather briefcase, gold rings on his fingers . . .
Claudius stops at the door, listening to the tune, then softly picks up the refrain. Imaro looks up, sees him, but does not stop till the end of the song, that is, till he comes to "When will they ever learn?"

Claudius. *(Coming farther in)* Beautiful! But do they ever learn?
Imaro. Do we ever learn, you mean? Welcome.
Claudius. Sorry I'm . . . *(notices the empty office)* Hey, what's happening?
Imaro. What? Oh, this. *(pointing to the cartons)*
Claudius. Moving to a new office?
Imaro. I suppose you could put it that way.

Claudius. Downstairs?

Imaro. Maybe downstairs. Into a dungeon.

Claudius. What?

Imaro. I'm just pulling your leg. *(takes a bottle)* Drink?

Claudius. Wait. I brought you this. *(takes out a bottle from his case)*

Imaro. *(takes the bottle, whistles)* You'll never die!

Claudius. At least not before you, you drunkard!

Imaro. Where did you get this?

Claudius. The old man. He brought it back from Europe last week.

Imaro. *(opening the bottle, preparing to pour the drink into glasses)* Trust his taste! *(looks at the glasses, then tears some toilet tissue to clean them first before pouring the drink)*

Claudius. *(bringing out cigars)* And these.

Imaro. Drink. And cigar. And women. Your old man's talents are a legend!

Claudius. That's why I didn't take after him.

Imaro. *(drinking)* No, you have only surpassed him.

Claudius. I'm sure you've not forgotten that we have a law against slander in this country?

Imaro. Chip off the old block, as they say! But the chip has grown more adept than the original rock.

Claudius. I very much appreciate your manner of saying, "thank you," Imaro.

Imaro. Oh, I'm grateful, can't you see? And to tell the truth, Claudie, I was feeling so depressed. In fact, I had thought you weren't coming any more.

Claudius. Why wouldn't I? Our rehearsal's for this morning, isn't it?

Imaro. Yes. But what with all our crisis this past week . . .

Claudius. What crisis! What of the crises—in the plural, mind you—the numerous terrible crises that we go through outside everyday?

Imaro. Well . . .

Claudius. Life goes on, my friend. As Pozzo will say!

Imaro. Yes, I suppose so. Pozzo will say that. Life goes on. Except that you're playing Vladimir, not Pozzo. And he wanted to hang.

Claudius. Don't you believe it. I've studied that character thoroughly. He talks and talks about hanging himself, but come tomorrow, he'll still be there. Waiting. For Godot.

Imaro. Like all of us.

Claudius. Yes. Like all of us.

Imaro. Cowards!

Claudius. I beg your pardon?

Imaro. Forget it.

Claudius. Well, when are we starting? *(He starts some physical exercises.)*

Imaro. Estragon's not here yet.

Claudius. What! That is so unlike him!

Imaro. Yes, I know. If he doesn't come, I'll play the part myself. At least to rehearse you. *(moves to join in the exercise)*

Claudius. Very strange. He's never late. Or absent.

Imaro. Never, not before now.

Claudius. You don't think something may have happened to him?

Imaro. His sister's gone to find out.

Claudius. Who? Oh, Moni.

Imaro. Yes. I've sent her to his house.

Claudius. So, what do we do? *(briefly stopping the exercises)*

Imaro. We wait.

Claudius. For Estragon.

Imaro. Who will come and wait . . .

Claudius. For Godot! *(They laugh and resume the exercises.)* And you know, it was because of him that I walked.

Imaro. Walked? From where?

Claudius. From the gate.

Imaro. But why?

Claudius. Police.

Imaro. Police?

Claudius. Yes, at your gate. Didn't you know?

Imaro. So, they're still there. *(The exercise stops as he moves away.)*

Claudius. Lorry-loads of them. Checking every car coming or going. And causing a bloody hold-up.

Imaro. You see? Even though we've shut the place down and sent the students home.

Claudius. Well, when I checked my watch and saw I was already late, I decided to leave Salawu in the car and walk down.

Imaro. Sorry. All that distance.

Claudius. It wasn't too bad. In fact it was pleasant!

Imaro. What! You don't say! You mean, even for a millionaire? Such as you!

Claudius. Even for a capitalist! Don't disappoint me by changing your vocabulary . . .

Imaro. And all for what, I ask you? All that dust and sweat, just to come for a rehearsal! A rehearsal, not a contract! You're not behaving to type, Claudius! You're a disgrace to the rest of your class!

Claudius. So that makes two of us, ehn? Look at you puffing away at that cigar, and drowning yourself in Chivas Regal! *(mock salute)* Comrade! Revolutionary greetings! *A luta continua!*

Imaro. I'm glad you admit that you corrupt me.

Claudius. And it's so obvious that you're resisting it! See, your stomach's beginning to sag!

Imaro. Signs of kwashiorkor, maybe . . . ?

Claudius. Oh, I'm sorry! How absolutely inconsiderate of me! Poor, starving man, would you like a drink? Take *(offers the bottle)*—it will relieve it!

Imaro. Thanks. Thanks, my friend! *(pause, then, bitterly)* It shows, doesn't it?

Claudius. What?

Imaro. The falsehood of our lives! So easily it shows!

Claudius. I don't know what you mean. I'm a businessman. I make money . . .

Imaro. And I'm an intellectual. As they say, I make words . . .

Claudius. So, each one to his profession . . .

Imaro. It's a masquerade, Claudius! And you're right to laugh. Everybody laughs at us, except the Police.

Claudius. I'm not sure I understand . . .

Imaro. A masquerade! Gogo. Didi. We intellectuals, whatever labels we give ourselves. We're just as privileged as the rest.

Claudius. What's this? A confessional?

Imaro. Since I woke up this morning, I've been thinking. Asking: What's the value of my life? Since they brought me the terrible news, I have been . . .

Claudius. Wait! What news?

Imaro. Well, I'd better tell you, Claudius. Estragon may not be coming today.

Claudius. I see. Why?

Imaro. It's most likely they took him too.

Claudius. Who? Who took him?

Imaro. Our friends from the Police.

Claudius. What! You mean . . .

Imaro. They came knocking in the night.

Claudius. Last night?

Imaro. The news is all over the campus now. They took away Oloko and Dejumo. And Peter. They wouldn't even let them call the Veecee.*

Claudius. Christ! And you?

Imaro. I don't know. We were all in this thing together. I don't know why they missed me out.

Claudius. It's strange . . .

Imaro. Unless they made a mistake. In which case they . . .

Claudius. Yes?

Imaro. They will be coming back.

Claudius. So what are you going to do?

Imaro. You can see that I've packed. Everything I'll need is in that bag. I'm ready, whenever they come.

Claudius. I'm sorry.

Imaro. Why. It's got nothing to do with you. You didn't cause it.

Claudius. No. But it must be hard, waiting. Not being sure. Listening for footsteps.

Imaro. But that's it, Claudius! That's what I'm trying to say! We've been waiting all our lives! You said it just now. We the so-called intellectuals, we're just professional waiters we've just . . .

Claudius. Come, let's start the rehearsals. Take your mind off it.

Imaro. But it's true, isn't it! We wait. We talk. We fiddle with the props. Sometimes even, we relish the leftovers. Like Estragon, nibbling bones . . .

---

* The vice chancellor of the university, equivalent to college president.

Claudius. Let's talk of something else, Imaro . . .

Imaro. . . . like the cigar. The wine. The car. The deejay. Or maybe it's Mozart, Beethoven, or the unending conferences. All the props of our empty lives . . .

Claudius. Imaro . . .

Imaro. Oh yes, of course, I haven't forgotten. We're capable too of pity. Claudius! The sensitive ones among us have abundant tears for those of the race of that unlucky man, whom Beckett cynically calls Lucky. The wretches born with a rope round their neck. Who suffer and continue to suffer mainly because they are incapable of shedding their burden. Because, absurdly, they have been persuaded to accept patiently the lavish whips of their oppressors . . .

Claudius. You're harsh on yourself . . .

Imaro. Look at us! Just look at us! We shed tears. We write poetry. Articles in the journals brimming with eloquence! But meanwhile the Pozzos of this world ride on, unchecked. While we continue to pray for God, for almighty God. Even though we know already that his second coming will be just as bitter as the first, a nightmare of anguish . . .

Claudius. Enough! Enough of that! If you need a shoulder to cry on, go home to your wife! Or wait till Moni comes back! I'm not here for that.

Imaro. *(after a pause)* I'm sorry.

Claudius. That's all right.

Imaro. It's just that, at the moment, I don't like myself very much.

Claudius. Just because the Police came . . .

Imaro. Because they came. Because they can come and go at will. And because they know it, that we're so vulnerable, that we have no defense . . .

Claudius. You made a choice. Like all of us. You made a choice about your life . . .

Imaro. Yes.

Claudius. And you knew the risks.

Imaro. Claudie, I'm ashamed to say it, but I'm frightened.

Claudius. And me? Who says I'm brave? If you live in this country, in this generation, then you know you have to get used to fear. If you must survive, you learn to live with it.

Imaro. Don't give me that! Shit! Is it the same kind of fear? Which policeman will dare lay his hands on you? Tell me!

Claudius. Because I made a choice, long ago . . .

Imaro. Yes! You chose to join the Pozzos, the exploiters . . .

Claudius. Call it what you will. I chose to survive. I chose to live beyond fear, to conquer power. I wouldn't go and stretch out my neck now to talk to rioting students . . .

Imaro. Ah, so they told you!

Claudius. Didn't you? Deny it! I can't think of anything more reckless!

Imaro. Of course, we spoke to the students . . .

Claudius. Your Veecee says you incited them.

Imaro. That's it! That's the irony of history, isn't it? It's always the version of those in power that's believed.

Claudius. But you've just admitted it, that you spoke to the students . . .

Imaro. You were a student here too, once. You even led a riot. Which lecturer incited you?

Claudius. No lecturer *spoke* to us.

Imaro. This time somebody had to act. Somebody had to prevent a massacre. And the campus authorities were in flight, in hiding . . .

Claudius. So what happened? Tell me the story . . .

Imaro. We went to try and calm the students, to dissuade them from violence. *(sign of disbelief from Claudius)* But you see, you won't even believe me!

Claudius. Of course, I don't believe you!

Imaro. But it's the truth.

Claudius. Rubbish! Come, Imaro, whom do you expect to believe you? You and your friends, you're quite known for your fiery talk. You've been on television, lots of times. You've written in newspapers, spoken at debates and symposia. Violence! Revolution! Uprising! Those are your commonest words! And now you're telling me that suddenly, on a day that students were up in arms, there you were, speaking to them of peace . . .

Imaro. Because they were outnumbered.

Claudius. Don't be funny . . .

Imaro. You know the saying yourself: in a gathering, where only one man carries a gun, that man is the majority.

Claudius. And so?

Imaro. So we went to speak to them, to make them see the odds. They were armed, as usual, only with their youth and innocence. With their anger. With the righteous anger that their cause was right. But as you know, right alone does not win a war. Especially not when the other side is better armed.

Claudius. Go on.

Imaro. They were going to face troops that were armed with guns. Armed, on horseback, and accompanied by dogs. That's how our nation deals with its youths. Man, it would have been a one-way fight. But luckily, after booing us and heckling us, the majority of the students listened. They agreed to be peaceful. And most crucially, to remain within the campus.

Claudius. Is that what happened?

Imaro. That was just the beginning. Students had been arrested, and no one knew how many, or in what condition they were being kept. The appropriate authorities, as I said, had melted away. So we formed a delegation to talk to the Police. Surprisingly, the officer was very reasonable and cooperative. It was later on that we found that his son was a student here too. He agreed to restrain his men and keep them strictly at the gate. As for the detained students, he would release them, he promised, as soon as the students released the policeman they too had kidnapped.

Claudius. Yes?

Imaro. So we went back to the students. They said they had released the policeman. The Police said they had not seen him, that the students must have killed the man. Then they gave an ultimatum: the students must bring him or his body by a certain hour or they would come in and get him. Crisis again! Who was lying now? It looked like all the efforts we were making, to prevent bloodshed, would be in vain.

Claudius. So what happened?

Imaro. Then the funny part of the episode. I don't know who thought of it now, but someone suddenly suggested that we should go to the man's house ourselves to find out. Well, we got there. It was empty, locked up. Wife and children, nowhere to be found. So we asked for his hometown. We discovered that the man was from a village, far away in another state. Undaunted, we drove there. And you won't believe this—as we arrived, there the man was, drinking with his friends, celebrating his "lucky escape from death" as he put it!

Claudius. *(laughing)* What?!

Imaro. In fact, as we found out, he had been hastily released by the very student supposed to be guarding him. I think the boy was frightened by the possible consequences of his action. So, without telling his mates, he had "carelessly" left the door open, and gone "to urinate." And the policeman, seeing that, quickly changed into one of the boy's shirts in the wardrobe and made his escape. But he wasn't going to go back to the barracks. No, not until the whole thing was over. He wasn't going to risk being sent back on duty to the dangerous campus . . .

Claudius. So he ran straight to his village, clever man!

Imaro. Can you blame him? In a place where there's no reliable insurance, no security whatsoever for his family! Anyway, we persuaded him to come with us, and everything was settled. All that time, three days in all, I think, no single campus official showed his face! Even the Registrar, whom we sent to at first, declined to intervene, saying the students deserved to face the consequences. You see? So we had to act alone, all by ourselves. And that was our error, our "crime." By doing all that, shuttling between the students and the Police, we had exposed ourselves. For those who needed scapegoats afterward, we had cast ourselves well for the role . . .

Claudius. It's strange to hear all this. It's completely different from what people are saying outside.

Imaro. Outside? What of inside here on campus? Two days ago, we were summoned to the Veecee's house. I don't know if you've been there before. Huge colonial mansion, an extensive fruit garden, all surrounded by a high wall. It was my first time of entering the place. You should have been there! The man didn't even get up when we entered. He just went straight into it, an hour-long tirade, telling us off and making all sorts of threats. With his wife as the primary witness. And you should see her eyes, such malevolence! We never had a chance to answer back. When the man had finished raving, he just stood up abruptly and climbed up the stairs! It was hard, hard, my friend, restraining myself from climbing up after him!

Claudius. But what did he accuse you of?

Imaro. What else? That we incited the students! That there was evidence that we planned their strategies, served as their emissaries! And that we would be dealt with!

Claudius. And so last night, the Police came knocking on your door . . .

Imaro. At three in the morning! Can you imagine! Oloko's houseboy came to wake me and we ran to find our lawyers. But you know how it is. The Police say it's a security matter and won't answer them. The lawyers got the message and left, defeated. So I came back to pack my things, to wait.

Claudius. *(trying to make a joke of things)* For Godot.

Imaro. No. Say rather, for Pozzo. He's the one with the whip. Godot never comes.

Claudius. *(abruptly changing his tone)* Imaro, maybe the Police won't be coming for you after all.

Imaro. *(nodding, not noticing his change of tone)* Maybe not today. Maybe tomorrow. But one day, I know they'll be there, knocking on my door. As long as we keep on the fight for justice in our land.

Claudius. But is it worth it? Why not go away?

Imaro. To where?

Claudius. Anywhere. Take a holiday. Go on a sabbatical. At least for a few months. A few years.

Imaro. That will be like running away.

Claudius. So, what's wrong with that? What's . . .

Imaro. This is our homeland. There is nowhere else to go.

Claudius. You know, it's exactly the same answer you gave me . . . twelve years ago?

Imaro. Twelve years ago? I don't remem . . .

Claudius. Yes, when we were students! Remember the day we stood by the Registrar's office, when we were summoned before the Disciplinary Committee . . .

Imaro. Oh, yes! Over that rice issue, wasn't it?

Claudius. Exactly! And you know, it's funny but that's what I was thinking about as I was walking down just now. Everything seemed to come back, like a film being replayed. Especially with the Police around. It was like—like walking back along a corridor of memories. Everything was so familiar.

Imaro. Yes, I know. Sometimes life is just like that. Some new experience becomes like the photo album of a past trip.

Claudius. Such a long time ago, and yet . . . You know, I said to myself: Claudius, you've not really been away, have you? Here's where you belong! How long was it! How like yesterday! I was away, making money in the world outside, fighting the vicious battles that had to be fought, for survival, but, here, all the scenes have remained as they were. Like patient mothers. The stones, the lawns have not gone away. All just as I left them. And I walked close to the cacia trees along the avenue . . . You know, that tree by the crossroads, that huge araba? I went to look. And yes our names are still there, white on its stem, where we scratched them, you, me, and Chike! Remember that rainy day when we waited for the Prime Minister with those placards? And the placards gradually got wet and soggy in the rain, and started falling off . . .

Imaro. You old rascal! By the time the Prime Minister arrived, all we had left were the bare sticks and wooden frames! The placards had all been washed away!

Claudius. And the boys began to shout at the convoy, hurling abuses. And the Prime Minister, who couldn't hear a thing, since the glass was all wound up, went on grinning and waving back, thinking that we were cheering him . . .

Imaro. Ole! (Claudius, playing the Prime Minister, will wave back cheerfully and shake his handkerchief at each abuse.) Fascist pig! Imperialist stooge! African Nigger! Traitor! Bastard! (They laugh.) God, the whole scene was so funny that in the end, the boys collapsed in laughter, rolling in the wet mud . . . (They laugh on briefly.)

Claudius. All those memories, they accompanied me here as I walked down. And I thought of you, and I said, "My God, but how could he live daily among all these fragments and still complain?"

Imaro. You're wrong, Claudius. I do not complain about memories. It's not the past that bothers me, can't you see? It's the squalid present, turning and turning upon itself, refusing to move on, to go forward.

Claudius. Why be impatient? The soldiers now ruling us will soon fade away.

Imaro. When Claudius? Can you give me a date?

Claudius. I don't know. Soldiers come. Soldiers go. It can't last forever.

Imaro. Wasn't that what we said about the civilians, ehn?

Claudius. And where are they now? They went to the grave . . .

Imaro. And did poverty go with them? Did exploitation go to the grave? Tell me! Are the poor folks not still having their heads ground in the dust, their screams muffled in the sound of sirens? And the rich ones, are they not still selling our people into slavery, while they go smiling to the Swiss banks? Pass the hat . . .

Claudius. What?

Imaro. You're Didi, and I am Gogo. Look, this is the hat that the poor miserable Lucky wears. The hat of slavery. Here . . . *(He gives "it" to Claudius, who examines it, weighs it, then puts it on, to replace his own, which he hands over to Imaro. They play "Gogo and Didi passing on Lucky's hat" throughout the following speech.)* And they continue to sell our people. Once it was for mirrors, for cheap jewelry, for cowries. The rich men raided the poor, captured them, and sold them off to the slave ships. Then came the age of palm oil, of cocoa, timber, and cotton. The rich men made their slaves work on their plantations, carting off the products of their labor into the white ships. Always into the white ships. Then came the age of mineral ore, of tin, marble, and gold dust. And the rich now have policemen. They have soldiers, with numbers and uniforms. They make their numerous Luckys go down into the mines and bring out the ore. And then straight into the white ships. Always, always into the white ships. Into the insatiable white ships. While they send us their second-rate experts, their second-rate machines, their mind-destroying music, their corrupting culture, their consoling bible. Put all our best products into the white ships, the richest resources of our land. Always, always into the white ships. And now, it is the age of oil, of uranium. And we still pass the hat . . . hoping that one day, perhaps, Godot will come, and we will be saved.

Claudius. And of course, he will not come.

Imaro. And the middle man, the one who profits from it all, he knows. And he goes on laughing, and strengthens his Police. *(throws the "hat" down and tramples on it)*

Claudius. *(after watching his angry gestures for a while)* Imaro, Estragon will not be coming today.

Imaro. What? You know?

Claudius. He won't be coming. And they'll not come for you.

Imaro. How do you know?

Claudius. Since last night. I knew all about it. And I intervened to save you. You can unpack your bag.

Imaro. *(speechless)* You . . . You . . .

Claudius. Last night, some officer phoned my father. They'd got instructions to take you all in. I spoke to him, made him read out the list. You know, he was clever. He tried to jump your name. But not fast enough. There was something in his voice that I caught. So he confessed. You were on the list.

Imaro. And you told him: "Remove it." Just like that!

Claudius. Well . . .

Imaro. How does it feel, ehn?

Claudius. What?

Imaro. To be clothed in power? To have such wealth that nothing can touch you or those you protect. Not even the head of state! Tell me, it must be wonderful!

Claudius. You made your choice. So did I. And now, I am in a position to save you.

Imaro. Thank you, Claudius. You've ruined my life.

Claudius. Listen, I . . .

Imaro. You did what you thought was proper. I thank you for that. But you've pushed me to the middle ground, alone. Oh God, you should have let me suffer with the others!

Claudius. Nonsense! As if by merely suffering, you achieve anything. If you . . .

(enter Moni)

Moni. Imaro!

Imaro. Yes, I know. Estragon will not be coming.

Moni. You know already?

Imaro. Claudius told me.

Claudius. I'm sorry, Moni. There was nothing I could do for him.

Imaro. Claudius knew of it last night. They had a list out for all of us.

Moni. His house is all in a mess. I tried to tidy it up as best as I could.

Claudius. Christ, did he struggle with them?

Imaro. Or maybe they just ripped the place apart, out of spite. As they've done before.

Moni. Yes, they enjoy that.

Claudius. Why?

Imaro. It's not difficult to understand. Look at them, how little they earn. Their miserable wages. They can't understand why we, so comfortable in our university chairs, can still "make trouble" as they see it. They get so bitter. They can't understand that we're fighting for them too.

Moni. One day, they will. One day, the rabbits will turn on their hunters.

Claudius. *(hastily)* Ima, I'll be going. We'll have to fix the rehearsals for another day, when all this is over.

Moni. Do you know when it'll be over? When my brother and the rest will be released, Mr. Claudius?

Claudius. No, I'm afraid I can't say. But it should be soon.

Moni. Thank you. Bye then.

Claudius. Bye-bye.

Imaro. Moni, let's see him off to . . .

Moni. No! Don't touch me!

Imaro. What? What's the matter?

Moni. Aren't you going with him? Aren't you going with your master?

Imaro. What do you mean, Moni?

Moni. *(to Claudius)* I hope you're taking your dog along.

Imaro. *(stung)* Who? What are you saying? Who's a dog?

Moni. Yap, yap! The clever dog! Yap, the master's got a bone! You think it's not clear now, the game you're playing!

Imaro. Are you crazy! What game am I playing?

Moni. I must congratulate you anyway! You know how to play the game! You made the right noises with the rest. You egged them on, you shouted slogans, you could paint flaming placards. But you knew how to dodge at the appropriate moment! You had taken out the best insurance for yourself!

Imaro. What's she talking about? What insurance?

Moni. Go on pretending that you don't know what I'm talking about. But the rest are gone, all our comrades, and you are here. You alone, and Claudius.

Claudius. Moni, that's not . . .

Moni. Deny it! Deny that it's because of you that he's here untouched . . .

Claudius. I won't deny it. But you're being unfair to him. He knew nothing about it.

Moni. He knew! He's always known! Haven't you, Imaro? That's why you carefully planned out your insurance, isn't it? You were cleverer than the rest of us, and I didn't understand. Until today! Until now, that you've laid yourself wide open!

Imaro. You see now, Claudie!

Moni. Don't call Claudius! Is he the only one? What of the others with whom you've carefully surrounded yourself? The Johnsons! The de Gamas! The Bioyes! The Chukwuras! Shall I go on? The rich, powerful people you preach against but who are always guests at your house? Whom you abuse, but dance around, and fawn for? Is it a lie? You're there when their wives give birth; when their uncles die and are being buried! When their sisters wed you're the master of ceremony! And on Sundays you put on a jersey and accompany them to the squash court. . . . God, how I've been deceived! How I loved you! . . . all that talk about revolution, war, exploitation, the masses . . . but you had built your escape route . . .

Claudius. Moni, maybe it's not my business, but it's not true, all you said just now. Ima and I, and all the others you mentioned, Bioye, Johnson, Chukwura, and the rest, we've been friends from youth. We all grew up together, went to the same schools, shared our vacations and, sometimes even, our girlfriends. It is true that later, each of us went his own way. Are you saying that because of that, all the past should be forgotten?

Moni. You can't understand, Mr. Claudius. And I don't expect you to. You're a business man. You live by sucking on others. You cheat and extort and ruin others, and you call it making profits. So I have no arguments with you; you've made your choice. But he had always claimed to be different. He knows what it means to run with the hare, in the morning, and then at noon, to change skins and hunt with the hounds.

Claudius. Moni . . .

Imaro. Enough, Claudius. She is only saying things I've been telling myself since morning. Maybe I made the wrong choice, gave my life to a cause that I could only end up by betraying. Maybe I am just too much on the other side . . .

Moni. At least you're sincere . . .

Imaro. Please let me finish! *(angry)* You know, I'm just sorry for you, because, in a very short time, if you're not careful, you would have changed so much that no one would recognize you anymore, Moni. Not even your closest friends.

Moni. I won't be a traitor at least.

Claudius. No. But will you be a human being?

Moni. Not by your standard anyhow.

Claudius. I've met your type before. Those who fight for a cause so blindly, that in the end it maims them, turns them into an ogre, a machine of hatred, and hatred alone . . .

Moni. You're frightened, that's all. Frightened! You and others like you, you know your days are numbered. The revolution that's coming . . .

Claudius. Yes, tell me! What is it like, this revolution I hear so much about? This Godot that will sweep everything away and bring paradise? A scene in a play? All the words you throw about, your savage gestures, your wild-waving fists in the air, what do they all amount to? To a room in a prison cell? Boots in the crotch? Or electrodes on the nerve centers? You think those will make you more of a revolutionary and less of a fake?

Moni. I don't have to convince you, sir. When the day comes, it will have enough words to describe itself.

Imaro. *(stopping Claudius)* Wait, Claudie, wait. Let me handle it. You're right, Moni . . . but not for the reasons you think. I wasn't trying to build myself an escape route. These people, these capitalists you mention, they are indeed too close to me. Maybe because I watched them grow up, came to know them so intimately. I know their crimes, but I also know their grotesque fear of poverty, of insecurity, of death. I know how they built up their wealth as a bulwark against this fear, with such desperate determination, and through such short-cuts, that without knowing it, many of them have ceased to be human . . . Yes, but they're not all like that. Claudie, Claudie here, he isn't like that. Nor is Chukwura. You know him! Nor Abioye whom . . .

Moni. You see how you make exceptions for your friends. If we were all to do that, what would be left of the revolution?

Claudius. But Moni . . .

Imaro. You're right. She's right. Maybe I'm just making excuses. Maybe it is time to choose, again, and be honest with myself.

Claudius. What kind of choice now, after so many years?

Imaro. You, Claudie, I've thought of it, there's no other way out for me. By your act of kindness last night, you turned me into an outcast, denounced by my friends. Now it is left to you to rescue me.

Claudius. Me? How?

Imaro. There's only one way I can go now.

Claudius. Where?

Imaro. Out of all this. Somewhere I can learn to start anew.

Claudius. I don't understand.

Imaro. *(almost to himself)* Perhaps this is the chance I've been seeking all these years, to find out what breaks them. Even our best students. Why they never come back except to show off their Mercedes, their glittering lace garments and gold teeth, their bejeweled mistresses. Perhaps this is the occasion at last to quit the ivory tower, and learn also to dirty my hands.

Moni. Yes, grasshopper! Time to fly, and learn the antics of locusts.

Claudius. You want to quit, Ima?

Moni. Why not? Don't you know the oriki of a grasshopper? When the forest heats up, in a hot season . . .

Imaro. Try me, Claudie. Take me out of here. Into your company for a start. It's as good a place as any to begin my life anew.

Claudius. Into our company! Do you know what you're saying?

Moni. I'm going . . .

Imaro. Why the hurry? Won't you even hear the post he'll offer me?

Claudius. You're not serious, are you?

Imaro. Of course, I'm serious. I want to start all over again. I'm giving all this up, all this preaching, all this empty talking into the air. I'm going to leave the ranks of the losers . . .

Claudius. It's all because of this girl that you're saying this?

Imaro. I'm tired, Claudie. I told you I've been thinking, didn't I?

Moni. He's betrayed us. He's betrayed me. Now he wants to chicken out.

Imaro. I don't blame you for being so cruel, Moni. I can see for myself that my life's in shreds. What have I achieved? I have talked and talked. Like the others. I've tried to teach my students that we can build a new world. That a brave new world is within our grasp. But to what purpose? Our society has marked us out as eccentrics. Worse, as felons! And I am tired. I can't live my whole life as a fugitive . . .

Moni. God, is this the man I loved?

Claudius. Imaro, if you'll listen to me . . .

Imaro. . . . a losing war! And perhaps we've been teaching them lies! There must be much more out there than we know. Something that breaks these students totally, changes them, corrupts them, so that later, when you see them again, they're totally different men . . . totally altered.

Moni. You forget, I was your student too.

Imaro. That is different, you were in love with me. And there was always your brother too. No, Claudie, I'm serious, help me. Give me a job.

Claudius. As what? What can you do?

Imaro. What do you mean, what can I do?

Claudius. You have no qualification . . .

Imaro. Don't be funny. I have a Ph.D., remember? I've written books and essays. I produce plays . . .

Claudius. Useless, I'm afraid. All that's no qualification for a job in our company.

Imaro. Oh, come off it. Not even for PRO work?

Claudius. Not even for PRO work.

Imaro. You don't want to take me, that's all.

Moni. Please take him, Mr. Claudius. His forest's burning, can't you see?

Claudius. Look, the PRO is a professional. You're just an academician, even though a brilliant one. You're useless. And what shall we pay you anyway? The PRO post is eighth rank to mine . . .

Imaro. What does that matter? It's still double my present salary anyway. If I survive. Help me!

Claudius. And it's not that alone. It's . . . It's . . . can't you understand? I'll have to give you orders . . .

Imaro. Who says I won't obey?

Claudius. Stop kidding yourself. The orders won't even come from me directly. I'll give instruction to some boys who will pass it down to someone else, who will then pass it on to someone else . . . and so on, eight rungs down, before it is passed to you. And your direct boss, from whom you'll take the orders, do you know who he will be? One of your former students, who graduated maybe three years ago! Who was in his diapers when you took your first degree! When you wish to talk to me, you'll have to go to his Secretary, who'll then pass it on to him, to see if it's worth passing on. Ah! If you wanted to quit, you've left it years too late!

Imaro. You're afraid, aren't you? You're afraid to give me orders.

Claudius. Don't be funny. Giving orders, that's mere routine. Something you wear and adjust, like a tie or a belt. In the office, whatever you may have been outside, when we reach the office, you'll just be a pair of hands, to work, or ears, to take instructions, that's all.

Imaro. I understand, Claudie. Employ me. I can be all that too.

Moni. Jesus Christ! Must you degrade yourself like this?

Imaro. Answer me, Claudie.

Claudius. You think the ability to speak English is all it takes, don't you?

Imaro. What else? Isn't it an advertising job?

Claudius. You see! You'll have to go out and bring in contracts. Can you do that?

Imaro. I could try . . .

Claudius. You!

Imaro. Yes! Why not?

Claudius. Right, let me see you try. Go on. Let me see you go to a Minister now for a contract. For you know, it's the government that gives all of us most of our jobs. Now go on, show me. Start at the door, where his Secretary is waiting, like a guard. He is a public servant, don't forget. He is paid out of your tax. He is supposed to be polite. So come on, approach him. Ask your question.

Imaro. *(Coming forward. They will begin to playact now.)* Good morning.

Claudius. *(Takes a sitting position, pretends to be writing. His tone is hostile, exaggeratedly so of course. Greater effect is obtained by playing in one of the heavily accented local dictions.)* Yes, what do you want?

Imaro. *(his most polite tone)* Can I see the Minister, please?

Claudius. Which Minister?

Imaro. Or isn't this the office of the Minister?

Claudius. Are you deaf, Mr. Man? I said, which Minister?

Imaro. Are there two Ministers here?

Claudius. Go on! Lawyer me!

Imaro. Oh, I'm sorry. Please that's not what I mean . . .

Claudius. No, I know I don't understand English. I've not been to England like you . . .

Imaro. But please . . .

Claudius. Look here Mr. Man! I'm busy!

Imaro. The Minister . . .

Claudius. Is busy! Engaged! Or do you have an appointment?

Imaro. No, but . . .

Claudius. But what! I say he's busy. Come another day. Stop wasting my time, my friend! *(turns his back, resolutely)*

Imaro. I give up.

Claudius. You see? You can't even get past the Secretary! I wonder in fact if you would have got past the messenger! So how will you win us the contract, Mr. PRO?

Imaro. I'll go back, the next day.

Claudius. *(reverting to his role)* You again! Didn't I tell you yesterday to book an appointment?

Imaro. Well, how am I to book?

Claudius. How are you to book! Ask me!

Imaro. How can he give me an appointment if I don't see him?

Claudius. And how will you see him without an appointment? Man, I'm busy. It's not because of your *wahala* that I was employed here. Goodbye.

Imaro. But . . .

Claudius. I said goodbye! Or do you want to be thrown out? Messenger! Call me the . . .

Imaro. All right, all right, I'm leaving . . .

Claudius. That's your second day. And it won't be different on the third. Or the fourth. Or even the seventy-fourth. And meanwhile your workers must be paid. Your family will eat. Your relations will come to you with problems that only money can solve. So what will you do?

Moni. He knows what everybody does. We all know what it takes to fight through to that inner door. And that's what our movement was all about, and he was a leader, the loudest among us. Until today.

Claudius. Oh, it's all beautiful to shout and denounce! Corruption is evil and dirty and all that. Paradise must come where everyone will be clean. Where doors will be automatically opened to knocking hands, because angels hold the key. But in the interim what happens?

Moni. Are you asking me, or the grasshopper?

Claudius. A hungry man, they say, is an angry man. Your workers, your children, your wife, they are all hungry. Tell me how you'll hop away.

Moni. *(giggles)* If you have the right legs . . .

Imaro. Claudie, these things are all rumor to me. It's a world I hear about, but I've never really been there. What is the process? Tell me, let me hear it from you, how does it feel?

Claudius. *(proud to demonstrate)* It's all a game, a riddle, and it has a formula. Every contractor knows it. Poverty is like that; it has fenced our lives round with so many riddles of deceit. And you cannot advance past them without the right response. But it's not hard to learn. So the next time you get the Ministry, you know what to do. Stand before him, that stubborn secretary, or clerk, and open your wallet with a crack. Crack! And see him raise his head! He notices. An instant, startling, and sickening transformation *(leaping up)*, "Yes, sir. Good morning , sir. Can I help you, sir? Is it to see the Minister? Oh, he is around, sir . . ." A few notes on the table, and he's your slave forever . . .

Moni. Estragon, munching bones . . .

Imaro. No, I couldn't do it. I'll never get past that secretary at the door.

Claudius. But suppose you do? What happens next? You'll find, my friend, that inside, the story's no different. Except that—careful!—the man may be an illiterate, more cunning, more suspicious, and far more savage. You've got to watch it. Build your circle around him, slowly. You know what he wants . . .

Imaro. Do I?

Claudius. You must! And it's vital: you must know which item on the list is his current headache, or you'll be paying more than you could afford. An account in a foreign bank. A palace in an exclusive estate. A car with a singing horn. A holiday in the Bahamas. But careful, don't go charging into him! Circle him like a bull in the ring, till he lays open his weakest point! And then drive in, sir, sharp and quick! Crawl, cringe, and fawn. If your children saw you at that moment, they must not recognize the grinning monkey on the carpet! Flash the party card. Mention a few acquaintances. Show the references they've written for you, if you've been lucky. Chief so and so. Alhaji this and that. A Managing Director. A Company Chairman. A member of one Board or another. The party big wigs. And all the time watch his eyes. Watch the widening glint behind them . . .

Imaro. Oh, God! Of course, it's our country!

Claudius. And is that all! I could tell you of other occasions, of other riddles to crack. Such as when you catch your worker stealing, and you sack him and the rest go on a rampage, burning up the costly equipment. And you have to bribe their leaders! Or such as collecting your payment from the Ministry when finally you manage to complete the assignment. And your file disappears, and reappears and disappears again and again like a conjuring acrobat. And the man paid to sign your check is mysteriously never "on seat" when you call. And it's another round of handshakes. You understand? Expensive handshakes . . .

Imaro. I understand all too well, I'll be quite useless for such a job.

Claudius. So stay where you are. And continue to do what you alone, and people like you, can do.

Imaro. What is the use, Claudie? Only the Police will be calling. No one else understands.

Claudius. Who's telling you that? Man, the world you dream of is still the best, however remote it may seem. And how we envy you! We've made money, as you can see. We've stolen, some of us have killed even, to arrive where we are. We've colluded with aliens, betrayed our land, to fill our pockets . . . but Ima, I'm not proud of what we've become. Certainly I would not like our children to be like us, to be likewise ringed in crime . . .

Imaro. I'm not sure I understand you . . .

Claudius. No. Do I myself, do I really understand? I mean, dear Teacher, that I still love this country, in spite of everything. In spite of having had, again and again, to betray it, just like every other businessman. I make no apologies; in a country of cats, only the fiercest survive. We were born into a world where, to survive, we must feed on one another, and I have grown to be one of the survivors. That's why Moni here cannot stick my guts, and she is right. But my hope is that the time will come when a new generation will replace us and wipe everything away. When it will be possible to live without having to eat your neighbor . . . and I know that hope will be in vain, that there will be no new generation, if the real teachers quit. If no one remains to nurture the fresh minds . . . have I made myself a bit clearer now? That was the only reason I intervened, yesternight. Why I've come down this morning to see you. If I could have saved your comrades, I would have done so. But my father has promised to do his best to look to their welfare while they're in detention. But don't think nobody cares, that nobody listens. Please do not give up the fight.

Imaro. *(after a long pause)* You rascal! I'd forgotten that you were once the President of the Debating Club!

Claudius. Well, I'm off now. Please don't forget what I said.

Imaro. How can I forget? You've given me a new lease on life. Thank you.

Claudius. Well Moni, bye-bye. Take care of our . . . grasshopper. See you at the next rehearsal.

Imaro. I'll phone you. When all this is over.

Claudius. Moni, I'm sure you can still shake the hand of a capitalist? *(proffers his hand)*

Moni. *(taking it, still moody)* Bye, Mr. Claudius.

Claudius. *(to Imaro)* No, don't bother to see me down. All those stairs! See you soon. *(goes)*

Moni. *(clapping)* Clap for him, Imaro. Don't let him leave without an applause.

Imaro. Moni, I thought . . . I thought that now that we're alone, we'd be able to talk.

Moni. About what? I said you should clap for your generous and eloquent friend. How his words shone like diamond rings! He was well chosen; he has done his job well, has given you a new lease on life! Now you can rise and straighten your back.

Imaro. Will you now listen . . .

Moni. It would be grotesquely funny, too, if one were not already past the age of pranks. To think that it's a capitalist—a flamboyant, unrepentant capitalist at that! He is the person you have to rely on to restore your socialist ideals! I wish the comrades were here! *(laughs)*

Imaro. Claudius restored my faith not in socialism, but in myself.

Moni. And where's the difference? You know, Imaro, if I closed my eyes, all this would fade into nightmare. I would not see you as you are now, a wreck, but only as I first knew you and grew to love you—tall on so many platforms, talking, laughing, waving your arms, especially your arms, affirming. On many nights your voice has come to my pillow, like an echoing dream, your voice urging us not to despair, to rise up and carry the burden of our destiny. Teaching us that . . .

(Imaro's voice joins hers now as she goes on.)

Both. "We, the young and the gifted of Africa. Of all the black world. We, the educated and the articulate. Rise! Rise up now and shake off your slumber. History waits for our footsteps, for the command of our voices, for we have a special role to play . . ."

Moni. . . . oh, how sweet your voice . . .

Imaro. *(alone now)* " . . . yes we have a special role waiting for us, and the future must be different because our forefathers knew . . .

(Moni joins him.)

Both. ". . . knew the bitter taste of chains, the savage experience of the Middle Passage. And we, their children, must redeem that past! Must turn our arid history into an oasis, a refreshing folktale. Rise! Fill your muscles with the energies of a creative YES-S-S-S!"

Moni. It was your voice, Imaro!

Imaro. *(continuing alone)* ". . . time is in our hands! Let us seize it and shape it into our glory!" *(His force is spent. As she goes on, he seems to collapse, turning in a wild circle like a trapped beast.)*

Moni. All those beautiful things. Oh, how many words in your voice! And I would reach out and pull it close, I would cuddle your voice jealously, till it turned to endless dreams of hope, of forests shaping into radiant cities, into schools, hospitals, factories, and fertile farmlands, of slums yielding place to skyscrapers. . . . Aah, is it that same voice I hear now, filled with such dirges of defeat?

Imaro. Moni, dreams are a wall that every man builds to lean his life on. But I did not promise to be strong all the time, at every hour of the day. Sometimes, because we are only human, sometimes the wall cracks.

Moni. This is worse than anything I had imagined, Imaro. You, leaning on Claudius for . . . for . . . oh God!

Imaro. You're young. You do not understand.

Moni. I needed someone who could fly. And you gave me a promise of wings. But alas, you're only a grasshopper, powerless before the wind. When the forest begins to burn, you're just as trapped as all the crawling things.

Imaro. And you? What are you?

Moni. I know what I do not wish to be. I've had enough of this.

Imaro. Love is for the rainy day, as well as for the dry season. It isn't only on those days when a man is strong that he deserves to be called a comrade.

Moni. You don't need me. You've taken your life and folded it carefully on the lap of . . . Claudius. The genuine comrades have a name for that.

Imaro. Moni . . . (*moving toward her*)

Moni. No, don't touch me!

Imaro. (*raising his voice*) That's right! Run away then! And shout it to all the comrades! Imaro has turned tail and joined them! The tall socialist obelisk has crashed down in the market place of capital, and broken into fragments! Imaro is down! Three cheers for capitalism, hip! hip! hip! All because I spoke to Claudius, my friend, in a moment of stress—and I allowed him to comfort me! Bring them! Bring all your friends with axes and shovels! With their shit and spittle, so we can truly bury the corpse of the traitor!

Moni. (*shouting back*) Rave on, but it's the truth. Whether you scream or foam at the mouth! You're their servant! Even if you pretend not to see! They take away the others and leave you alone. Untouched. Then they send their spokesman in the morning with words to comfort you. With cigars and a bottle of Chivas Regal! And you still say you don't know. You don't know. You don't know what? Whom are you kidding? You're the Establishment's token Marxist, my dear! Nobody will ever touch you. Never! Because it's good for them that you are here. Screeching like a cricket, but unable to bite! You are their ever . . .

Imaro. (*furious, approaching to strike her*) Enough! Enough you hear, or by God, I'll . . . (*She screams, terrified, and he* *stops, his hand in the air. Then he backs down into a chair. Long silence. Then she takes her bag and rises.)*

Moni. Poor man.

Imaro. What?

Moni. I said, you poor man. You're so filled with contradictions!

Imaro. I suppose there are many of us, waiting for Godot.

Moni. *(going)* Well, bye-bye. I'm going to try and get in touch with my brother.

Imaro. Let me come along then.

Moni. No. It has to stop.

Imaro. I love you, Moni.

Moni. Please let's not go back to that.

Imaro. You too, you used to dream. And those dreams filled me with strength. So now it's over; you're no longer my fairy queen, owner of a thousand dreams. You've become just another woman, prone to hurt and . . .

Moni. What do you want me to say? Yes, I've grown up. I used to think of you as a god, but I've come to see your weaknesses, and your feeble attempts to cover them up, to justify them . . . I don't love you any more. I don't want to be contaminated.

Imaro. And so nothing remains at all?

Moni. No, I . . . listen, I know what I wanted. Not marriage, no. You're married already, and I've always accepted that. You've got kids. So it wasn't because of marriage that I've followed you, loved you, loved you for, oh, so many years. Not for a wedding ring . . .

Imaro. But I know that, don't I? I've celebrated it in songs . . .

Moni. That's just it! Songs are not enough.

Imaro. There's always a place for those who have nothing else to share but their dreams.

Moni. Not anymore. I must start putting my life in order . . .

Imaro. Well, if that's the way you see it . . .

Moni. You know, it's not just what has happened. It's what you are. I don't think you can really love anybody apart from yourself. All that revolution talk is just a drug to you. I'm not saying that you don't believe it, but the fact is, that deep, deep down, you're a man alone. You're alone,

desperately, and you'll always be alone. It's like a perma-
nent ache, and everything you do is just a way of relieving
it. You must fill your loneliness, and that is why you need
companions. We're all there to help you pass the day . . .

Imaro. Maybe you're right, as you always are. Maybe we're all
alone in the end. How did Beckett put it? *(quotes)* "Astride
of a grave and a difficult birth. Down in the hole, lingeringly,
the grave-digger puts on the forceps. We have time to grow
old. The air is full of our cries. *(He listens, as in the text of
Beckett's play.)* But habit is a great deadner. *(He looks, as if
at the sleeping form of Estragon.)* At me too someone is
looking, of me too someone is saying, he is sleeping, he
knows nothing, let him sleep on." *(pause)* I can't go on!
(pause) What have I said?

Moni. It's like a game to you, isn't it? It doesn't matter if others
suffer?

Imaro. You say you're going away, and I can't stop you. I can
offer nothing, except perhaps my loneliness, which you
knew so well how to share. I need you, but not as you are this
moment. Only as you are when you dream, when you turn
the world into fairyland . . . Owner of a Thousand Dreams,
don't go away! Teach me how to dream! . . .

Moni. *(in a great emotional difficulty)* I'll help you, you hear?
But only for the last time! You must not try to stop me. I
don't want to be trapped in your failures. Whatever you
wish to make of your life, please count me out. I'm opting
out, and the world won't be the less beautiful because of
that. You hear?

Imaro. Yes, yes.

Moni. We're just two friends parting, remember? *(She forces
herself out.)* Just two friends shaking hands, standing in
the light. And it's a fine morning, look! Just look! With a
touch, like this, everything withers into gold! Ooooooh,
what is this? Take, hold it. Carefully. To others, it's just a
book. But don't you believe it. You have better eyes. It's a
box, isn't it? Emerald, filled with dreams! Don't let us
open it; one man, that magician down the street, has put
all of his life inside it . . . And that! Handle it gently,
gently. Fools call it a chalk! But we know better, don't we!

It's a chip off an ivory tusk, which the prince was taking down to the sea-maiden. It glitters; it has memories of forests and lakes . . . *(She sees that his eyes are shut.)* and now, bye-bye my love. It's a fine morning, and I don't know why I'm crying. I don't know why I'm afraid . . . *(She is sobbing.)*

Imaro. *(opening his eyes)* It's a dream my dear. Don't wake from it; it's young and fragile! It can break into fragments! Where's your hand? Take, hold this. Wipe your eyes with it. You see now how soft and wet it's become? It sometimes feeds on tears, and they say it's a handkerchief. But you and I, we know that's a lie! Shake it, and you'll hear the wind sing in it. Fold it, like this, and it turns into a flower, fluttering in your palm . . .

Moni. No, no let me go, please . . .

Imaro. . . . And I, who am I? Tutuola gave me a hundred names! When I am like this *(flapping his arms)* I am known as Featherman of the Jungle. *(She begins to smile in spite of herself.)* Then I change, without announcement, like this *(on all fours)* and I am the unknown Television-handed Lord of the City of Glow-Worms! *(He pursues her and she flees, giggling.)* But not for long. No, my triumph does not last, alas! For at moments, I am just a helpless fetus, like this, curled up and afraid. Afraid of the sun, of eagles and talons in the air, of the sound of boots and sirens, and I need a hand around me at such moments . . . someone to sing to me . . . for I am afraid . . .

Moni. *(down by his side)* Don't worry, I have arrived. I've got hands like wings, you see . . . Tell your fear to go away . . . I've brought my voice to shield you . . .

> And I shall sing, my love,
> Of a shield called Freedom
> Against which the talons of eagles break;
> Of a nut impervious
> To the knocking of boots, in which
> The kernels are ancient songs
> Set ablaze;
> Words felonious as the poet

And dangerous to the sword
Of tyrants. Rise, my love,
Like a scream in which history
Is summarized to a savage
Cry: AMANDLA!
Let Freedom come!
To the Forest of thorns and

(Imaro joins her at this point.)

Brittle things, of elephants
And butterflies and grasshoppers. Shout:
MANDELA! AMANDLA!
Let freedom come!

(Moni stops and begins to go out slowly. Imaro, not noticing, goes on like one transfixed.)

Imaro.

To all the lands
Withering in the harmattan
Of hate;
To the numerous hands
Pounding without pause
Against oppression,
Against leaders with fingers of greed,
Those always turning our people
Into slaves
On their own farmlands.
So, come, my dar—

(He turns, only to find that Moni is gone. A pause, in which we see his pain. Lights begin to fade. He walks round slowly, like one searching for something in the sand. His voice is broken when he speaks again.)

So, come my darling,
Take my hand
And with the other,
Hold the next comrade
Who shall also hold

The next man, till
We form a wide ring of wishes
AMANDLA!
Let freedom come . . .
Let freedom come . . .
Let freedom . . .

(The lights fade out.)
THE END

ESU AND THE VAGABOND MINSTRELS

A Fertility Rite for the Modern Stage

CHARACTERS
(In Order of Appearance)

Chief
Ade
Youth Corpers
Minstrels
Omele
Epo Oyinbo
Jigi
Sinsin
Redio

Worshipers:
Priest in Loincloth
Women with Baskets
Man

Spirits:
Esu
Esu's followers
Pregnant woman
Male leper / Orunmila
Female leper / Yeye Osun
Obaluaye

FROM THE PLAYWRIGHT

The late existentialist philosopher and writer Albert Camus provided the theme for this play. He wrote: "Principles are needed in great matters. Compassion suffices in the small." So this play is on a theme as simple as that—COMPASSION, a sentiment now considered a sign of weakness or "effeminacy" in today's macho world of tough American gangsters, super-Bonds and Supermen, and Kung-fu experts. Just see what our world has become, with kindness so out of date. Alas, the road toward "civilization" and "development" takes us daily farther and farther away from our humanity. But should this be so?

Esu and the Vagabond Minstrels is the second of my "Magic Boon" plays of which, hopefully, there will eventually be ten. Common to these plays is a central dramatic motif borrowed and adapted from the world of folklore—namely a group of persons in a moment of desperation (caused by some social or political crisis) suddenly obtains, from some mysterious agent they come across, a magical power capable of altering their circumstances, provided of course that they use the power according to expressed injunctions. The play then is essentially a map of their adventures as they exploit this wonderful boon, teaching us in the process about themselves, their lives, and their society.

Once Upon Four Robbers was the first in the series, and its action was located in a market, which has many meanings in the Yoruba worldview. Now we have *Esu and the Vagabond Minstrels*, located in a crossroads, another significant place to the Yoruba, as richly metaphoric as the market. Each of these locations has its god, of course, but as we shall see, Orunmila always turns up, alone or accompanied, ever the repository of wisdom and symbol of reconciliation and replenishment. His appearance should be taken therefore as what it is, as a pledge from me that these plays at least will be performed in a context of delight, with song, dance, and spectacle, to please and enrich you. This one is a simple morality play, but it is also intended to be a rite of fertility, a celebration of the clashing and the fusing of the sexes. Somehow—and here I invoke the mystery of creation—the play is not as raw and primitive as I would have wished. But forgive us, we have done our best, at least to steer away from mere sentimentality. For what else, but sheer sensual ecstasy, can sufficiently contradict, and compensate, these images of brutality and violence that fill our daily life? Let the actors answer that question with the melody of their movements. . . .

Femi Osofisan

ONE: ORCHESTRA

Lights come up on a festive scene. A community in obvious celebration. The community in the author's mind is a National Youth Service Corps camp, but note that, in production, this could be substituted for—an end-of-year school's gathering, a village assembly at the close of harvest, a tourists' holiday camp, a workers' commune, a military barracks, a gathering of beggars and/or criminals in their usual havens after a heavy haul, or prison inmates or seminarists on an "open" day—any community will do, and the appropriate vocabulary adjustments should then be made. Community leaders sit on a slightly raised platform, while the rest are on mats, stools, etc. Each holds a calabash cup, while younger men and women, bearing large gourds, go around serving. Noise of conversation, chanting, quarreling, bantering, etc. Some musicians can be picked up here and there among the crowd, although they are not all necessarily playing. Soon the community leader—whom we shall name Chief for convenience—calls for silence.

Chief. Thank you, everybody, thank you! I believe you're all well served? Good! May we continue to have days like this, when happiness and prosperity sit so solidly in our midst! *(responses)* Before we close, however, I think this an appro-

priate moment to ask our players what they have ready for
the competition next week. *(noises of assent)* Okay, Ade,
where are you? Ade! Has anyone seen our lead singer?
(Voices rise, calling Ade, till he answers, offstage.)

A Voice. But, chief . . . the competition, is it still on? I mean,
with the coup d'état and the change of government in the
capital . . .? *(He is interrupted by some voices, some laughing, some hissing.)*

Chief. The competition is still very much on, my friend! What
do they say? "The government changes, the people remain!"
Let them go on with their fighting over there in the capital!
It doesn't concern us, does it? *(A thundering response of
"Noooo!" Then someone starts the "Song of Khaki and
Agbada," which everybody picks up.)*

The Song of Khaki and Agbada

Chorus: *Jo mi jo!*

Olufe, wa gb'akara
Ma d'olosi lohun
Wole, ko ti'lekun!
Khaki toun t'agbada
Awon lo jo nrin
Ti khaki ba gba power
A fese bi agbada!
T'Agbada ba gb'agbara
A tunse bi soja
Agbara dun tabi kodun?
"With immediate effect."
Non fi nkowo ilu mi
"With immediate dispatch!"
Won nwo jet lo Mecca
Won a lo Rome fun "shopping"
Ko ni sonje loja
Aiye o ni le gbadun
Won ma so'lu d'ahoro
Awon Oje lu pansaga!
But, Khaki o gba'ru e
Ani, Soja o gba se!

Chorus: *Jo mi jo!*

Darling, chop akara!
Make you no mind de rumors
Shut de door and window
Khaki and Agbada
De two dey waka together
Khaki come to power
Imitate Agbada!
Agbada come to power
And go dey do like Khaki
Power de sweet man pickin!
"With immediate effect."
He don chop de treasury
"With immediate dispatch!"
He buy jet for Mecca
Fly to Rome for shopping
Food go dear for market
Man go suffer—suffer
Farm go dry like desert
Still Agbada no go care
Then Khaki go thunder
Soldier don vex finish

Adie ba l'okun tan	*Na fowl tanda for rope*
Kiniun gb'o de l'ehin	*Hunter dey for lion back . . .*
Aroye ni mo wa ro!	*But, I too dey talk—talk*
Emi ele nuso biri	*With my mouth like shovel*
Bi mba dake ma ro'ran!	*And I go henter for trouble*
Olufe, tilekun!	*Darling, make you shut de door!*

(They end the song in great laughter.)

Chief. Thank you, thank you! I wonder why many of you here are not in the acting troupe! *(Ade enters.)* Ah, Ade, there you are! Your players, are they here?

Ade. *(looking around)* Yes, I should think so. Except for Leke.

Chief. Well, what play are you people taking to the competition? Or is it not ready?

Ade. Not quite, but have no fear at all! I promise everyone here that we shall not fail you! *(cheers)* We have an excellent play that we are working on seriously. It's going to beat anything our rivals may bring up! *(cheers)*

Chief. That is the kind of thing I love to see in the community! A winning spirit! But . . . is it possible . . . I mean, can we see some bit of it before we disperse today? Just to give us a foretaste?

Ade. Oh yes, why not? I'm sure the Players will love it. It will give us a chance to test it out before a live audience. That is, if you don't mind our doing it without costumes and the necessary props.

Chief. Come on, what are costumes? What are props? Are they not just embellishment? It's the story we want, not so? *(responses)*

Ade. Okay, we have some costumes and props anyway. If you give us your go-ahead, we'll get started. Players, where are you? *(They assemble round him.)* Taju, run and fetch Leke. Tell him it's a rehearsal, and he's needed. Now let's see . . . ah, yes, clear the center here, please; that will be our stage. Right here, at the center. We are putting a crossroads there. A crossroads, which as you all know is Esu's homing ground! Where's Esu! Come on, take position here with your followers. Er, Chief, you won't mind, will you, if we borrow the signpost over there? Dele, go and fetch it and put it up in the center here. Yes! This will be the spot for Esu's homing ground.

(looking out) What! *(laughs)* Okay, Chuks, run quickly and give Dele a hand with the signpost. Meanwhile, Esu, where are you again? Let's have you and your followers to this side. *(Dele and Chuks appear with a large signpost that has crossed arms.)* Here! Good. Esu, come on, take position now, with your men. *(Esu and the followers sit or squat around the road sign. Then one of the players whispers in Ade's ears.)* All right, all right. I think I'll ask the women present to help us. Can you please lend us your shawls? Thank you. Thank you. These people, or what shall we call them? Gods? Esu and his followers need them. When they wrap themselves, as they are doing now, they turn to stones. Yes, just like that. See? Ah, there's Leke! I know you'd fly here, once you hear the word *rehearsal! (to the crowd)* He doesn't want to lose his part to another player! Even though he's going to be a mere vagabond! Well, ladies and gentlemen, here are your lead players, these five. They are what I said before, vagabonds! Vagabond musicians. They've been jobless for months—since the change of government actually, and the proscription of entertainers like them. And they've been forced therefore to trek from town to town, village to village, searching for work, all in vain, till they arrived here, at this crossroads. That's where our story will start. Please watch well, and let us have your comments after the show. Ah, what changes, what unexpected changes, a new government can bring to people's lives! *(The crowd starts the "Song of Khaki and Agbada" again, as they disperse into the orchestra. The sitting arrangements now must be such that, except for the open space at the center, there is no real separation between the players and the assembled audience. Players not directly needed onstage, or in the orchestra, should mix with the audience. Lights dim gradually, till the next scene is ready.)*

TWO: OVERTURE

The lights come up on a crossroads. Dawn. Later clearing into morning. Sounds of cockcrow. Five bedraggled minstrels—three men and two women—come wearily onto the stage.

Omele. This is the place.

Epo Oyinbo. Where?

Omele. Here.

Jigi. This crossroads?

Omele. Yes. Where the roads meet. You can put down your things. We've arrived.

Sinsin. At last! My poor feet!

Epo Oyinbo. But . . . where's the food?

Omele. Put down your things.

Epo Oyinbo. I said, where's the food?

Omele. I don't know Epo Oyinbo! Are you the only one hungry here?

Epo Oyinbo. Well show us then!

Omele. You mean you can't wait?

Epo Oyinbo. Wait for what?

Omele. Look, I'm tired . . .

Epo Oyinbo. You hear that!

Redio. Now, what's the game, Omele?

Epo Oyinbo. He's tired!

Omele. All I'm saying is that . . .

Epo Oyinbo. Nonsense! What are you saying? A feasting house, that's what you promised us! Food in abundance! That's why we dragged ourselves through the dust and followed you all this distance! And now, see, you are "tired," and the place is as barren as a graveyard!

Omele. And so what! Are you better than a corpse anyway?

Epo Oyinbo. *(furious)* You hear him, Oga Redio? You hear his filthy mouth!

Jigi. But he's right, isn't he? Corpses, Epo Oyinbo! Is that not what we've become! We crawl from one hole to another, scrounging. And the smell of the grave follows our every step.

Epo Oyinbo. You too, Jigi? You too?

Jigi. Hunger, my friend. Hunger makes a life meaningless!

Epo Oyinbo. And all those words of rubbish that you keep mouthing, is that what will feed us?

Jigi. Corpses, my friend!

Sinsin. Yes, but living corpses! The dead don't have a stomach howling for food.

Redio. Stomach! You must be damn lucky! What I have here *(pointing at his stomach)* is a furnace of rioting embers! I don't know where you fellows find the strength to quarrel like this.

Epo Oyinbo. But that's just it, Oga Redio! Eggs! Yams! Palm oil! Bananas! What else did he promise us? And now this—a forlorn crossroads!

Sinsin. I can't even curse him! My voice is swallowed in my aching belly.

Omele. If only you'll be patient . . .

Epo Oyinbo. I should have known! After the prank you played last week! Only last week! But here I am, an imbecile, following you again! Don't I deserve it!

Omele. *(angry now)* It wasn't a prank, and you know it! Or would I play a prank on myself too?

Jigi. You're going too far, Epo Oyinbo. Raking up such memories.

Epo Oyinbo. I'm starving!

Jigi. And him? Has he eaten more in the last three days than the groundnuts we scavenged from that poor woman?

Omele. *(bitterly)* A prank! I wanted to help! It was my hometown, wasn't it? Where I was born and raised! How could I have known that the place had changed so much? How? That was my mistake . . .

Epo Oyinbo. Which almost killed us! A mistake!

Omele. Charity! That was the creed we were all raised on, and the whole village practiced it! Not even a stranger passed by without finding a roof, or a warm bed. They taught us to always give, freely, like Mother Nature. They said God owned everything, and that every man was a creature of God. Created in his image! So, how was I to know that in just five years, five years since I left, all that would have changed? How could I have foreseen it, that a day would come when these same people, my own people, would see men in torment, and drive them back into the wind?

Jigi. And how they drove us! Omele ran like a squirrel, when the hunters suddenly emerged behind us!

Sinsin. And you! You didn't run?

Jigi. I was the first to turn, I admit it! And then I saw Epo Oyinbo zooming past, with his scattered legs . . .

Epo Oyinbo. Who? Whose legs are scattered? *(Jigi flees, laughing.)*

Jigi. *(to Omele)* Don't blame your people, my dear. In those days you talk of, there was a different God in this land. The locusts had not come to power. The priests of austerity, drought, and perennial shortages. The greedy men with their gleaming teeth, calling themselves politicians . . .

Epo Oyinbo. But is this the time for sermons! What's wrong with all of you? I'm starving!

Omele. If only you'll be patient! I told you . . .

Redio. Tell us, Omele! Tell us again! If there's no food, why have you brought us here?

Omele. There'll be food. But Oga Redio, you all agreed to follow me, remember, because no one else had a better idea?

Epo Oyinbo. What! I suggested the bridge! We would have found shelter at least under it, instead of having to roam around like this, like beggars!

Jigi. That would have been all right for you! No doubt. You would have been quite comfortable. They're your type, the scum who live under the bridge. You would have been comfortable with them!

Epo Oyinbo. You'd better watch your tongue, Jigi!

Sinsin. I suggested the market. The stalls are warm and empty in the night.

Omele. Empty? Where do all the roaming lunatics go to roost at sundown?

Jigi. And the soldiers on patrol! Who wants to wake up with a gun pointing down her throat?

Sinsin. Oga Redio suggested the beach! We could have stayed there with the aladuras.*

Omele. And feed on what, Sinsin? On sand and salt water?

Sinsin. On fish!

Jigi. But we went through all these arguments before! We all agreed Omele's idea was the best.

Epo Oyinbo. Yes! But did he say it would be a barren crossroads?

Omele. It isn't a barren crossroads, Epo Oyinbo! Has any of you never heard of Sepeteri?

---

* Members of a Christian evangelical sect.

Sinsin. Sepeteri?

Redio. What is Sepeteri?

Epo Oyinbo. It rings a bell, let me see ... *(shouts in alarm)* Yeeh-pa! Sepeteri! Is that where we are?

Omele. Yes. This is the crossroads of Sepeteri.

Epo Oyinbo. Sepeteri! My friends, let's go quickly! Let's go!

Sinsin. Why?

Epo Oyinbo. You're strangers here, to the legends of the land. You don't know where he's brought you, this crazy man. But just follow me quickly out of ...

Redio. Wait. Let him explain to us.

Epo Oyinbo. No, not here! Later! Please heed my advice!

Redio. *(laughing)* This is getting intriguing. To see you trembling, Epo Oyinbo! You, who used to laugh at death as you turned somersaults on the dashboard of lorries, before I brought you into the band! So something can turn you into a woman!

Epo Oyinbo. You don't understand! You don't understand at all, Oga Redio! This place ... Sepeteri! This is the home of Esu himself! Esu, the dreaded god of mischief, this is his homing ground! We are standing on his head! *(Jigi and Sinsin scream in alarm.)*

Redio. Indeed! Calm yourself ...

Epo Oyinbo. I swear it to you! Tales are told of ... of people going mad here! Suddenly losing their senses and beginning to bark! Like dogs dying of rabies! Of men suddenly transfixed and having to be carried stiff to the home of herbalists! And of course they never recover to recount their experience! Or of women turning into screaming monsters! Of ...

Omele. Calm yourself, Epo Oyinbo. I know these stories too.

Epo Oyinbo. So why did you bring us here? And at this time of night?

Omele. It's already morning as you can see. You heard the cocks crow.

Epo Oyinbo. What does that matter? Is there any time of day or night when it is safe to share Esu's bed?

Omele. We're not sharing his bed. We're only going to share his food.

Epo Oyinbo. *Soponna O!* What did you say?

Jigi. Can you explain to us, Omele? Now, I'm getting frightened.

Sinsin. And I! What's this about Esu and his food?

Omele. Those stories, my friends, they are for children. Or those with the brains of kids. But it's all going to be a boon for us, as you'll see.

Redio. I'm not afraid of Esu. I know he can be kind too to those he favors. But what precisely is this story about sharing his food?

Omele. I'll explain. This place . . . this crossroads, I used to live here. After I left the village, they brought me here, to train as a mechanic. My master's workshop was over there, by that tree. So I saw a lot of things, here. People used to bring a lot of food and leave it at this crossroads.

Sinsin. Why? What for?

Omele. As offering to Esu. From those looking for children, or for riches, or for a long life. You see, Sepeteri is the last point between the town behind us and the sacred grove of Orunmila, over there. So Esu, the lord of Sepeteri, is regarded as a kind of intermediary, between men and their wishes, between destiny and fulfillment. If you wait, in a short while you will see. They will soon begin to arrive with their baskets and pots, to placate Esu. The whole place will be laden with food!

Sinsin. And then what happens?

Omele. What else? The feasting will begin!

Epo Oyinbo. Have I gone mad, or am I hearing you correctly, Omele? Are you telling us to steal food from a god?

Omele. Steal! Is it stealing to eat food that will only go to rot, or at best will be devoured by stray dogs and goats?

Epo Oyinbo. But . . . Omele, that's an abomination! Have you thought of the god himself, how he will take it? Or are you going to risk the wrath of Esu?

Omele. With a full belly, yes! Go and sit down my friend. If your god does not object to vermin eating his food, why should he be angry that human beings, driven by hunger, feed themselves?

Epo Oyinbo. You're mad! Completely insane! Your hunger has turned your head!

Omele. Well, that is my plan anyway. And I am going to wait here for those baskets!

Epo Oyinbo. Oga Redio, you've heard him. Let's go away and leave him alone to dare the anger of Esu if he wants to.

Redio. Wait, Epo Oyinbo. Let's think about this.

Epo Oyinbo. Wait? Think? You mean it's not obvious enough this crazy plan? Oga Redio! Sinsin! Jigi!

Sinsin. How do I know? How can I think on an empty stomach?

Jigi. I think I'll stay and eat. Yes, I'll eat first, and then repent afterward. The god will understand.

Sinsin. He definitely will. I'm sure he knows that we have no other choice. It's not our fault after all that we're jobless.

Redio. I think I agree with you. At worst, we'll repay it all when we find work again.

Epo Oyinbo. When, Oga Redio? Speak now, as our leader. The band has been proscribed. They said we played too much for the politicians. We were banned, and all our assets seized! So when do you think the new government will change its mind about us?

Redio. Governments are not eternal. Someday there'll be another one, with its own ideas. But first, we must survive, which means we must eat. Who knows in fact, there may come a government tomorrow, headed by a fellow musician!

Sinsin. I like that! His Excellency, Commander of the Charmed Voices!

Jigi. Ah, to have a governor who will dance *bata* with me! On television!

Omele. *(laughing too)* Dreams, my friends! That will be the day! What do you think a government is? A musical jamboree?

Sinsin. Hear him! Haven't we seen worse?

Jigi. Better to have a musical jamboree than a dance of corpses!

Sinsin. Yes! Better to have singers than slayers.

Jigi. Better storytellers than treasury looters!

Sinsin. Better leaders than murderers!

Omele. I'm sure you understand me. The leaders the people need must provide, not music, but food. Food!

Jigi. Wrong, Omele. They need music too!

Omele. They do? So why are you complaining of hunger? You're the best singer in the band. You've got music. Eat it!

Redio. *(chuckling)* I like that! And it's her song too, you know!

Jigi. What?

Redio. Your song! The one Omele wrote for you: "The Maiden and the Music Man"!

Omele. *(laughing)* Oh yes! How appropriate! *(He begins to sing the "Song of the Maiden and the Music Man." They all join, except for Epo Oyinbo, who turns his back in disgust.)*

The Song of the Maiden and the Music Man (I)

1. *And the Music Man, he said*
   "I've brought my band:
   See, my songs are mellow!
   I've cooked them well,
   Put in your names like sugar-ah-ah
   Oh, like sugar!"

2. *But the broken girl, on her bed*
   Was crying, and
   The tears poured down on her pillow:
   "You sing so well,
   But you don't see the hunger around,
   Oh, the hunger!

3. *"You've helped me, to shred*
   The magic wand
   Of blind love, so adieu!
   Lock the door well
   As you go, Mister Singer-ah-ah
   Oh, Mister Singer! . . .

(Epo Oyinbo, unable to contain his anger, finally shouts them down.)

Epo Oyinbo. Just look at you! Look at you! Singing, at a time like this! *(But none of them seems affected by his anger.)*

Redio. *(merrily)* Ah Omele, that's a cruel song! No one told me anything like that in my youth! And now! I mean, how can an old man like me suddenly begin to change profession now?

Omele. We learned the trade our fathers taught us. And we learned it well. Pity, that the season turned bitter, and the leaders grew corrupt. We had to eat! And how those politicians sprayed when we sang for them!

Jigi. They loved the sound of their names! My voice wrapped them in lovely fantasy!

Sinsin. No one! No one could have known that times would change like this! That the feasting would end, the dancers would go to prison. And we, the singers, so many times decorated, would turn to vagabonds.

Redio. "Go back to the land!" "Go and farm!" Crows the government radio. But with hands like these, made for drumming? The hands that have felt the trembling skin of a drum, how can they condescend to hold a hoe? Is there no limit at all then to the vulgarity of the age?

Jigi. *(laughing)* Ah, soldiers! You remember that one, that night at the police station . . . ? He came up to me . . . They'd just picked us up at the hotel . . . yes, I had just finished one of my numbers, and the audience was clapping, when . . . suddenly, soldiers everywhere . . . the stampede, ah! . . . so, at the station, where they took us, the man said to me—"Why don't you go and farm? Why waste your life away in the corruption of the city?"—That's what he called it, corruption! *(hisses)* Well, I told him. I said, "Soldier, what do you mean? How can I go and farm, when I myself, I am a farm already?" He was puzzled by that. You should see his face. "I beg your pardon?" he asked. "You don't understand? No? Well, it's like this . . . the man brings his shovel where I am lying. He digs. Yes, he digs! And I respond, like this! *(makes a suggestive movement with her buttocks)* Soldier, don't turn away. Let me tell you . . . how the seeds pour in!" *(They all laugh, except for Epo Oyinbo, who has been looking around furtively.)*

Epo Oyinbo. God! God! To see all of you laughing like this, with all the problems on our hands! I'm going! I won't . . . *(At that moment, from offstage, comes the sound of a bell, followed by incantations. The actors freeze.)*

Sinsin. What . . . is that?

Omele. *(in whispers)* A bell . . . shhh, listen! *(The bell and the voice of incantations become more audible, approaching.)*

Epo Oyinbo. You see! It's beginning!

Omele. *(taking command)* Okay, quick! Let's hide! I think they're beginning to come! *(They scramble for cover behind the stones. Enter a priest, in a white loincloth, ringing a bell, holding a pot in his other hand. He puts down the pot at the center of the crossroads, kneels briefly, chanting. Then he rises and exits. As soon as he goes, the musicians rush out to the pot—then recoil, in disgust.)*

Redio. Omele . . . what's this?

Omele. *(baffled)* I . . . I don't know . . .

Epo Oyinbo. You see? You see now?

Redio. You goat! You accursed animal! This is what you call food!

Sinsin. Cow dung! What an insult! *(Omele carries the pot and throws it away.)*

Jigi. Leave him. Let's not be so hasty. That was only the first man to come after all . . . let's wait . . .

Omele. I don't understand . . . I just don't understand . . . *(Esu and his followers laugh out suddenly, briefly.)*

Sinsin. *(cowering)* What's that?

Redio. I'm beginning to hate it all, you know. The whole bloody setup! Let's listen again. *(They listen. But now it is the voice of women, chanting, from offstage. Omele signals again, hurriedly, and the musicians scramble for cover as before. Now some women enter, with baskets. They put the baskets down at the center of the crossroads and go out again, chanting. The musicians come out to look, cautiously now, and apprehensive, and are again disappointed.)*

Redio. *(angry)* I can't believe it! This is obviously a rubbish dump! Rubbish, Omele! You've been playing tricks with us!

Sinsin. Oh, my stomach! My stomach!

Omele. But I don't understand! They'll not dare . . . Things could not have got as bad as that! They can't bring rubbish to Esu!

Redio. No, it's food! Food! Eat it! Eat! *(He plunges Omele's face into the basket. When Omele stands up, he is covered in sawdust. Jigi comes to help him brush it off.)*

Sinsin. Let's go, *jare!* I've had enough of this!

Epo Oyinbo. If only you'd listened to me! *(He kicks the basket away savagely into the bush.)*

Jigi. *(quick to defend Omele)* Quiet! Are you any better? Were you not expecting food too? All you said was that we should not eat it, not that it would be sawdust!

Redio. Let's go! Let's leave this place at once! *(They try, but find they cannot move.)*

Sinsin. What . . . what's happening?

Epo Oyinbo. I . . . I can't move! My legs are stuck!

Jigi. And me too! As if there's a clamp on my feet!

Redio. We're stuck! Stuck!

Omele. What's happening? It's not possible!

Redio. Go on, move then!

Omele. I can't! My legs, they're . . .

Epo Oyinbo. I warned you, didn't I? I warned you, but no one would listen to me!

Redio. Omele, do something! You brought us here!

Omele. I don't know what to do!

Sinsin. We're lost! We're going to die here!

Jigi. Omele, you must remember! What the men used to do when they came here. You must have seen them from your workshop.

Omele. I can't remember . . .

Jigi. Think! There must be something!

Omele. Maybe . . . ? A song! Yes, a song! There's a song that every one of them sings when he come here.

Redio. A song!

Jigi. How does it go? Maybe we can sing it?

Omele. It's Esu's song of supplication. You know it. One of those we sang before. Maybe if we try it?

(They begin to sing "Esu's Theme Song." Slowly, as they sing, hooded figures begin around the signboard to come alive and the static figure of the signboard begins to shake, till a man gradually emerges from it in a cloud of smoke and fire. It is an old man, and the now animated figures gather round him, singing too. There is a brief dance round the Old Man, although the musicians, stunned, have stopped singing, to watch in fascination.)

Esu's Theme Song

Esu O, Esu O!   Esu O, Esu O!
Esu O, Laaroye   Esu O, Laaroye

Se oun gbo'gbe, baba!	*Father, please hear our prayers,*
Araiye de'ri wa mo konga	*We've been pushed down the well of despair;*
A o ti se ka yo o!	*We long to surface again;*
Awa ti de gboin gboin	*We have our backs pinned to the wall;*
Dede'eni kongun, baba o!	*Completely lost and undone!*
Eranko o inu iboji	*The mighty beasts, who rule the jungles,*
Won ra ma ko s'omi lo o!	*How can they drown at sea!*
Akere e—ema ik'osa	*Will the crab leave his home in rivers*
Ko poun k'ori b'oko!	*And then take to the bush!*
Gbawa o, we de sim'edo,	*We call you, and crave your pity*
Ko gbo t'eni o!	*Please do not shun our prayers!*

(The Old Man stops the song abruptly.)

Old Man. *(stern)*

    The Owner of the World
    Has created balance between the forces of Good
    And those of Evil. He appointed Esu
    To watch over them, and I am his priest.
    But everywhere, Evil is in the ascendant!
    My ears fill daily
    With the woes of the afflicted.
    Speak! Tell me your wishes, you who would eat
    The Offerings of Esu!

(Epo Oyinbo runs forward and prostrates.)

Epo Oyinbo. I warned them, sir! They would not listen! I told them it was sacrilege!

Jigi. We were hungry. Please, forgive us. We do not normally live by stealing.

Omele. The times are desperate. We've not eaten for days. It was I who brought them here. If there's to be any punishment, let it be mine alone.

Old Man.

    Those are fine words, such as
    I seldom hear from human beings.
    But I know you:
    You used to eat in abundance, yes!
    At the feasts of the wealthy, once,

You sang the praise-songs,
While their victims perished at the door.
Sinsin. We were earning a living, like everyone else! Sir, we did
not make the laws, we only tried to live by them.
Old Man.
You learned to live
Like pests. Feeding on other pests.
Omele. We did, but we have paid dearly for it. Look at the
condition we are now in! Pity us!
Redio. Old Man, we've come to the end of the road. And it
looks like you can help us, as a priest of the gods.
Old Man.
Esu loves to help men, but only
When they show that they can live
Happily among other human beings.
For human beings are greedy . . .
Jigi. Help us, servant of the King of the Crossroads! We've
learned our lesson!
Old Man.
Esu does not see into the hearts of men,
Only their actions.
Are you ready
To help those among you, who are in distress?
To bring redress to the wronged?
And justice to the exploited?
All. Yes! Yes! We're ready!
Old Man. If you are, I can change your lives! I can make you
really prosperous again!
All. We are! Priest of the Crossroads! Help us!

(Again, they begin Esu's theme song, the "Song of Supplication.")

Old Man.
That is enough. Songs alone
Do not prove a man's sincerity.
But I am going to give you a chance
To help yourselves. Come forward.

(The retinue begin a soft chant and dance.)

I am going to give you a power

That can raise you from dust
Onto a throne of gold! But, careful!
If you misuse it, you'll be punished
Heavily! It's a power, and it's also a test.
Take these seeds, one for each of you.
Eat it. Swallow it. Done?
Now, let each one find a suffering man,
Someone unhappy, and sing to him.
Sing to him your favorite song,
And make him dance with you. That's all.

(He sees their puzzled looks and smiles.)

As you sing and dance, whatever his pain,
Whatever his suffering, it will end!
If he is thirsty, he will be satisfied.
If crippled, he will walk. Whatever
His agony, your song will relieve it,
Your dance will bear it all away.
Are you listening to me? Sing and dance,
Let the suffering man heal, and
Afterward, ask for anything.
Anything you wish! His gratitude
Will make you rich, or make you poor.
It depends on what you ask. Find a man
This morning, and by evening
You become a millionaire,
Or return to the gutter!
So, now it depends on you. Choose your targets
Carefully, according to your personal wishes
Choose those truly capable of gratitude.
And you will be well repaid!
As for me, I'll be back here tomorrow
To see the result. And whatever you have
Won, Esu will double it for you!
You hear? Esu will multiply by two,
Whatever you have used the power to acquire!
But if you have gained nothing,
If you have misused the power,
Chosen the wrong targets, I promise,

You will be severely punished.
So I leave now. You have all eaten
The seed of wishes. Good luck to you.

(The Old Man leaves, with his retinue chanting and dancing.)

Sinsin. *(after a while)* A song and a dance! Do you think it will work?

Omele. We'll soon find out, won't we?

Epo Oyinbo. Hm, Esu, god of mischief! I don't trust him! Or his priest!

Jigi. But he's also a god of justice, remember? And a friend to Orunmila. On the tray of divination, he takes a forward place. I don't think he'll deceive us more than we deceive ourselves.

Omele. You're right. Esu is not destiny, only the way to it. He is like a loom in the market of fate. But we each hold the shuttle, free to swing it the way we like.

Sinsin. Anyway I've eaten the charm, and I am ready to sing! Strange how my belly no longer feels the pang of hunger!

Redio. And mine too! I feel heavy with hope. I know I shall choose the right person.

Epo Oyinbo. Well, how do we begin? Shall we go and look for them?

Omele. No. I think this is a good place to wait.

Sinsin. You think so?

Omele. Look at it. A crossroads! One way to the market, there. This one to town. And that to the stream, and beyond, to the sacred grove. Think of it. Anyone in trouble must pass by here.

Jigi. Yes! Besides, this is the shrine of Esu, isn't it? This is where you say all those invalids come with their offerings?

Redio. You're right. We'll wait here.

Sinsin. Ah, let them come quickly! I'm dying to be rich!

Jigi. Fortune, please smile on us today! *(They spread out, relaxing, and sing the rest of the "Song of the Maiden and Music Man.")*

The Song of the Maiden and the Music Man (II)

4. *As the man turned, she shouted*
with command:
"Listen, Singer, to the willow:
The trees can tell

How winds wake to anger-ah-ah
Oh, to anger!

5. "And the waters have repeated
On the sea-sand,
On the ocean breeze and the billow:
They all can tell
That wars breed on hunger-ah-ah
Oh, on hunger!

6. "And the voices of the wretched
Of the land,
While your songs are so mellow,
They speak of hell,
And they scream of danger ahead,
Oh, of danger!"

(The lights fade slowly here, to indicate the passage of time.
End of Overture.)

THREE: OPIUM

Same situation. A few moments after the last scene. The musicians are apparently sleeping, as a man, middle-aged, enters
carrying a basket of fruits. The man looks round carefully, does
not see the musicians apparently, and then goes to put down
his load at the center of the crossroads. He kneels to pray. The
musicians stir and stand up at the sound of his voice. Mistaking
them for armed robbers, however, the praying man leaps up, his
hands in the air.

Man. Please! Please, spare me! I'll give you anything you want!
   Anything!
Sinsin. What's the matter with him?
Man. (falling on his knees piteously) Sir . . . Madam . . . I beg
   you! In the name of Orunmila! Spare my life!
Redio. Stand up my friend! We've not come to harm you.
Jigi. You see, Epo Oyinbo? You see how your evil face scares
   honest people!

Epo Oyinbo. Nonsense! Oga, don't be afraid. We've come to help you.

Man. *(uncertain)* To . . . help me?

Redio. Yes. We're musicians, as you can see. We're not robbers.

Man. *(still unconvinced)* Yes, yes . . .

Jigi. Put your hands down. And tell us your problems. Maybe we can help.

Man. *(putting his arms down, but scornful)* You! You can help?

Sinsin. Yes. Why not try us?

Man. Thanks. I thank you all. But . . . my problems, you see . . . No one can help. Except the gods! No one on earth can help! Especially not musicians, if you don't mind my saying so . . .

Omele. You may be right, but I'll advise you to try us first. We may not look like much, but we do have the power to help those in need. There's no harm in trying.

Man. I have been to . . . how many herbalists! I've been to doctors all over the world. All of them made me try one thing or the other. Even prayer houses, how many! But all in vain, my friends! My manhood won't come back!

Sinsin. *(laughing)* So that's it!

Man. Yes, laugh, dear lady! That's how they've been laughing at me for five years! My manhood! I've lost it and become a husk, an empty husk! *(sobbing)* Ah, the shame of it! I can't even get it up anymore! I'm only an empty, walking shell!

Omele. Calm yourself, mister. We can help you, I'm sure.

Man. You can't imagine how bad it is! To have so much wealth but not to . . .

Epo Oyinbo. Eh, repeat that. You are wealthy?

Man. Yes, alas! Perhaps more than wealthy. Houses! Cars! A private jet! What don't I have? I've bought them all. But all for what, I ask you? *(sobbing again)* For whom? I cannot father children to inherit them. My life's a waste!

Epo Oyinbo. I will help you! Now! Come with me!

Sinsin. *(with others)* What! Why you? Who says I myself, I don't . . .

Epo Oyinbo. *(turning on them)* Now, no interference from any of you! This one is my own. I saw him first!

Jigi. But we all saw him together!

Epo Oyinbo. Well, I am the first to volunteer to help! And he's mine!

Sinsin. Nonsense! You have no right to claim him!

Epo Oyinbo. Are you going to fight me then? Come on! We can decide it that way, if that's what you want. *(Takes out a knife. The women flee, screaming, toward Redio, who also backs away.)*

Redio. *(finally)* Shut up! Shut up all of you! And put that knife away. I'll decide.

Sinsin. Yes, good! Let the band leader decide.

Redio. There's no need for us to begin to quarrel like this. The day is still young, and this is only the first man to come along. Who knows, the day may still bring richer prizes! Let each wait his turn then! Okay? *(sees the knife again)* Right, Epo Oyinbo, since you want this one, go ahead. He's all yours.

Man. Wait a minute! What do you mean, I'm all his? Am I some meat to be shared . . . ?

Epo Oyinbo. My dear man, all it means is that your troubles are over! I can cure you of your impotence!

Man. Look, look, swear you're not joking! You really can?

Epo Oyinbo. Yes, I can. But what are you ready to offer?

Man. Everything! I'll give anything to be cured of this disgrace! Anything!

Epo Oyinbo. Talk, man! "Anything" is not definite enough!

Man. What do you want? Houses? Lands? Take them all! You'll be one of the wealthiest men in the land!

Epo Oyinbo. *(exultant)* You hear, all of you? All his property! *(hesitates)* But how do I know I can trust you?

Man. Take, here's my ring! Gold, all of it! Just rid me of this shame, and I'll show you who I am! Please!

Epo Oyinbo. You are cured! You'll be fit and prancing again, like a festive drumstick! Just sing with me!

Man. *(disappointed)* Sing! At a moment like this!

Epo Oyinbo. Sing! And dance!

Man. Can't we do all that afterward? I mean, I don't see why I should begin to celebrate before I can . . .

Epo Oyinbo. You're wasting your own time, my friend. This is no celebration. It is the cure itself. Join me! *(He beings to sing. The others first refuse to join him. He begs them.)*
Redio. Let your knife sing with you!

(But finally they yield to his entreaties and sing "Let the Snake Rise.")

Let the Snake Rise *(led by Epo Oyinbo)*

1. *Eyin ero, mo fe korin*
   —Yes, a ngbo, Epo Oy-
   inbo!

1. *Listen to me, I have a song*
   —Yes, sing your song, Epo Oyinbo!

2. *Mo fe korin, mo fe sure*
   —A ngbo, Epo Oyinbo,
   Sise sise o ni talakose

2. *I have a song, I have a prayer*
   —Sing your song, Epo Oyinbo,
   May your prayers, may they come true

3. *E ba mi gbe, eyin ore mi*

   —A mo e, Epo Oyinbo
   Orin aladun ni tire

3. *I need your help, sing along with me*
   —Start your song, Epo Oyinbo,
   We are willing to sing along.

4. *Eni lowo lowo*
   ti o bimo o
   O ti gbe s'aiye.
   Ka sise sise
   Ka si romo fun logun
   B'ogede ba ku,
   soun fomo ropo ni,
   Ile o to,
   Aso o p'eniyan
   L'ojo ale,
   Omo nikan lo le sin ni!

4. *Any man of wealth*
   Who has no children
   Wastes his life on earth,
   May we have a son
   To inherit everything,
   Like the banana
   Whose tree dies to be reborn;
   When the clothing
   And the money have gone
   With our dust,
   Children will prolong our name!

5. *E ma pe ko se—Ase!*
   Igi wa a ruwe—Ase!
   Igi wa a ruwe—"
   Konga wa a ponmi—"
   Ojola a dide—"

5. *Say after me: Amen!—Amen!*
   Say after me: Amen!—Amen!
   Our trees will be green—"
   Our wells fill to brim—"
   And the snake will rise—"

A dide a s'ogbe—"	*Snake will rise and strike—"*
Ekun iya aburo—"	*Then a mother's cries—"*
Ekun omo a so—"	*Welcome, new baby!—"*
Layo n'igbehin orin—"	*May sweetness end our song—"*

(As they sing, the Old Man's retinue, apparently unseen by the minstrels and the Impotent Man, return to dance along. They gradually involve the Impotent Man in a kind of ritual and then dance away. As soon as they disappear, the man, as if awakening from a trance, shouts out in surprise.)

Man. Soponna O! By God, it's working! I'm coming alive!

Sinsin. *(laughing)* Look! It's working!

Man. *(We now see a bulge under his cloth. The man runs after Sinsin, who flees, then after Jigi. Finally he grasps Epo Oyinbo.)* My friend! Your name is Epo Oyinbo, isn't it? Your fortune is made, you hear me! I have to hurry away now, you understand? It's five years, and I just have to be sure! Excuse me, I'll be back! (He rushes out. Epo Oyinbo, recovering from his laughter, makes as if to follow him.)*

Omele. No, let him go. He'll be back.

Epo Oyinbo. You think so?

Sinsin. You have his ring.

Epo Oyinbo. Yes, a golden ring! Am I not lucky!

Sinsin. It's going to be my turn next, Oga Redio! I insist!

Redio. All right, you can have the next person. Meanwhile, as for me . . . *(He moves to the basket abandoned by the Impotent Man, takes out fruits, and begins to eat. The others join him. They eat, humming their theme song. Soon, a new sound is heard. A woman, wailing. They hastily drag the basket to one side and hide. A woman, heavily pregnant, but half-nude, her hair disheveled, enters. She looks truly wretched, and carries a small earthen pot, crying. She kneels with great difficulty and begins to pray.)*

Woman. *(through her sobs)* Onile Orita! Esu, god of the crossroads! I have been bearing this burden now for nine years! Nine years with this stone inside me! It won't let me stand, it won't let me sit! I can't even lie down, it's all pain, pain, pain! What have I done? Which god have I offended? Priests, herbalists, doctors, I've seen them all! I've undergone, oh, how many operations! Various men have opened me up! All kinds of fingers have probed inside me! Why? Why don't you let me die and forget it all! Orisa, why not kill me! . . . *(As she prays, the musicians are discussing at the other side of the stage.)*

Omele. A truly pathetic case!

Redio. Well, here you are, Sinsin. Here's your chance.

Sinsin. No, I don't want it!

Redio. What? I beg your pardon?

Sinsin. It's a trick, and I won't have it!

Jigi. But you yourself insisted, just now!

Sinsin. So what? Why don't you take her yourself? Just look at the woman. Look at her condition! What kind of reward do you think this one will be able to offer?

Omele. Sinsin!

Epo Oyinbo. She's right! Can't you see? The woman looks really wretched. She can't have anything. Let her go.

Omele. I'll help her then!

Sinsin. Don't be a fool, Omele!

Omele. We can't let her go like this! Look at her! She's in torment.

Jigi. Listen to me, Omele. I know how you feel about the woman. I am a woman myself, and I should be the first to step forward. But remember, it's the only chance we have, this song, to make something of our lives at last, to cease our wandering in the slums of the world, give reality at last—Oh God—to our dreams . . .

Omele. I know, Jigi. Thank you for caring. But money is not the only road to happiness. I cannot let her go like this.

Redio. Omele, maybe I should stop you. After all, I trained you, made you into the accomplished musician that you are. I am also responsible for your future. I won't be happy to be rich, while you take the wrong turning at this crucial crossroads, and walk back to wretchedness . . .

Omele. Thank you, sir. Now step back. *(Redio is offended.)* I'll carry my own future in my hands. *(calls)* Woman! Wipe your tears, I'll help you!

Woman. *(startled, seeing them)* Sir? . . . I beg your pardon, sir?

Omele. Orisa has listened to your prayers. I'll help you out of your pain.

Woman. Sir . . . whoever you are, let me beg you, sir, not to make a jest of me. I'm a poor woman, you can see. Since I've been carrying this curse around, I've lost everything! Everybody has run away from me! My friends, my relations, and my husband! My relatives were the first to stop calling. And then my husband went across the threshold one day and has never returned! Sir . . . you say you can help me?

Omele. Yes, I can. Trust me.

Woman. This baby, my first pregnancy . . . but it has stayed inside me for nine years! Nine years! And you mean, sir . . . you mean you can . . . can . . .

Omele. Yes, I mean it, poor woman. Stand up.

Woman. Oh God, I dare not! I'm afraid! No, I must not dare to hope . . . Sir . . . Sir, perhaps you do not understand. I have *nothing*. I won't be able to pay you!

Omele. *(helping her up)* Will you be able, at least, to say "thank you"?

Woman. I'll crawl at your feet! I'll be your slave forever!

Omele. A small "thank you," that's all I'll need. Now are you ready?

Woman. Oh God! Oh God! I don't know how to answer! Will it hurt very much?

Omele. It may be hard a little. You have to dance.

Woman. Dance?

Omele. Yes, I'm afraid. I'll be singing, with my friends.

Woman. Is that all I have to do?

Omele. Yes. Will you try?

Woman. Try, sir? Ask me to jump! To run over to the stream and back! What's all that compared to the relief that's coming! To be able to bring this baby to the world at last, and rest . . .

Omele. All right then, let us begin.

(He begins to sing, his friends accompanying him, at first reluctantly, then enthusiastically. The chorus of Esu followers appear, as usual, as Omele leads the woman in a slow dance.)

The Child Inside Is Calling *(led by Omele)*

1. *Ba mi se o, Yeye Osun*
   Jowo gbo temi, Yeye Osun
   —Jowo ba mi se o, Yeye Osun
   Dakun gbo temi, Yeye Osun.

2. *Ebe la be e o, Yeye Osun*
   Dakun gbo temi, Yeye Osun.
   —Jowo ba mi se o, Yeye Osun
   Dakun gbo temi, Yeye Osun.

3. *Oh please hear my cry, Yeye Osun*
   Don't abandon me, Yeye Osun
   —Will you hear my cry, Yeye Osun
   Don't abandon me, Yeye Osun.

4. *Fill me with your love, Yeye Osun*
   Fold me in your arms, Yeye Osun
   —Will you hear my cry, Yeye Osun
   Don't abandon me, Yeye Osun.

5. *Iwo lo l'oyun, to tun l'omo*
   Iwo lo l'ekun abiyamo
   Iwo lo l'erin yeye omo
   —Fill me with your love, Yeye Osun
   Fold me in your arms, Yeye Osun.

6. *Iwo lo ni wa, ki la le se!*
   Yeye ma ni t'atare
   Pupo pupoo l'omi okun
   Dakun ba mi se o, Yeye Osun
   —Fill me with your love, Yeye Osun
   Fold me in your arms, Yeye Osun.

7. *Eni gb'omo pon lo le so'tan*
   Iwo to l'oyun, iwo la pe
   Dakun wa gb'ohun abiyamo o
   K'oloyun s'amodun o tomotomo
   —Fill me with your love, Yeye Osun
   Fold me in your arms, Yeye.

(The woman collapses suddenly.)

Woman. He-e-elp! *(The chorus of Esu followers dance hastily off.)*

Omele. *(anxious)* What? What is it?

Woman. The baby! I can feel it! It's moving!

Jigi. It's working again! The power works!

Omele. Come on, let's sing harder! *(They sing. The woman rises, painfully.)*

Woman. My dear sir, I must be going now . . . I think I have to find a midwife quickly—it's my first time, you see, and I don't want to make a mess before you . . . I shall return, you'll see, with the baby! We'll come to thank you . . . But, just in case it takes a while—for it's my first time, you see, and I don't know how long I'll be down—just in case I don't come back by tomorrow, sir, please come around, if you can do us the honor. My house is not hard to find. It's the only one opposite the market, with a half-fallen roof. And everybody knows the house of Mam Oloyun, the Ever-pregnant Woman . . . I'm talking too much, I'm so excited. I'm going to be the first mother of the season! *(pausing as she goes)* Can I beg you sir, for a token? Something to hang on the child when he comes? . . .

Omele. Oh yes, of course! Here's my chain, take it!

Woman. *(going)* Thank you sir. Thank you all! Until tomorrow!

Omele. *(watching her go)* What a woman! What a woman!

Sinsin. Omele! Even your chain into the bargain!

Omele. She was so happy! I wish I could be there, when the baby comes!

Sinsin. You're just a fool, that's all! Who's stopping you from following her?

Epo Oyinbo. Since you've so stubbornly gone ahead and blown your chance, I hope you're not depending on me to help you in the future! You won't get anything! I will not share a kobo of the fortune coming to me! Everyone must reap his own harvest.

Redio. Of course, he knows that. He pushed me back! Me! Nobody here is going to bail him out when the time comes!

Omele. I accept. I won't complain.

Jigi. Poor Omele.

Redio. Well, two gone, three more to go! Who'll be next now?

Sinsin. What do you mean, Oga Redio? You know of course that I'm next!

Redio. No, I think I'll go next, or ask Jigi. You lost your chance.

Sinsin. No! No! It's me, I insist. *(beginning to wail)* It's me next!

Redio. Come on, don't be childish . . .

Jigi. Let her go next, Oga Redio. I can wait; I'm not in a hurry.

Redio. Well, if you say so. But only because of you.

Jigi. Take the next man, Sinsin.

Sinsin. Of course, provided he's not a wretch like the last one!

Jigi. *(smiling)* Ah, Sinsin! Anyway, you're lucky! Look! The man coming looks like he owns the Central Bank! Take him; he's all yours!

(Enter a tall, richly dressed man, limping. He is also coughing badly at intervals. But his looks are fierce and arrogant.)

Man. *(with difficulty)* Good . . . day to you all!

Sinsin. Good day to you, sir.

Man. Tell me . . . young lady . . . is this the way to Ife?

(Baffled, Sinsin turns to Omele, who nods.)

Sinsin. Yes, sir. You're right.

Man. And the hospital? Can you direct me to the hospital?

Omele. He means the Specialist Hospital in the town. *(to the man)* Sorry sir, the hospital is closed.

Man. *(in alarm)* Closed! Since when?

Omele. For some months now. There was a riot there. Some policeman died, under treatment, and his colleagues came and stormed the place. So the doctors withdrew their services, pending an apology from the police. The place has been closed down since then, because the doctors won't work.

Man. Oh, God! Oh, God!

Omele. The government has ordered an inquiry, which is still going on. The hospital won't reopen till they submit their findings.

Man. *(hoarsely)* And when will that be?

Omele. Who knows? Maybe another couple of months . . .

Man. Months! I'll be dead by then!

Sinsin. Dead!

Man. Yes, alas! Look . . . *(He unbuttons his shirt. It is all splattered with blood. The musicians scream.)* It was fierce! Fierce! They must have pumped a hundred bullets inside me, the hounds! . . . But I still managed to escape, you see . . . thinking that if I got to the hospital here . . . They have a good reputation don't they, the doctors at the . . . ah, at the hospital . . . ? But now . . . *(He falls gradually, groaning.)*

Jigi. He's going to die! *(running to him)*

Sinsin. *(pushing her back)* No! He's mine, remember? I'll save him!

Redio. That's all right, Sinsin, but first, who's he? Let's find that out first! This talk about fighting and bullets . . .

Sinsin. It doesn't matter. I'll save his life if he's rich.

Man. *(on his knees, battling bravely)* Rich! What a joke! So . . . none of you . . . none of you knows me!

Sinsin. Talk quickly. Are you a rich man?

Man. *(laughing weakly)* It . . . must be a joke! Fate is . . . is . . . playing pranks on me, in my dying moments! To think that . . . that there's a place in this land where I am unknown, and imbeciles . . . imbeciles ask whether I am rich!

(The angry minstrels are held back by Sinsin.)

Sinsin. So speak! Are you rich or not? Your life hangs on it!

Man. Well . . . what does it matter anymore? Let me go like this then, unknown, among ignorant fools from some unknown planet. I have lived a life of fantasy, chasing adventures, daring death itself! I anchored my name to the winds, so that everywhere, whenever I touched down, I arrived like fear itself! Yes, when I found that men had made money their god, I conquered it! . . . You know how? With the blood of virgin children, the sperm of virile men, a pair of succulent breasts, such as yours . . . *(reaches toward Jigi, who slaps his hand)*

Jigi. Keep your hands off! I thought you were dying!

Sinsin. Sh! Let's hear him. Gently now . . .

Man. . . . Yes, bye bye! *(regretfully, to Jigi)* Breasts like yours, they could have fetched a fortune! But no more! *(laughs* *weakly)* I've reaped more than my share of the commerce in human seeds! Ah, yes, I made gold my servant, built a palace of gems . . . so well, now . . . *(His voice is now very feeble.)* . . . no matter. Adieu, fools! My candle has burned out . . .

Sinsin. Wait! You say you built a palace of gems! I'll save you!

Man. No, dear lady. It's too late.

Omele. Sinsin, didn't you hear him? How he made money? *(She is not listening to him.)*

Sinsin. Try! All you have to do is sing, and you'll recover! Don't laugh!

Man. *(laughing)* A miracle, eh? If anyone can save me now he can have all my wealth!

Sinsin. I won't forget that! Now, let's see you try. *(She goes to help him.)* Rise a little. Yes, hang on to me. That's it! Hang on! I'm going to sing now. And dance. No, don't shut your eyes yet! All you have to do is just sway along. No, Omele, don't help me, I'll manage. Don't give me your bad luck. Hang on, man, for God's sake! *(She begins to sing.)*

I Sing to End Your Pain *(led by Sinsin)*

1. *Sekere yeni ola*
   Sekere yeni owo
   Oloomi o ba dide o jo
      sekere o
   Sekere yeni ola o

1. *Sekere beats for the rich,*
   Sekere sounds just for kings;
   My sweetheart, it's for you
      gourds are rattling,
   Celebrating your wealth!

2. *Ikoko omo aiye le o*
   Erupe ponmi oro—

   Olojo oni ma ma je Ka
      mu nibe o
   Ikoko omi oro o!

2. *The pots of men can deceive;*
   You drink from them at your
      risk;
   May bad luck not descend
      upon us
   When we drink with our
      friends!

3. *Oro l'eiye ngbo*
   Oro ase iye
   Eiyekeiye gberu l'orule o

   Oro l'eiye ngbo o

3. *Bird of death in our sky;*
   We dance to drive you away;
   You will not alight on our
      rooftop;
   Bird of death, fly away!

4. *Arun l'orin nle lo o*	4. *I sing to end all your pain,*
Aisan l'orin nle	*My song commands your relief*
Ore mi tete jijo ajomole o	*My friend, dance along with abandon,*
Aisan l'orin nle lo!	*And that will cure your disease.*

(For a more dramatic effect, as discovered in the Ife production, Sinsin and her friends sing the English version first. At the end of it, the chorus of Esu followers do not disappear, but stand trembling like leaves, shaken by a silent laughter. The Wounded Man, who seems revived, rushes forward in joy toward Sinsin, only to collapse and die. There is general consternation. Wailing, Sinsin begins the Yoruba version of the song, like a dirge now, and the others gradually join in. The Esu chorus then dance away, as the Wounded Man finally recovers, carries Sinsin up, and dances with her.)

Man. *(setting her down finally)* Lady, what's your name?

Sinsin. They call me Sinsin.

Man. Sinsin! You saved my life! You actually did!

Sinsin. Yes, and you remember your promise?

Man. Of course, how could I forget! But we can settle all that tomorrow. Let me go and deal with those rascals first, or you may find you have nothing to receive! If I know them well, they'll be busy sharing my inheritance now among themselves! Let me go quickly! Tomorrow, let us meet here again!

Sinsin. Right, sir, but give me a token. Something to assure me you'll be back.

Man. I'll be back! I never break my word! *(He sees that his path has been blocked by Epo Oyinbo with his knife out.)* All right, take this anyway. It's my necklace, and it's got my insignia on it in diamond. I'll see you tomorrow! *(He runs out.)*

Sinsin. *(dancing)* I made it! Dance with me! I made it! I'm going to be rich!

(They crowd around her, hugging her happily. Then she starts the "Song of Rejoicing," which they pick up.)

The Song of Rejoicing (led by *Sinsin*)

1. *E wa ba mi jo*
     Ke gberin
   E wa ba mi yo
     Ke korin

2. *E wa ba mi jo*
     Ke korin
   E wa ba mi yo
     Ke gberin

3. *Mo royin nita*
   Mo riyo nita
   Keregbe mo fi bu lo le

   Solo: *Keregbe mo fi*
     bu lo o-ee
   Chorus: *Keregbe mo fi*
     bu lo le!

1. *Come and dance my friends*
     Sing my song
   Let your voices ring
     Like a bell

2. *Stand and dance, I say,*
     Sing my song
   Come rejoice with me,
     Ring my bell

3. *Where I found honey,*
   And discovered salt,
   I carried calabashes home.

   Solo: *I carried calabashes of*
     them
   Chorus: *I carried calabashes*
     home

(Dancing lustily, they do not notice the three businessmen who enter, apparently in a hurry, until one of them coughs. Three different accents of local speech—e.g., Hausa, Yoruba, Igbo— are suggested for these strangers.)

First Stranger. We're sorry to interrupt your celebration. But we need help urgently.
Redio. You need help! All three of you?
First Stranger. Yes, all of us. We're searching for a man. And if we don't find him by sundown, we hope to find death.
Jigi. Death! This is such a beautiful day!
Second Stranger. Not for us. A man has swindled us. And because of him, the new government has tied a noose around our throat.
Third Stranger. Don't bother them with our problem! Just go to the essentials.
First Stranger. Has any of you seen a short, yellow man, with side whiskers and mustache? He has greyed a bit at the temples . . .

(The Second Stranger takes a photograph around.)

Epo Oyinbo. No, no man with such a description passed by. And we've been here all morning.

Second Stranger. Then all is lost, my friends! Lost!

Third Stranger. Let's not waste more time. Better death than public disgrace!

First Stranger. Please, can you show us the way to the house of death?

Omele. Tell us first, what is the problem? We may be able to help.

Second Stranger. Thank you, but there's nothing you can do. The man we are searching for was our Manager.

Third Stranger. We own the Lagbaja Trading Company, you see!

Epo Oyinbo. *(whistling)* So you're the owners of LTC!

Redio. I'm sorry, Jigi, you'll have to wait. This is definitely going to be my case! *(Jigi tries to protest.)*
Quiet! *(pushes her back)* Please go on.

First Stranger. Six months ago, we were able to win the bid for an import license. To bring in two million bags of rice.

Sinsin. Two million bags!

First Stranger. A paltry number, my dear, considering what we paid out for the contract. And then our Manager vanished with the license! Can you believe that! No one has seen him since! Not even his family!

Third Stranger. Six months now! Six months since he disappeared! But we're probably boring them with our . . .

Redio. No, please, go on! I am interested!

Second Stranger. Well, the Manager disappeared. At that time, with the old government, it didn't seem to matter at all. They had all got their kickbacks and didn't care a hoot for rice. Even the Minister told us not to bother ourselves, to simply put in for another license. For fertilizers.

Jigi. Indeed! Just like that!

First Stranger. Yes, just like that. We did, and it was approved, through the same process.

Third Stranger. And then, the coup came, and with it, a new government! Go on with the story; make it brisk!

First Stranger. And the soldiers have said—Produce the fertilizers, and the rice, or return the money!

Second Stranger. Three hundred and fifty million!

First Stranger. Within seven days!

Second Stranger. Or pay the price!

Third Stranger. Friends, today is the seventh day!

First Stranger. And we haven't got the rice! Or the fertilizer!

Second Stranger. Or the license!

Third Stranger. And the Manager is still missing!

Redio. Well, is that all?

First Stranger. Yes, except that our wives and children, they've been taken away, to detention . . .

Second Stranger. Our passports have been seized . . .

Third Stranger. Our property confiscated . . .

Second Stranger. Our accounts frozen . . .

First Stranger. All our friends have fled . . .

Second Stranger. All our mistresses . . .

Third Stranger. And today is the seventh day!

Redio. I can help you!

First Stranger. I beg your pardon?

Redio. I can help you, I said.

Second Stranger. You know where he is, the Manager?

First Stranger. You know about the license!

Third Stranger. You have friends in the new government?

Redio. No, no. I don't know where the Manager or the license is. And I know no one in the cabinet. But still, I can help. You can recover your license!

First Stranger. When?

Third Stranger. How?

Redio. You can have it back right now!

Second Stranger. Impossible!

Redio. And you won't believe it, merely by dancing!

Third Stranger. Let's go. The man is mad.

Second Stranger. He's mocking us, the devil!

Third Stranger. Let's go. Quickly!

Redio. I am the last chance you have. Today, as you said, is your final day. You can try me, or go on to find your death.

Sinsin. He's offering you life! Your whole life back! Will you refuse?

Third Stranger. Can you imagine such frivolity, at a moment like this! To begin to . . . *(demonstrating a dance)*

First Stranger. Maybe, if he explains . . . ?

Redio. And I must have your solid promise first. You'll have to offer me some reward if I succeed.

First Stranger. Oh that's no problem. Ask for anything you want.

Second Stranger. Well, I suppose there's no harm in trying?

Redio. What will you give me, if I save your honor and your life?

Second Stranger. I have a newly built estate in Lagos. It has thirty-five flats. You can have it all.

First Stranger. I own the majority shares in the Magna Profit Bank. What does it yield now? Some few millions a year, after tax. I'll give it to you.

Redio. An estate and a bank! What lovely prizes! Omele, you see what it means, not to be in haste, to use one's head *(to the Third Stranger)* And you, sir, I'm waiting! What are you going to give me?

Third Stranger. Well, what do you want? I own the Imole Shipping Line. The biggest in the country, but I'm ready to forfeit it. Will you want that?

Redio. It's not bad—for a start. From anybody else, that would be quite substantial, I confess. But from you, sir, come, that's rather miserly!

Third Stranger. Okay, add the Wilson Associates. We sell furniture worth—er, how much now? Some millions a year. Take it, and tell us quickly how to recover the license!

Redio. Don't worry, it will come straight into your pockets. I am going to sing now with my friends. As we sing, you will dance along with us. As best as you can. Okay? It's as simple as that. Now come on! *(He sings and dances, with the three strangers copying his footsteps rather badly, their looks showing great scepticism. The Esu chorus appear and join the dance.)*

Na Money Rule de World *(led by Redio)*

1. Awon eniyan lo wa saye
   Taye dun mo won lara
   Sebi eniyan lo ngbaye
   Taye ro fun won jare
   Oba Naira, Iwo la nsin o
   Ma kehin si'gba wa o
   Wa pese s'oja ta wa

1. Some men we know today
   Belle dey sweet for dem
   Dem chop better so-tay
   Dem mouth na honey oh!
   God of Naira, we your worshipers
   Beg for your favors now
   Come to our stalls today!

2. *Awon miran wa saye*
   Won tosi lo ma ni
   Awon yen o je kogbon
   P'Owo, Oba osi ni

2. *Some others waste away*
   Dem die in misery!
   Dem never learn at all
   Na money rule de world!

3. *Iwo Esu lo wa saye*
   Pelu ogun orin kiko
   O si ti seleri
   Lori esun ibi kibi
   Awon meta wonyi,
      daakun o
   Ma kehin si'gba won o
   Wa f'ere soja ta won

3. *Esu, na you talk am*
   Say song be medicine,
   You tell us make we dance
   And play for all disease;
   Dis three people, we dey beg
      you oh,
   Ask for your helping hand,
   Carry their problems away!

4. *Awon ijoye lo nfole*
   Laye oni, se mo yen!
   Tori eniyan o nilari
   Bi ko le jale o.
   Tani o mo p'Owo lo laye
      Aje ni iranse re,
      Ofin ni!
      A si gbodo sa
      Ka bowo fun!

4. *The chiefs na dem be thiefs*
   Nowadays no be lie!
   For man wey be somebody
   He find money first to steal.

(Finally, touching his pockets, one of the three strangers exclaims.)

First Stranger. I feel something! There's something in my pocket!
Second Stranger. And me too!
Third Stranger. And me!

(They reach frantically inside their pockets and bring out documents.)

Third Stranger. By God, it's . . .
Strangers. The LICENSE!!
First Stranger. *(embracing them childishly)* It's true! It's the license! The license! We're saved!
Third Stranger. Yes! Hurry! We must beat the deadline! *(Redio runs to stop them.)*
Redio. And what of me? How do we settle our bargain?

Third Stranger. *(in a hurry)* Here, take my card. Call tomorrow in the office.

Redio. A card, after all I did! Do you think . . .

First Stranger. Have my wristwatch, as a token for now.

Redio. Now that's something!

Second Stranger. *(irritated)* Have my lighter and cigarette case. Gold, both of them, and inscribed. Just show them at the gate!

Third Stranger. He won't need to show anything. We ourselves will be back here, tomorrow. Then he'll see how we keep our promises! Meanwhile have this too, as a token. *(He gives him one of his coral beads.)* You say your name is . . . ?

Redio. Redio! That's what they call me, sir.

First Stranger. Right, Radio, or Television. It doesn't matter. We'll see you tomorrow! *(They hurry off.)*

Redio. *(dancing)* You see? You see! My friends, rejoice with me also! My fortune is made!

Epo Oyinbo. Congratulations! The ball we shall have after this, you and me!

Redio. You and who? Insult! With what's coming to me I can employ you as a houseboy!

Epo Oyinbo. Me, houseboy! What of Sinsin then?

Sinsin. Sinsin's going to be a billionairess, you just watch! And if I hear any nonsense from you then . . . *(They laugh.)*

Jigi. Poor Omele. How bad you must feel!

Omele. I won't be rich, I know. But perhaps . . . perhaps . . .

Jigi. Perhaps what?

Omele. Perhaps I can be happy . . . ? I know I will be happy!

Redio. Happy! What can be happy in: "Come here, boy! Have you swept the carpet this morning? The cars, you've washed them? And madam's dirty clothes? Yes? You've bathed the kids? What of the dog, have you taken it for a walk? And, God, all this dust on the furniture! Why do you think I'm paying you all that money? As soon as you take your pay tomorrow, you leave! You hear? You are sacked! Pack your load and leave the boys' quarters! Don't ask me where you're going, idiot! Go to hell if you wish! . . ." And so on! For you know, don't you, that that is the only future waiting for you?

Omele. Yes, but even amid it all, even as I pack my load, I'll remember and say: "One woman came to me in great pain, and she left smiling."

Epo Oyinbo. I don't know why you even bother yourself with him, Oga Redio. There's obviously a curse of poverty on his head!

Sinsin. Ah, tomorrow, when I collect! When I collect!

Redio. Hey, wait! I'm going after them!

Sinsin. I beg your pardon? After who, Oga Redio?

Redio. Those three businessmen.

Sinsin. Why? What's the need?

Epo Oyinbo. They'll be here tomorrow and . . .

Redio. Tomorrow! That's just it! I don't trust the words of the rich!

Sinsin. Well, there's nothing you can do about it now. You have to wait at least till Jigi gets her own chance.

Redio. Who says so? Does she need my mouth to sing her song?

Omele. Ah, Oga Redio! Are you the one saying this!

Redio. I've just thought of it. All this premature rejoicing! Suppose the men fail to turn up?

Epo Oyinbo. We have their tokens, don't we?

Redio. I see! You have their tokens! Wait for me! *(He goes out.)*

Sinsin. What! After him, Epo Oyinbo! We can't abandon Jigi like this!

Epo Oyinbo. Come with me, Omele! We'll force him back!

Omele. You wait here, Jigi. Something's gone wrong with the old man. But we'll not abandon you!

(They run out after Redio, leaving Jigi alone on stage. She goes to wait for them, withdrawing to one side of the stage, so that her back is turned when the next man enters. The man looks around furtively, then tiptoes to the road sign. He stops when he finds a rope, which he picks up and tests. This could be his trouser belt. He makes a noose quickly, to string it on one arm of the road sign. Putting the noose round his neck, however, he finds the rope short, even when he jumps. He searches around desperately for something to stand on. At that moment Jigi turns, and sees him.)

Jigi. What are you doing!

Man. Please . . . don't make a noise! Come and help me!

Jigi. Help you do what?

Man. Please, it'll take maybe a few seconds of your time. But you must help me! Just a brief ride . . . on your shoulder . . .

Jigi. Indeed. You think I don't know what you're trying to do!

Man. Please! It's a matter of honor.

Jigi. I won't be an accomplice, sir!

Man. Just a little ride, and then you can run from here!

Jigi. Hear him! My friend, I am a dancer, not a donkey!

Man. I'll make it worth your while.

Jigi. Besides, how am I sure I can hold your weight?

Man. You can, I assure you. I know about such things.

Jigi. You do!

Man. Yes, . . . I was born into it, you see! I've ridden on shoulders more fragile and more gaunt than yours. I am . . . er . . . I was a prince, you see . . .

Jigi. *(laughing)* Ah, Kabiyesi! Greetings, Your Majesty! But you'll have to find someone else to give you her shoulder!

Man. *(stern)* It's no laughing matter, young woman! I must kill myself before they get here!

Jigi. Who? Before who gets here? And why must you kill yourself?

Man. Will you . . . promise? Promise me! Say you will help me, if I explain to you.

Jigi. But of course! That's what I've been trying to make you see! I can help you. But not to hang yourself! I can help save your life.

Man. No! No! I don't want it! You'll have to promise to help me die. I cannot live in dishonor. The women will strip me naked, put hot ashes in my . . . hair . . .

Jigi. They adore you that much?

Man. Listen. They will burn my hair with ashes. Then they will lead me in a disgraceful procession back to the town. Through the open streets, while they beat me with their pestles and cooking spoons, and mock my dangling manhood! I will be the butt of every filthy urchin on the street! After which they will chain me and sell me off at the border! Do you hear? Slavery! That's the fate pursuing me hotly down here! Do you want me to face it, or will you help me simply to die?

Jigi. But why? Why would your people want to treat a prince like this?

Man. Barbaric, isn't it? A pagan custom. But no one in the town will listen to me! Not even the Christians and Muslims among us! When it comes to brutality, we are all united! We call it keeping our traditional customs! *(laughs bitterly)* But one day I said, no, no more! The past must end, so we can clear the way for the future! Why, other men elsewhere are sending astronauts to the moon! We too must march into the future! . . . So I seized the royal python, symbol of the whole decadence! I poured petrol on it! I set it on fire! And was I sorry for the poor thing, as it writhed to death! But, well, it died! Yes! The immortal serpent, whom they said could never die, I turned it into ashes.

Jigi. You mean you . . . you dared to . . .

Man. I wanted to free my people, liberate them from superstition. Just think of it! A mere snake! How can it be the harbinger of harvest? Why should adults, balls in their pants, consent to dance for it year after year, in the stupid belief that the ritual will bring rain? That a python can exercise power on the spirits of the soil, make them nurture seeds into exuberant crops? I turned it to ashes! . . .

Jigi. And . . . what happened?

Man. At the news . . . my father, at the news, died from shock! Yes! Just fell back and died! Only the priest, the old priest, was strong. He alone was stronger than me. He told the people: "He is Evil! He is the scourge foretold in our prophecies! You must kill him!" And you should see the people swaying to his words as he ranted!

Jigi. So what did you do? You ran?

Man. Not then. I tried to buy time. I had to say something, fast. I said—oh, I am ashamed to confess it. It was the only thing that came to my mind. I promised them a miracle! Another superstition. I told them the snake would resurrect, today!

Jigi. And they believed you?

Man. All, except the old priest. He was not fooled. His bread was at stake! But, well, my father was dead now, and I was already heir apparent. There was little he could do. He had to wait, like others. But he told them: "We'll see! If the day comes, and there is no miracle, you know what to do! The Prince must be treated as a carrier, as is the custom!" So that's the story, young woman. The day has come, with no miracle. I must die!

Jigi. Suppose I save you? Suppose the serpent resurrects?

Man. It can't! That was only a ruse I thought up.

Jigi. But suppose it does? You become the king, don't you?

Man. Yes, of course.

Jigi. And you'll have lands?

Man. I'll give them up! Back to the people, to whom they originally belonged!

Jigi. And jewels?

Man. Thousands of them in the palace collection! We were once a mining people, you see . . .

Jigi. What else will you inherit?

Man. Lots of other things. But I am not interested. They were all accumulated through exploitation.

Jigi. Will you give some of it to me?

Man. Why? What for?

Jigi. Because I am poor, and I want to be rich. I want to change from these rags into the best finery available! I want princes like you to see me, and be filled with lust! I want you to smell my scented breath, and swoon in the perfume of my mouth! I want to sing, and dance, and I wish to see powerful monarchs grovel as they watch! All the dreams that have followed me all my life, laughing at me, because I was poor, and they could not be fulfilled! Prince, will you give me your wealth, in exchange for your life?

Man. Wealth, that is immaterial. You can have all you want. But how will you give me back my life?

(*The other musicians return, holding on to an obviously displeased Redio.*)

Jigi. I'll resurrect the serpent for you. Look at my friends here. We're all musicians, and we've got some magic from some passing old man, a priest. Believe me, it works! All I have to do is sing and dance, and your serpent will come back to life!

Man. No, I don't want the serpent back. It will mean that those superstitions have won!

Jigi. Well, what then?

Man. Well . . . let me think . . . The priest, yes! The priest is leading the women down here! Without him, the rest are nothing. Kill him! Let him tumble and fall dead!

Jigi. That's easily done then. As you wish! Just come forward and dance with me as I sing! Come, my friends, this is Jigi's chance to rise from the gutter! Sing with me!

(They begin to sing and dance, accompanied by the unseen chorus of Esu's followers, as before.)

My Beads Are Jingling *(led by Jigi)*

Ise aje o	*Road of business*
Ona toro f'erin	*Opens wide for lions,*
Ise owo	*Road of money*
Ona fere f'ejo	*Narrows down for rabbits;*
Bi o se o	*If you walk it*
Owuro re a ro	*Pain will fill your morning,*
Bi we se o	*And if you don't*
Ale ojo a le	*Hardship for your evening;*
Owo baba Orisa	*Business, prime Orisa*
Aje, oko okunrin	*Money, husband of men!*
E maa pe Jigi—Jigi Aro!	*Announce my name—Jigi Aro!*
E maa mi jigi—jigi ileke	*And bend and ripple—to my rhythm*
Ileke sa so—sa so Oyinto	*My beads are jingling—like Oyinto*
Oyinto dara—o di wura	*Oyinto the maiden—a song of gold*
Wura a mi jigi—jigi ileke	*The gold of beauty—like singing beads*
Ileke Jigi—Jigi Aro!	*The beads of Jigi—Jigi Aro!*
Aro nro gboun—gboun bata	*A name like music, a call of drums,*
Bata olota—ota kongo	*When drums are throbbing, who can sleep?*
Kongo a dun keke— keke bula	*You dance in the blood, like fire,*

Bula a ke roro—bi ti soja	*The fire of battle, you pretty soldier,*
A ke roro titi—ebi gbode	*You eat our insides, like a hunger,*
Ode Eleko—ilu Owo!	*The hunger of Lagos, town of riches!*

(Suddenly there is a scream, from offstage, followed by the noise of wailing. The singing and dancing stop abruptly, and the chorus of dancers disappears.)

Man. What's that?

Sinsin. A scream! I heard it!

Jigi. *(smiling)* I think someone here has just lost an important enemy and is going to become king!

(The noise of keening women approaches. Then the townsmen arrive—this may be a large or small number, as is convenient for the Director. They fall on their faces before the Prince. Their spokesman speaks.)

Spokesman. Ka-a-a-bi-ye-siii! King-to-be! We've been sent as emissaries from the homeland. The people have asked us to tender their apologies and bring you back. We now know who the forces of evil were, and they're dead! You must come back to sit on the throne of your fathers!

Second Spokesman. We are sent with these—sandals, so your feet will always go forward henceforth on steps of ease.

(Each of these gestures is henceforth punctuated with a shout of "Ka-a-biyesi!")

Another. And this wrapper for your waist, as only splendor can robe you!

Another. This shawl, for your shoulders! Grace becomes them.

Another. Finally, this sparkling cap, for your royal head. Only the crown can henceforth displace it!

All. Ka-a-a-a-bi-ye-siiiii!!!

Spokesman. Come, your majesty! Now to lead you home!

Man. *(to the musicians)* Goodbye, my friends. At least for a while. You have helped me so much!

Jigi. And my reward, Prince?

Man. Sh!! Tomorrow, at the palace! Come and see me! Everything will be settled!

Jigi. And how shall I enter? Who'll show me in?

Man. Take this, my royal bangle. It's heavy, but you can carry
it. When they see you wearing it, they'll open the gate!

Jigi. Goodbye then. Until tomorrow!

*(The townspeople, singing the royal praise-songs, follow the
Prince out. Jigi dances.)*

Jigi. My friends, my friends, rejoice with me!

Sinsin. Jigi! So you too, you made it!

Epo Oyinbo. You've joined the league of the big spenders!

Redio. We'll all see tomorrow! Tomorrow, when we will say
goodbye to poverty forever!

Omele. *(pointing out suddenly)* Hey, look!

(They look and shrink back immediately.)

Epo Oyinbo. By God, they're not coming here!

Sinsin. Drive them away! Don't let them get near!

Jigi. How? How!

*(They run to one side, except for Omele, as two lepers enter.
Male and female, they are badly deformed and look hideous.
They stop, however, at a good distance, making no attempt to
go near the musicians.)*

Male Leper. Good day to you all.

*(There is a brief silence, when no one answers. Then Omele
steps forward.)*

Omele. Good day, children of the earth.

Male Leper. We know how you must feel, just to look at us.
We've seen ourselves in the mirror, and we see each other
every minute. But that's why we need help, my wife and I.
We've walked here from a far country, and hopefully, this
will be our last stopping point. And if we don't get help here,
we'll have to give up, for it will be too late anyhow. Can you
help us?

Omele. You need help! Oh God, it's too late! We've used all our
powers! Why didn't you come five minutes before?

Female Leper. We walked as fast as we could. But hunger, and the blisters on our feet, slowed our progress.

Male Leper. The help we need will be useless only after mid-day. So it can still be done, if you wish.

Omele. What do you mean?

Male Leper. Last season, the drought came, bringing a terrible wind. That was when the epidemic swept our land. At the height of the ravaging disease, one day, a priest came by. He said—"There's a way you all can be cured. If you can find a man bold and selfless enough."

Omele. Yes? What will the man do?

Male Leper. That's what I asked him exactly. And he replied; a simple but rather difficult thing. He will come forward and take you in his arms!

Sinsin. What! You hear that!

Male Leper. Those were his very words. "The man will embrace you, and thereby confirm to the gods that you're still one with the living, that your humanity is intact! That's all you need to be cured!"

Epo Oyinbo. You mean . . . you want someone to embrace you!

Redio. Not on your life, sir! Not for all the riches in the world.

Omele. How I wish you had come earlier!

Male Leper. It's a gamble I know. Is none of you brave enough, to step forward, in the name of humanity?

Sinsin. A gamble he calls it! It's a summons to suicide!

Epo Oyinbo. I'd rather drink a bucket of poison!

Male Leper. *(to his wife)* It's just as I feared, Lewa! Just as I feared!

Female Leper. Well, we must keep walking.

Male Leper. But to where?

Female Leper. Today is the last day he gave us, remember?

Male Leper. Well then, let's go quickly. We may still find someone, who knows?

Female Leper. *(desperately)* Friends . . . look at us! We were beautiful too, once, like you! We had ambitions, dreams . . .

Male Leper. Let's go, Lewa. They are healthy, young. They have their future before them! They cannot listen to such arguments . . .

Omele. Wait! *(He is visibly disturbed.)*

Jigi. *(apprehensive)* Let them go Omele! Why are you calling them back? You're not going to do something rash again?

Omele. I'm thinking—the Old Man, he gave us each this tremendous power. He said nothing about using it twice . . .

Sinsin. He did! He warned us not to even try!

Omele. Why not? Why not, if it's to help people like these?

Redio. Well go ahead. I'm tired of trying to talk sense into your brain. Go ahead, it's your own funeral!

Jigi. Omele, you're crazy!

Epo Oyinbo. I can even understand, if it's to try and repair the chance you bungled the first time. But, look, they haven't even told you that they have anything to offer.

Omele. It doesn't matter. I don't want anything. Come here, my dear people. I'll do it! I'll take the risk!

Jigi. I'm going! I don't want to witness this! *(She's nearly in tears.)*

Sinsin. And me too! I don't want to see it! I know what will happen.

Epo Oyinbo. We don't have to be back here anyway, till tomorrow.

Redio. That's right. Let's go.

Omele. You won't stay, to help me with the song?

Redio. Help yourself! Idiot! *(They go, Jigi sobbing.)*

Female Leper. Young man, maybe after all . . . maybe you shouldn't try. I'm afraid suddenly, afraid for you! Look at you. You're so young! We're older at least. We've known life, given birth to children, made something of our lives! Even if death comes now, it cannot come with too much regret. But you . . .

Male Leper. Yes, Lewa! You're right, he shouldn't do it!

Omele. It's my choice!

Male Leper. Yes, but it's our disease! Look, your friends have all fled. You're alone, and you're young. Leave us to our plight.

Omele. It's no use now. If I let you go, I'll never grow old. For I'll never know happiness again! I'll be thinking only of this single moment of cowardice, when I turned away some human beings in need. So come on. I'll do it, even though I'm trembling! I've used my chance up, Old Man, but I'm going to try again a second time! If your power was good, it should work always, wherever suffering is found! But we shall not know that, shall we, unless we take the risk! So you, sir, you first! Like this! *(He embraces the male leper.)* And you, dear lady, like this! I'll hold both of you together now while I sing and dance with you. See if you can sing with me! *(He holds them and begins to sing, slowly, till they join him in the singing. The Esu dancers do not appear for this song.)*

When Others Run *(led by Omele)*

Bo ba ya o ya	*If the time comes*
Bo ba je ewo	*When sympathy's wrong*
Iranlowo le pa ni	*And to help a friend can kill,*
Ka s'okunrin	*Cowards will run:*
Bo ba ya se	*If courage fails*
Bo ba je ese	*And tears are treason,*
Igba kan l'okunrin nlo	*Pity helps a man to stand*
Ka s'okunrin	*When others run:*
Omele ti rubo	*Omele takes the risk,*
Mo rubo nile Orin	*Dares to fight leprosy,*
Eru oje k'eniyan sere	*Fear never lets some men*
Fun eni to nwa're	*Feel compassion when they can.*
Onile Orita!	*Onile Orita!*
Ajantala Orun!	*Ajantala Orun!*
Esu ma tan mi o:	*Esu, weave your spell*
Adete o ye'ni	*Leprosy disappear!*
Se'wo lo fun wa l'agbara	*Invoke a magic remedy,*
Orin kiko:	*My melody,*
Eru o je k'eniyan se're	*Fear never lets some men*
Fun eni to nwa're	*Feel compassion when they can.*

(Soon, the changes begin. The limbs of the lepers begin to stretch out again, the spots disappear from their faces and skin; they begin, literally, to glow. They shout out joyously.)

Male Leper. Lewa! Lewa! Look at you!
Female Leper. *(incredulous)* Love, it's you! Your old self again! You're cured! *(Omele collapses in great pain.)*
Male Leper. We're cured! We're cured!

Female Leper. My dear young man—*(She runs forward, only to see Omele writhing on the ground. A transformation has also taken place in him: his limbs have retracted, and there are spots all over him. The woman screams, while her husband stands, trembling.)*

Male Leper. Lewa! What have we done?

Female Leper. *(sobbing)* He's got it, love! We've given him the disease!

Omele. *(in panic, his voice changed)* My God, I've got it! I've been marked! Help me!

Female Leper. *(shaken)* What have we done? There's no help we can give!

Male Leper. We've passed it to him! The priest tricked us!

Female Leper. We've ruined his life! We've ruined another man's life. Oh God, what shall we do?

(Omele stand up, hideously deformed. But he is calm now.)

Omele. It doesn't matter. I accept. Don't blame yourselves, it was my decision. What was I before now anyway? A corpse! So what does it matter? I remain a corpse. I accept . . .

(Blackout)

FOUR: HANGOVER

Same situation. Next morning. On one side, the four lucky singers, eating and drinking merrily, all finely dressed. On the other side, alone, the leprosy-infested Omele, driving flies off his body.

Epo Oyinbo. Yes, my friends! That's how I got the food. I walked up to her in the stall and said: Give me, on credit! And she looked up at me and said, yes sir! Without any argument, just like that!

Redio. Yes, incredible, isn't it, Epo Oyinbo? Money, even just the promise of it, gives you power! Walk, and everybody catches the smell of it! Dance, and the world tumbles down at your feet.

Sinsin. It was the same story at the clothes' store. *(She throws* *a bone across to Omele.)* Take that. *(Omele turns disdain-fully away from it.)* Yes, at the stores. They let us pick the clothes and dresses we wanted! All on credit!

Jigi. When my Prince comes this morning—ah, when the Prince arrives, I don't want him to find me still unkempt! So I went to the hairdresser's. I said, Go on, the Prince will be paying! And see, they turned me into a fairy queen!

Epo Oyinbo. I hope you're listening, Omele? We warned you, but you would not listen! You see now!

Omele. I'm not complaining.

Epo Oyinbo. No? You can have the leftovers. *(laughs)* Here, have this . . .

Jigi. No! Don't give him anything!

Epo Oyinbo. Why, Jigi? It's only a bone!

Jigi. He doesn't deserve anything! He made his choice. He wanted to stand alone. He didn't care for any of us. So don't give him anything! Let him also eat his own reward!

Sinsin. She's right! He doesn't deserve any pity! Always that holier-than-thou attitude! Let him pay for it!

Jigi. He doesn't even deserve to remain here! His presence alone infuriates me! He contaminates the air!

Redio. That's true, you know! Staying by him, any of us could get infected!

Sinsin. Good God, you're right! This vermin could ruin the rest of our lives, just as he's wrecked his own! We must drive him away!

Omele. But Sinsin! My friends . . .

Jigi. Shut up and go away! You have no friend here!

Omele. Jigi!

Epo Oyinbo. You heard her! What are you waiting for?

Omele. You can't drive me way. This is a public place. I have a right just like any of you, to . . .

Jigi. A right! Look at the leper talking of rights! Are you going to go, or do you want us to treat you the way lepers are treated?

Sinsin. Torches! Let's burn him out! *(They rush to find matches and dry sticks.)*

Epo Oyinbo. No, that will only bring the government down on our back. But stones! Use stones to drive him away! *(picks up a stone and throws it at Omele)* Go!

Omele. *(hit)* Epo Oyinbo! It's me!
Epo Oyinbo. Go away, leper!

(The others also pick up stones and begin to throw them at Omele, shouting for him to go away. He calls them one by one, in pain as he is hit, but the rain of stones only increases. He falls down and begins the "Song of Tomorrow," to which the other musicians reply in antiphony.)

The Song of Tomorrow *(led by Omele)*

Omele.

1. Remember tomorrow,
   For evil will sprout,
   And like seedlings grow,
   Your deeds will come out.

2. You'll pay back with pain
   When you cause people sorrow
   But you'll reap the gain
   From the good you sow.

Others.

   In vain we talked to you,
   You shunned all our warnings,
   Whoever calls Sango,
   Sango, Oba Koso o,
   Sango, voice of thunder,
   Brings him home for lunch.
   If lightning wrecks your house,
   You cannot complain.

Omele.

3. You hassle for glamour,
   For material gains,
   But money does not endure,
   Friendship remains,

4. To others be kind,
   And think of tomorrow,
   The actions of humankind
   Bear fruits to show.

Others.
> In vain we talked to you,
> You shunned all our warnings,
> Whoever calls Sango,
> Sango, King of Koso,
> Wears rainstorms for clothing,
> Brings him to your farm,
> And floods destroy your crops,
> You cannot complain!

(Omele falls down, the stones rain on him again. Finally he turns and runs. The other minstrels return laughing to their feasting.)

Jigi. Good riddance to bad rubbish!

Redio. Yes! His sight would have driven back my business tycoons! Just imagine that!

Jigi. Now, my Prince can come! Ah, even if he doesn't pay any more! If he merely twists his finger, and says, Come along! What happiness! What a promise of luxury!

Redio. It's the only song people like us live our lives for, the song of wealth! Otherwise, when we reach the crossroads at last, at a place like this—we may choose the wrong direction. But, Edumare, you created this jungle we live in, and you made some animals with teeth. Don't forget us, listen to our song!

(They begin the "Song of the Jungle.")

Song of the Jungle *(led by Redio)*

1. Obangiji o, oba to laje,

   Feti sebe mi:
   Kiniun l'oba, gbogbo
     aginju
   Nitori ehin
   Iwo lo ma fun, Edumare
     O!

2. Aje wu'niyan, ise aje pe

   Nitori owo

1. Obangiji o, the owner of
     wealth,
   Listen to my plea:
   The lion it is, who rules the
     jungle
   Because he can kill:
   You gave him his teeth, Edu-
     mare O!

2. We cheat and scramble, be-
     cause business pays,
   Money in the bank,

Nitori afe, aiye to l'ero,

Nitori aje,
Iwo le se o, Edumare O!

Money in the hand, and a life
  of ease,
Lots of luxury
Make me rich today-o, Edumare o!

3. *Ko fun mi l'ehin, to mu*
     sasa
   Feti sebe mi
   Se mi n'kiniun, l'oja
     araye
   Nitori aje
   Iwo le se o, Edumare o!

3. Give me teeth, I pray, sharper
     than the blade,
   For this is my plea:
   Make me the lion, in the busi-
     ness world,
   With the power to kill,
   Make me rich today-o, Edu-
     mare o!

4. *Tantara!*
   Oro aje ni!—Tantara!

   O wu ni'yan—Tantara!
   Ise aje dun o Tantara!

   Aiye afe ni—Tantara!

   O wu ni'yan—Tantara!
   Aiye afe dun o Tantara!

4. Tantara!
   Money will be mine!—Tan-
     tara!
   World of luxury—Tantara!
   O what a golden dream—
     Tantara!
   Comforts will be mine—
     Tantara!
   World of fantasy—Tantara!
   O what a lovely dream—
     Tantara!

(But suddenly, in counter-chorus, Esu's theme song rises, as the Old Man and his followers, hooded, arrive. The musicians give them a rousing welcome.)

Old Man. *(smiling)* Good day, my children, I am glad to see you all gay and happy like this. That means you made good for yourselves!

Redio. Indeed we have, Old Man! The charm you gave us, it worked wonderfully! In a few hours, if you wait long enough, all the people we helped will be arriving here to repay their debts!

Old Man. I am glad to hear that! How you must all have helped to reduce suffering in the world!

Epo Oyinbo. The important thing is—because I hate beating about the bush—the important thing is that we have reduced suffering for ourselves! No more hunger and no more wandering for us! Finished, the vagabond life. We've planted our feet down firmly in fortune!

Old Man. Good! Where's your other comrade?

Sinsin. Gone, Old Man.

Old Man. To where?

Jigi. He alone, he wasted your power! He's always been foolish and pig-headed. As if an eternal curse followed him, never to let him make good! You see, with your power, he did not pick up prosperity, like us! He picked up leprosy!

Old Man. Leprosy! How? . . .

Epo Oyinbo. First, he wasted his power on a pauper. A woman with no money or means. And then, he tried again, a second time. Yes, despite your warning, he tried to use your power a second time!

Old Man. So where is he?

Redio. We drove him away, to avoid contamination. Because . . . *(enter Omele)*

Omele. Because of your greed! But I'm here. Here also to give account!

Jigi. Is that what brought you back, you shameless man?

Omele. Everywhere I went, they drove me away. So I returned here. Old Man, punish me. I have not grown wealthy like the others.

Old Man. All is set then! The hour has come for your reward, all of you. *(to his followers)* Reveal yourselves, my children. *(The hoods fall off, one by one, to reveal the same characters who had been helped by the musicians, all except the pregnant woman and the lepers. The musicians jump with shock.)*

Old Man. Look at them well. Don't say you don't recognize them?

Redio. But . . . but . . . *(Jigi runs forward in ecstasy.)*

Jigi. Prince! I know you're an adventurer! Still, what a spectacular manner this is of making a reappearance! *(The Prince laughs.)* Well, the Old Man is a magician, although you probably know that already, since I see you're friends. He was the one who gave me the power I used for you, to save you from that priest. Thank you for coming back to settle acc . . .

Prince. Woman! What are you talking about? Saved me! From what priest?

Jigi. Prince! Yesterday! Here, in this very place, when you . . .

Prince. Quiet woman! And move back! How you smell! Old Man, this is extraordinary! Is this why you asked me here, to talk with commoners like this?

Jigi. *(bursting into tears)* It's not possible! Prince, my beloved! This, this is your bangle . . .

Prince. Where did you steal it from?

Jigi. Oh God! Why are you . . . ?

Old Man. Stand back! Give way to the next person!

Redio. I come next, and I make my claim with these items. A wristwatch, a lighter, and a cigarette case. They belong to him, and him, and him. They gave me these yesterday, when I helped them retrieve a license. I know they are rich and generous and will reward me well, as they promised. So go ahead, Old Man, ask them. *(The strangers laugh.)*

First Stranger. Really! Where did these people get their fanciful dreams?

Second Stranger. Who did you help retrieve a license, my dear fellow?

Redio. You, of course! Yesterday!

Third Stranger. Was that when you woke up from your nightmare?

Redio. Please . . . please! You can't do this to me! These are your tokens!

Second Stranger. *(laughing)* Ours, those tinsels!

First Stranger. Old Man, this is past a joke! Why force us to come here to listen to riff-raff?

Redio. No! Old Man, I swear . . .

Old Man. Enough! Stand back! I warned you! I told you to choose well, and you all made your choice. So what about you, my dear? *(to Sinsin)* Are you ready to make your claim?

Sinsin. I don't know . . . I don't know any more . . . It all happened here, before our eyes. But now they're all lying, denying! So, I don't know. But he was here, all covered in blood. He was dying. Yes, you! You were wounded, and I saved you! You promised me half of your wealth!

Man. Indeed! Why would I do such a reckless thing?

Sinsin. But see! This is your necklace! The one you gave me for—

Man. Keep it, if indeed it's mine. Whatever next!

Old Man. Stand back then, woman! You—why are you drawing a knife?

Prince. Bandits! Old Man, you've brought us among bandits!

Epo Oyinbo. I'm not a bandit, but no one's going to trifle with me and get away with it! I've lived in prison before, and I'm willing to be hanged. But sir . . . yes, you! *(to the former Impotent Man)* You sir, say a word amiss! Say I didn't help you, one wrong word, and we'll both go to hell!

Man. Old Man, do something! The man is dangerous!

Old Man. This is childish! Put the knife away!

Epo Oyinbo. I want him to talk! He came here! He didn't have children. He couldn't even get it up! And I cured him! Yes, with your power, Old Man! I cured him!

Man. What vulgarity! But if you wish to know, I have forty-something wives in my harem! Children by the dozens! Grandchildren too numerous to count! They couldn't all have been born yesterday? So what are you saying, my dear fellow?

Epo Oyinbo. *(thundering)* . . . I've been cheated! He's lying! And by Sango, I'll . . . *(He lunges forward, but the Old Man stops him, with a gesture. Transfixed, he replies henceforth like a robot.)*

Old Man. Naughty boy. Go and throw that toy away! *(He does so mechanically.)* And don't let me see you repeat that foolishness again, or you'll be punished! Move back. Now, for the last man . . .

Omele. That's me, Old Man, but it's no use. I know I helped a woman, who is not here now. But even if she was, it would not change a thing, for she has nothing, and I asked for nothing. I was glad merely to see that she was happy. So I make no claim for myself. I too, I wasted your power. Instead of getting rich, I caught a disease. Punish me along with the rest.

Old Man. They tell me you were greedy. That you tried to use the power twice.

Omele. Yes, I confess. I tried a second time, but not out of greed. The people who came were really desperate, and I made them happy. I have no regrets.

Old Man. Where are they now? Will they be ready to give witness?

Omele. Who knows? Leave them alone. Let them enjoy their happiness.

Old Man. Well, I'll summon the woman at least . . .

Omele. No! *(But it's too late. The Old Man has already gestured toward the wings. Sound of a woman answering as if to a call. She enters, with her baby strapped to her back.)*

Woman. *(entering)* I heard my name and . . . *(sees Omele)* Oh God! Whatever happened to you!

Omele. *(evasive)* Congratulations! You've had your baby!

Woman. *(near tears)* Come with me! We'll find a doctor!

Old Man. You know him, woman?

Woman. *(angry)* No, I don't know him! *(hisses)* One of you, one of you here probably did this to him. And I swear the person is going to pay for it!

Old Man. But who are you? And where do you come from? You're not one of my followers . . .

Woman. And who would want to follow such an evil-looking man like you? Please . . .

Old Man. *(shouting)* You were not sent by Orunmila?

Woman. If you don't mind, you old man, I have no time for idle questions. *(to Omele)* Come, *jare* . . .

Old Man. All right, please don't be angry, woman. It's just that I don't know where or how you entered the game. And I should know, since I laid the rules.

Woman. But which game are you talking about? Listen if . . .

Old Man. All right, forget it. Just the suspicions of an old man, perhaps. But tell me now . . . why? Why are you sticking up for this man like this?

Woman. Because he saved me! Nine years, the child was inside me! And then he . . .

Epo Oyinbo. *(quickly stepping in)* It's a lie!

Woman. No! You, you were even singing and . . .

Epo Oyinbo. It's a lie! A conspiracy between you two! Isn't it, you fellows?

Jigi. It is! You're lying!

Woman. But . . .

Sinsin. Yes! It's a lie! A filthy lie!

Epo Oyinbo. Go away!

Redio. Get out of here, at once! Liar!

Woman. *(overwhelmed)* But . . . but . . .

Minstrels. Get out!! Go away!! Get lost!! Bitch!! *(They scream at her, frightening her, till she runs out sobbing.)*

Epo Oyinbo. Forget all about her, Old Man! They hatched the clever plot together, but it won't work. You've got to punish all of us together!

Jigi. Yes, let's all be punished!

Old Man. That was your witness, Omele. She's fled!

Omele. Yes, I know. They chased her away.

Old Man. So, what are you going to do?

Omele. Nothing. What shall I do against them? They were once my comrades. They taught me all I know. How to sing, and lie, and fight. Shall I turn all that against them? I am part of them.

Old Man. Do something at least. Put up a fight for yourself . . .

Omele. No. Not against them. *(enter the former lepers, now looking very healthy, although worried)*

Female Leper. Ah, there he is!

Male Leper. Young man, where have you been?

Omele. I . . . I didn't expect to see you back here!

Female Leper. We've been searching for you all over the place!

Old Man. Who are you?

Female Leper. *(sharply)* Please keep out of this, whoever you are! We are in a hurry.

Male Leper. We went and met the priest again. And he said we can take our disease back. Provided we embrace you again before noon. So, come . . .

Omele. No! Stand back!

Female Leper. *(surprised)* But what's wrong with him?

Omele. You've been cured. Stay cured!

Male Leper. Nonsense! Isn't it our disease?

Female Leper. We want it back!

Omele. Stay away from me! *(a short play, while they advance and he retreats)*

Male Leper. But be reasonable! Old Man, are you a friend of his?

Old Man. In a way, yes.

Male Leper. Well, judge for us. This man, to help us, did an extraordinary thing. He didn't know us; we had never even met before. But he saw us in our anguish, covered all over in leprous spots, and he had the courage to embrace us! Yes, he embraced us, and we were cured at once! Just as our priest had foretold, his embrace cured us of the dreadful disease! But alas, we could not rejoice for long. No! For he himself had become infected in the process!

Female Leper. So we ran back to seek the priest again. And we told him: No, Baba! We don't like the bargain! We'd rather take our disease back and let the young man go free! So that's why we have returned here. All we need, said the priest, is to embrace him again and he will return to what he was, in his sparkling health!

Omele. No! Let things stay as they are! *(another short chase)*

Old Man. I don't understand! How can you keep someone else's disease, if the owner wants it back?

Omele. Because it doesn't matter to me. I have only one life, and it's not worth much. I've always lived in want, as a vagabond. Oh yes, my life itself has been like a leprosy. So I am used to it, I can live like this for the rest of my wretched life. But look at them, aren't they handsome as they are? They have a name, a career; they have kids. They have money in the bank, an insurance policy no doubt. Their life is a hymn to the future. Society needs them, not dregs like me. I'll keep the disease!

Male and Female Lepers. We refuse!!!

Male Leper. Every life is as precious as the other. Including yours. It's not for you to give a value to any human life!

Old Man. I know what to do, but I think I need some advice first before I act. Who'll advise me? *(The minstrels eagerly volunteer.)* You, I don't trust. You've been caught in the mischief of my followers, and I can see you're hungry for vengeance! No. You'll wait there till I decide your punishment. So who will advise me?

Male Leper. *(exasperated, steps forward)* Look here, Esu! This is enough! You know what you have to do! Or why else do you think we came here?

Old Man. You? Who are you?

Male Leper. *(smiles, to the Female Leper)* My dear, how terrible you can be, even to a god! See, you've wrapped his mind so completely in your cobweb!

Female Leper. *(smiling)* Well, you know that when you play with the master trickster himself, you have to be ruthless. I put his mind in a season of drought, and Edumare obliged. But he can go now. *(gestures)* Winds, unfreeze! Roots, resume your growing!

Old Man. That voice! Those words! I've heard them before!

Male Leper. Close your eyes, Esu. Look deeply, where the gods look. Look below the surface.

Old Man. *(does so, recoils)* No, not you! Not you again, Orunmila! And . . . *(turns to Lewa)*

Female Leper. *(smiling)* Yes, its me, Esu. You forgot, didn't you, that even the cleverest fox can still be fooled.

Old Man. *(angry)* I see. I see now, Yeye Osun! Both of you, you sent that woman with the baby here.

Female Leper. You hatched your clever plot, Esu, as usual. And as usual, I am using it to retrieve my children.

Old Man. And to frustrate me, of course! All right, both of you! You think you've won, but I still have a last card. I'm going to throw the question to the audience and let their fellow human beings decide! *(to the audience)* You! Don't just sit there and let an injustice be done. Say something! Should Omele return the disease, or should he keep it? Speak up, we need your answers to decide! Yes, you sir? And you, madam! . . .

(A debate is now encouraged among members of the audience, while the actors freeze on stage. The lights come half down. The Old Man finally calls for a vote between the Aye's and the No's.)

Old Man. Again, please? Let's here the aye's, those who want the disease returned! Okay now, the no's! Well, I'm sorry—maybe my ears are failing—but no side has won! *(The Male Leper tries to intervene.)* No need, Orunmila, I know what you want. As well as the goddess Osun, by your side. These tricks you play on behalf of humanity! It's called cheating!

Male Leper. Decide quickly, now. It's not just what we want, but what you must do. You know you have no choice.

Old Man. *(sighs)* Yes. Let's end the play then, old spoilsport. And yet so much fun still to be had! Well, as you like it! Let the disease go to those who have won it, those who seek to be rich without labor. Who have put their selfish greed first before everything, including their humanity! I mean you, my dear fellows! Take your reward! *(The minstrels cringe in terror.)* Obaluaye, it's your turn now! They're yours!

(Obaluaye, the god of smallpox, detaches himself with a terrifying laughter from the retinue, and comes forward as his praise-song rises. The transformations begin: with Omele being cured, and his comrades writhing in agony as they are caught by the dreadful god, and are gradually covered in spots. Obaluaye finally leads them out in a dance.)

Old Man. Come, Orunmila, and you, mother of fertility. You know I am not unkind. We've all played the game. And now, it is time to reward the only man we have found truly worthy to be called a human being! Salute!

(Omele is led in, again, now decorated with cowrie beads. The once-pregnant woman holds him by the hand.)

Male Leper. *(as Orunmila, steps forward)*
    My son, this is no time for speeches,
    And I shall spare you one.
    Esu Laaroye, lord of the crossroads,
    Trickster, he set you a test, to see
    Whether between compassion and greed,
    You would know the road to take;
    Between hollow material wealth,
    So ephemeral,
    And the unseen riches of tenderness,
    You alone passed the test, you alone
    Pitied the woman we sent along
    Even in spite of her wretchedness
    So we said, let's test him again,
    Just to be sure, and we came down ourselves.

Me and Yeye Osun, disguised in
The frightful skin of Obaluaye, as lepers.
But again you did not let us down!
Again, you let your humanity
Yield to unusual compassion. Salute,
My friend! So, let's bring the play
To an end here. Let the parable
Come to a close. Let the gods disappear,
As we must, to where we came from,
In a fairy tale. The rest is for our audience
To learn from your example
For every man . . .

(The other minstrels, half undressed, burst in, and join, raucously, in completing the sentence.)

. . . has a lamp in his hand,
Waiting to be lit!

(The other actors onstage watch, in astonishment.)

Redio. *(in great laughter)*
"Every man carries the key . . ."
Jigi. *(same game)*
". . . To a door of happiness!"
Epo Oyinbo. *(to Orunmila)* Go on! Complete your speech!
Male Leper. But . . . what happened? I thought we just got rid of you?
Redio. Not tonight, my friend. Not again. Today the play's going to end differently.
Old Man. Indeed! And have you told the author about it!
Sinsin. Let him watch, like everybody else. But we're tired of taking part in deceit.
Female Leper. What do you mean? Where's Obaluaye?
Obaluaye. *(appearing)* Here. I am on their side. Let the audience know the truth.
Old Man. Which truth? Where has it ever happened before, that the characters in a play rewrite the script?
Male Leper. *(appealing)* Please, go back into the wings, and die as you've been doing before. Let's end the play.
Redio. That's the easiest way out, we know. But it's a lie.

There's just no miraculous answer to life's disasters. Even a play must face the truth.

Female Leper. For whom are you speaking?

Jigi. For ourselves, both as actors and as citizens.

Epo Oyinbo. There's no magic to the riddle of evil.

Sinsin. Kindness cannot be willed by the waving of a wand.

Redio. No incantations can cure the anguish caused by the greed of politicians.

Jigi. And prayers are not sufficient to counter the violence in the street.

(Some of the actors begin to gather from the wings.)

Epo Oyinbo. Neither prayers nor good wishes.

Redio. But only the actions of struggling men . . .

Epo Oyinbo. Only many fists, waving together . . .

Redio. For only the muscles behind a wheel can turn it.

Jigi. Only many voices rising together, to shout "NO!" this moment . . .

Sinsin. "YES!" another moment . . .

Epo Oyinbo. And "LET US MARCH!" all the moments . . .

Redio. And "LET US BUILD, FOR WE CAN BUILD!"

Minstrels. "FOR WE CAN BUILD!"

Jigi. Only such determined voices can change the course of history . . .

Sinsin. And bring the true compassion that people need.

Jigi. And bring the compassion that really endures.

Obaluaye. So, tell the audience, that I, Obaluaye, I do not exist . . . *(as he removes his costumes)*

Sinsin. *(doing the same)* The story you heard does not exist . . .

Jigi. And I, I do not . . .

Male Leper. Enough! Thank you! *(claps)* Fools!

Epo Oyinbo. What . . . !

Male Leper.
If only you'd waited for our last song!
Now the joke's on you. For, clearly,
You've missed the difference between reality
And its many mirrors. All of us,
What else are we, but metaphors in a
Fading tale? Just the props of a parable,

The drums on which the message is beaten.
But it is time to go. Call the others in the wings.
Let us end the play with our final song
As the author wants it. And remember,
Sing only as farmers plant seeds:
Sing well, And—please remove your costumes
And masks. Bring back the house lights!
Let us restore the audience back to reality.
Okay—are we set! After three!
One! Two! Three!

*(The actors, who have gathered round him in their own clothes,
as he requested, begin to sing the song "Esu Does Not Exist.")*

Esu Does Not Exist *(led by Orunmila)*

1. *HERE HE STANDS our dear friends*
   And as our story ends
   The man we call the hero
   He will now take a bow:
   All we have tried to say
   Through this gay storytelling
   Is that compassion pays
   Kindness has its own reward;
   Life's not all buying, selling,
   Cheating, amassing wealth;
   And greed is the way to death:
   God is one loving word!

2. *AND SO WE END our show*
   And we are about to go
   But don't take our story light
   Like some tale on moonlit night:
   All this magic we've shown
   All this miracle of healing
   They're devices that you've known,
   Spices to our narration—
   But though it's fascinating
   Till your mind can't resist,
   Esu does not exist
   Save in your imagination!

3. *ESU DOES NOT exist*
   And if evil does persist
   We must each search our soul
   What we've set ourselves as goal:
   If wealth is all we seek
   And don't care what means we're using,
   If our ways seem so sleek
   When we keep strange rendez-vous,
   One day we'll come to reason
   At some Sepeteri
   Where Esu—or History—
   Waits in ambush with his noose!

(The actors join the audience. The theatre empties. Life resumes.)

BIRTHDAYS ARE NOT FOR DYING

CHARACTERS

Mother
Kunle Aremo
Bosede Aremo, his wife
Chief Samuel Seminiyi, his father-in-law
Retired Major Peter Ajala
Councillor Lekan Bamgbade
Honourable O. O. Fakunle
Alhaji Nassir Kofoworola

The bedroom of Kunle Aremo. Fairly big and carpeted. Well furnished with a settee, armchairs, drinks trolley, a working table somewhat in disarray.

Kunle is seen before a standing mirror, combing his hair. He is in shirt and trousers, with socks only. In the course of the following scene, he will gradually dress up, choose a tie and put it on, put on a pair of shoes, and choose a coat.

The door opens, and his mother enters, pauses and knocks. He turns and sees her. Her face is solemn.

Mother. May I come in?

Kunle. Of course, mama. What's all that formality for?

Mother. *(shutting the door slightly behind her as she comes in)* Well, does one know with you anymore nowadays?

Kunle. You were in already, anyway. Ah, my head! *(crosses over to a drawer; brings out tablets)*

Mother. That headache again?

Kunle. Yes. I see you're all ready for the party.

Mother. I want to talk to you.

Kunle. Look at you. Just look at you! I hope some young man won't snatch you away tonight!

Mother. You and your sweet mouth! How old do you think I am!

Kunle. Whatever the case, you're not old enough to marry! As the current head of this family, I withhold my permission till you're eighteen!

Mother. Stop joking now and be serious. We must talk.

Kunle. *(takes flask and pours out water; swallows tablets)* Go on. Sometimes it's like my head is on fire!

Mother. My poor son. It's all these responsibilities, all of a sudden. You're not used to them.

Kunle. I'm learning.

Mother. But why not see a doctor, Kunle? Why do you keep dodging?

Kunle. I'm not dodging.

Mother. I can't understand. You have a choice of doctors. Our family doctor. Or the company's. I've called both of them, and they're only too willing to come. But they say you won't see them.

Kunle. I've been busy.

Mother. Too busy to take care of yourself?

Kunle. Later, mama, later. Maybe after my birthday party tonight.

Mother. Or maybe tomorrow. Maybe next week.

Kunle. *(grinning)* Maybe next week.

Mother. You think it's a joke, don't you?

Kunle. Don't worry, mama. I promise you, I won't die today. At least not till the party's over. Birthdays are not for dying!

Mother. You're frightened, that's all. You've always been frightened of doctors. Ever since you were as small as this. *(demonstrates)* I just hope your son won't be like that. I know he doesn't look like you, but who knows. His character may turn out to be like yours.

Kunle. His mother won't like that.

Mother. Will I blame her? You know, I once told Bose all about it.

Kunle. About what?

Mother. About you and that episode at the clinic. How we laughed and laughed! I think you were five years old at the time. Yes, five. I remember, it was a rainy day. You were very ill, and we took you to the clinic. The doctor prescribed an injection. The nurse had just cleaned your bottom for the injection when suddenly, a toad, a very big toad, jumped in through the window. You screamed, and . . . *(She looks up at his cry: he has half collapsed on the bed, gasping and clutch-*

ing his head. She rushes to him.) Kunle! Kunle! What's the matter?

Kunle. *(recovers gradually; brushes her hand off rather brusquely and goes to pour himself a drink from the trolley)* Ah!

Mother. *(in plain distress)* I'm sorry. I'm really sorry. It was . . . a childhood nightmare. I thought you'd forgotten, adjusted to it.

Kunle. Never again, mama. Don't bring up that scene again. Not even in jest. Now what's brought you here?

Mother. I want to talk to you.

Kunle. About what?

Mother. About . . . well, about other kinds of toads.

Kunle. Again! Mama, I—

Mother. Are you going to listen to me!

Kunle. Well, go on.

Mother. The Company lawyer, Mr. Jegede. I met him downstairs just now, as he was leaving your room.

Kunle. Yes?

Mother. He told me.

Kunle. *(angrily)* He told you what?

Mother. He told me everything.

Kunle. He's playing with his job! He's not supposed to be opening his mouth carelessly before every Tom, Dick, or Harry.

Mother. And is that what I've now become? Tom, Dick, and Harry?

Kunle. My discussions with him were strictly official! And confidential!

Mother. You're still my son. And your father, God bless his soul and preserve his memory, your father, who built up the Company, he was my husband.

Kunle. And you read his will.

Mother. Yes, I read his will. Unfortunately, he did not consult me before he made it.

Kunle. I know you didn't like it.

Mother. Of course, women don't mean much to you men. We're only good to nurse you, feed you, and wash your clothes. Never to be trusted. One would have thought that after so many years together, after so many things we've been through, side by side, he would come and seek my opinion on such a delicate thing. After all, it's my son too. But not him! And he's gone now, God rest his soul. All the same, I am saying that—

Kunle. Mother, if you've seen the lawyer, then you know I have an important meeting before the party starts. And I am the host; I shouldn't be late.

Mother. You're as pig-headed as your father! He too, he never listened to me, and they met him suddenly on the crest of his life's journey, just as I warned they would, and they stopped him dead—

Kunle. Mama, father died of a peptic ulcer. You read the medical reports—

Mother. Thank you. Thank you, Mr. Peptic Ulcer! When you meet your own share of it at the meeting you're attending tonight, it will be me, Bose, and Segun, your poor son, who'll be carrying the coffin. *(crying)* I supposed it's my fate. That all of my last days on earth should be filled with wailing. How I wish I could die, and rest from all this!

Kunle. *(clutching at his head)* God! You're making my headache worse! Worse! *(goes and pours another drink)* And I need all my senses now, all my nerves together, to face them. Is this how a mother is supposed to help her son?

Mother. They'll get you, I'm telling you. They're bastards, and they'll get you. They've always grinned at you till now. They've patted your head with fondness and shaken your hand and made jokes. They were all there at your wedding, gay and generous. They've always been nice. Some of them never come without bringing presents, expensive presents. That was all right. It was all a game. You were only the son of the Company Chairman. You were heir apparent, but as long as you were not of age, and were not on the Board, you posed no threat to them. They could fondle you and play with you as they played with toys. But I've known these men all my life. I was there when your father was putting the Company together. You're simply no match for them. For as soon as they learn of your decision tonight, everything will change. They'll come out in their true colors, loathsome and vile. And they'll get you—

Kunle. *(laughing)* One would think you were their paid agent!

Mother. Give up the Company, Kunle. Believe me, I know what I am saying. Sell off your shares to them.

Kunle. And disobey my father?

Mother. Your life, Kunle! That's all that matters to me. You're already more than rich, by any average standard. We have invested money for you. Bought you buildings and land both here and abroad. Your signature alone is worth thousands. You don't need the Company.

Kunle. Because you don't understand! Because you think it's only the money!

Mother. What else! What else could there be?

Kunle. My father wrote a will. At the age of thirty, his only son is to succeed him and take over the Company he spent all his life building. These were his wishes. He must have had a reason.

Mother. What reason? A dying man's unthinking gesture?

Kunle. Mother, I am thirty today!

Mother. You're thirty, and too young to die.

Kunle. I think my father knew me more than you do.

Mother. He did not think. He was too weak. But in life, acts of love, made in an unthinking moment, can be just like a death warrant.

Kunle. Mama, I am not saying I disbelieve you. But I am certain that my father was fully in his senses when he made his will. I've read his diary. It is not precise, but I think I know what he wants.

Mother. And what is that?

Kunle. That I should avenge him.

Mother. I knew it! Vengeance! He had planned your death for you! He sent you against them, and he knew you could not cope. That you're no match for them.

Kunle. How do you know?

Mother. You're my son. You ripened in my belly.

Kunle. But do you know me?

Mother. Give up. This is not your world. You're not like your father.

Kunle. My father! I think, after all, that he respected me. He knew that up till now, I've never lifted a finger to do anything. I am rich as you say, mama, because it was all bestowed on me. I think he wanted to give me a chance at last. A chance to prove myself, that I am really his son. Without fear. Like in a rite of initiation. I don't know what the world was when you were growing up, mama, but I know what you're saying. The world I've known since you sent me to school is a world of cannibals. Our people grow, sharpening their teeth on the flesh of their friends. Of their own relatives and children. We eat one another. And who says I don't know that only the toughest survive. The most brutal and heartless. Mama, calm your fears. The game is just starting, and all the hunters are alert.

Mother. But Kunle, you don't belong. You're not like them, are you? *(silence)* My son!

Kunle. Mama, why don't you look up. Look at me, as I am! I am no longer in the cradle.

Mother. But Kunle . . . my son . . . ?

Kunle. I will survive, mama. Father trusted me. And tonight, we will find out. Meanwhile, just wish me a happy birthday. *(The door is flung open suddenly, and Bosede rushes in.)*

Bosede. Kunle! Kunle! Where's Kunle o? I'm dead! Dead!

Kunle. Bose!

Mother. What's the matter?

Bosede. Ah, mama, you're here! I am finished! Finished!

Kunle. Calm yourself. What happened!

Mother. What happened, Bose?

Bosede. Segun! It's Segun o!

Mother. Segun!

Bosede. Yes! My head is done for!

Mother. What happened? Where's he? Bose!

Bosede. In the kitchen, mama! He's dying!

Mother. Dying! I'd better go and see! *(rushes out)*

Kunle. But dear . . . calm yourself. What's happened to Segun?

Bosede. Vomiting!

Kunle. Is that all?

Bosede. Is that all! Vomiting and vomiting! Four times in less than thirty minutes. Ah, I am dead!

Kunle. Why not call the doctor? *(moves to phone)* Oh, I keep forgetting it's dead. Get the driver to take you to the hospital at once.

Bosede. I can't find Lasisi anywhere.

Kunle. God, what's wrong with me? Of course, he's gone out. I sent him to Balogun, for the rest of the drinks. So he's not back.

Bosede. Can't you take us yourself?

Kunle. Are you joking?

Bosede. It's Segun, your son!

Kunle. And not yours? You can't drive any more? Or your hands have been cut?

Bosede. Kunle!

Kunle. You know I have a meeting now, don't you? With the Board of Directors of—

Bosede. Damn your Board of Directors! I say your son is ill, seriously ill, and—

Kunle. Don't shout at me, you harlot!

Bosede. What! What was that you just called me?

Kunle. Just wait till the meeting tonight, Bose. You're going to wish you'd never been born. You're going to be spread out, naked like a mad woman in the market.

Bosede. Kunle! What's all this? What's come over you? All I said was that your son is ill and needs—

Kunle. My son! All that fiction will end soon. Tonight! I swear it to you! You think I don't know, but by God, I'm going to bring out the truth at last, and it will smash you in the face like a brick!

Bosede. What truth? Kunle—

Kunle. Don't touch me, *asewo!* Don't ever put those filthy hands on me again. I am thirty today, and all that burden is ended. Those chains my father put on my feet because of his oath to your father, they will be broken tonight. And it will be all over at last between you and me.

Bosede. So that's it. You want a divorce.

Kunle. I'm going to have my revenge on you, my dear. I'm going to hurt you back!

Bose. But for what? At least tell me that. What have I done? I've never been unfaithful to you.

Kunle. *(laughs, shrilly)* Ha ha ha! No? *(clutches his head, in evident pain)* Oh my head.

Bosede. *(falls down)* I swear it to you. On my knees. Whatever you may have heard . . .

Kunle. Get up! Get up, you filthy lying bitch! Lest the earth denounce you forever! *(goes for tablets)*

Bosede. *(piteously)* Kunle, why are you being so cruel? Why are you calling me these horrible names? Especially today, on your birthday. I wanted it to be our nicest day. I wanted things to be good for you, so you could relax, so you could be like you always were before our marriage. You're always so tense nowadays, so easily irritable. But I thought it would be different today, when all your dreams are coming true at last and the sun is shining. I've cooked the best dishes for you. All our best friends will be coming—

Kunle. *(swallowing tablets)* Including Yinka? Tell me, is "Yinka-boy" not coming?

Bosede. *(Her mouth open, wide with shock. Slowly she sits on the floor, staring at him as if frightened. Her voice, when it comes, is almost a whisper.)* So you know. So you knew.

Kunle. *(bitterly)* I sent you to London. I myself, I paid the fare. Go round the shops, I said, my darling. Buy only the best things for our wedding. I wanted to come along myself, but there were so many details to see to, cards to print, drinks and food to be bought, cooks and stewards to find, several small things to ensure the success of the day. Our day. So I stayed behind. You kissed me, and the plane took off. And then what happened? Tell me, what happened over there?

Bosede. It was summer. There was madness all over. Don't ask me how it happened.

Kunle. Then the news began to reach me. You were no longer in London, but in Paris. Paris? No, you had left for Amsterdam. Then for Rome. Where else did you go? I sent frantic telegrams to my friends in London. They knew what to do. There are men over there who specialize in that sort of thing. They picked up your trail. In no time the full details were in my hands. Dates, places . . . photographs. Would you like to see them, Ehn? *(goes to the locker and brings out a fat envelope; throws it at her feet)* All the terrible scenes of your infidelity . . .

Bosede. Two years now! Two years and you still keep them.

Kunle. You thought it was a secret, didn't you? You thought I never knew?

Bosede. It was all madness. I don't know what came over me. I was never like that, you know that. You know you were the very first man I knew.

Kunle. And afterward? Who was the second? The third? How many others, since you met me? Since our fathers promised us to each other to cement their friendship and we agreed to be engaged?

Bosede. *(desperately)* I love you, Kunle. There's never been another man. Please believe me. Yinka was . . . nothing! He took me to all those places. They were like fairy lands to me; I was intoxicated. I was only nineteen, remember? But I swear it to you, nothing really happened between us.

Kunle. You call that nothing?

Bosede. Nothing . . . physical. Please believe me. I never slept with him. I was giddy for some time, but I quickly came back to my senses. That's why I came back to you. Why I married you. Because I love you.

Kunle. Love! How nice! I know everybody thinks that I am an infant. But we'll see! After the meeting tonight, we'll see!

Bosede. You don't believe me.

Kunle. Do you expect me to?

Bosede. Kunle, please—

Kunle. Enough. My advice is, pack your things. Before the storm breaks. Go away, you and your son.

Bosede. It's your son, Kunle. I'm not lying. Your son!

Kunle. I don't believe it, thank you. Born exactly nine months after your summer . . . er, "madness"!

Bosede. I was pregnant when I left here. I didn't know till I got there.

Kunle. Very good. It's my child: but does he even look like me?

Bosede. He's the image of my father, Kunle. You know that. Everyone says it. That is not my fault. But he's your son. *(From outside comes the cry of a child. Then we hear Kunle's mother calling. "Bose! Bosede o!")*

Kunle. Mama is calling you. *(The call is repeated.)* Go now. I don't want your son near me. I can't promise to control myself any longer! Go! *(The call comes again.)*

Bosede. *(rising, calls out)* I'm coming, mama! *(to Kunle)* Everything falls into place now. Your sudden strange ways since your father died some months ago. I thought it was just the grief. But I know now. It was your cowardice and your greed.

Kunle. You can't provoke me, Bose.

Bosede. Coward! You knew all that much. It pained you, but you could not discuss it with me. There could only have been one reason for that—your father! You were terrified of him! Terrified, because you never had the guts he had. You never could face up to men, but you were hungry for the possessions he would leave you.

Kunle. He loved your father too much, that was all. He wanted to keep his word to an old friend. I was the sacrificial lamb. I obeyed him because he was my father. I swallowed my pride. But all that is over now! Today is for the burying of ghosts.

Bosede. Words! You're not man enough for it. I know you. You should have been born a woman!

Kunle. *(incensed)* I have power, stupid! Power!

Bosede. You're just a toad, like the rest. A bloated toad, swollen with venom. But you've met your match. You think it's me you're going to destroy, but you just watch. Go to your meeting, toad! They'll take you and squash you underfoot till your belly bursts. And no one will be there to collect your scattered bits. I won't even shed a drop for you!

Kunle. *(almost beside himself with rage now)* Get out! Get out, you bitch. Or I shall—*(He flings his glass, just as she slams the door. The glass shatters against it.)* You'll see! You'll see! You and your father and all the rest! Smash! Like a hurtling brick! *(He staggers, clutching his head. Goes to trolley and pours himself a drink. He looks at his watch. Then sees the envelope on the floor. Goes to pick it up. There is a knock.)*

Kunle. *(straightening up)* Come in. *(The door opens, and in comes Bose's father, Chief Samuel Adejimi Seminiyi. He has a parcel in his hand. The unexpected visit throws Kunle into visible confusion.)*

Chief. Hello, happy birthday, my son. This is for you. *(hands the parcel over)*

Kunle. *(still confused)* Ah . . . thank you, sir . . . father. Thank you very much.

Chief. It's small, but I hope you'll like it. Thirty years is an

important milestone in anybody's career. I pray yours will
prove the beginning of many fruitful things.

Kunle. Thank you, father. You will still live long enough to
witness it.

Chief. I will. I will. And the secret of long life, as I always say,
is in that glass you're holding. If you don't mind, I'll use one
of that too.

Kunle. Father, you have not changed! *(goes to pour out a drink)*

Chief. *(sitting)* I don't really want to intervene. Storms are
things I hasten to avoid if I can help it. But I saw Bose just as
I was coming up. The way she rushed past me! My own
daughter, as if I was a stranger she'd never seen before. Not
even a "Good evening, father"! I mean, she could even have
pushed me down the stairs! What is happening? You haven't
been quarreling with her, have you?

Kunle. *(embarrassed)* Well . . . you know how it is. Women!

Chief. *(taking the drink from him)* Oh yes, of course. Are you
telling me! That's why I married eight of them. So each
has her own sparring partner, and I can watch from the
wings. That's the secret, my son. I learned it when I was a
boxer. You know, in my teens. Before—what do you call
him?—Momodu Aliu, or something like that. When the
contests heat up, it's always the referee who survives. Ha
ha ha. But I hope the matter between you is not too serious
though.

Kunle. *(recovered now)* No.

Chief. Good. Because I want to talk to you. Very seriously.
Before this meeting you have called.

Kunle. Go on.

Chief. I saw the lawyer, Jegede, as I drove in.

Kunle. That man again!

Chief. He told me what you wish to do. And frankly—

Kunle. He doesn't know everything.

Chief. He says you wish to step into your father's shoes.

Kunle. Yes.

Chief. It's not wise, my boy.

Kunle. Why not?

Chief. Legally, of course, nobody can stop you. But I am also
your father. And if you'd listen to me—

Kunle. Sorry, sir, but it's too late. All my life there has always been a father to push me. I am going to carry out his last wish. But only because, that way, I free myself.

Chief. But, listen—

Kunle. I've already signed the papers, sir. Since four o'clock this afternoon I have effectively become the President of the Company.

Chief. But we need to sell out. Fast! Otherwise we lose all our money. We're seriously in debt—

Kunle. I know. I also know the cause. And I intend to deal with it. This evening.

Chief. You! Excuse me, but . . . , it's a joke! What do you know?

Kunle. You'll find out, sir. And then maybe you won't be laughing anymore.

Chief. I know it's your father's wish. In all our life together, I never had cause once to disagree with him. Not once. But death I suppose is a funny thing. His mind must have decayed in those last minutes.

Kunle. Do you think so? Or are you just afraid?

Chief. What do you mean?

Kunle. I've gone through his papers. I've read his diary. My father was a very faithful and loyal man, but he was not foolish. He knew his friends thoroughly, even if he felt powerless to act.

Chief. I see. And you think you can act? That you have the guts?

Kunle. We'll see. *(Brief knock. Enter Major Ajala, with a parcel.)*

Major. My dear son! Ah, you're here already, Chief!

Chief. Welcome, Major.

Kunle. Welcome, sir.

Major. This is for you, my son. Many happy returns. Ah, when I remember how long ago it was, when I, myself, was thirty!

Chief. Hear the young boy talking. What of people like us then!

Kunle. You're not all that old yet, father.

Major. Chief, the young have all the luck, but can we grudge them? We had our time! However, I am famished. We came in straight from the airport, Mama Bola and I. She's waiting downstairs. I thought we'd walk in straight into the banquet.

But they say you want a meeting of the Board before the party. Hope nothing?

Kunle. It hasn't met since my father died.

Major. No, but what's the hurry anyway? Can't we eat first at least?

Chief. He's going to take over, Major.

Major. I beg your pardon?

Kunle. Wrong, father. Not going to. I've already taken over.

Major. Is this a joke? You, you wish to be Company President?

Kunle. I am Company President, Major. I've been, since four this afternoon.

Major. But . . . but that's crazy! You know absolutely nothing.

Kunle. You read my father's will.

Major. Yes, yes. Of course you're thirty now. How time flies.

Kunle. How time flies.

Chief. I was trying to persuade him to sell out his shares.

Kunle. To whom?

Major. To us, of course. Listen, I know that you're intelligent and all that, but you know nothing about how we operate. I mean, you're only a baby. You don't expect us to take orders from you.

Kunle. No, of course not, Major.

Major. You see!

Kunle. You won't be taking orders from me, Major. This afternoon I signed the papers removing you from the Board and from the Company. You'll have all your financial entitlements, of course. *(Both Chief and Major leap out of their chairs in surprise.)*

Chief. What!

Major. You . . . did what!

Chief. Is this a joke?

Kunle. Please sit down. I have—*(Knock. Councillor Bamgbade enters, with a small parcel, but seeing the situation, he tries to retreat, muttering apologies.)*

Kunle. Oh come in, Baba Councillor. Come in sir.

Councillor. If I'm disturbing—

Chief. No. Not at all, Councillor. In fact you appeared just at the right moment.

Councillor. *(shaking Kunle's hand)* My congratulations, son.

This—*(He holds up the parcel, but decides to pocket it.)*—it will wait. We will settle our score later. I greet you, Chief. And the Major! How do they say it? *(chants briefly)* "I remember when I was a soldier." Glad to see you again. You know, I thought I'd just sneak up and have my son to myself alone for a little while, but I didn't know you old crooks had beaten me to it! *(Remarking the silence suddenly, he stops and looks around.)* What's the matter? Has someone farted?

Major. *(still in a state of shock)* You know you can't do that, son. You know you can't. Not to me.

Kunle. I asked the lawyer. He advised me it was perfectly within my rights as President and principal share-holder.

Councillor. Wait a minute. What did I hear you say you are?

Chief. He's cooked us a nice dish, Councillor. Have your own taste.

Councillor. What does that—*(Two other people come in. They are Alhaji Nassir Kofoworola and Honourable O. O. Fakunle, also bearing presents.)*

Honourable. Alhaji, see? Here they all are, soaking away the drinks quietly, while we've been waiting for months in the study downstairs, dying of thirst.

Kunle. *(hastening to meet them)* I am sorry, I am sorry. All my fault. *(There are greetings all around.)* Welcome Honourable, sir. And you Alhaji. I forgot. My wife should have received you at the door, but she's off to the hospital with my mother. And all the servants are busy at the backyard. I'm sorry.

Alhaji. Hospital *ke!* What happened? Somebody is ill?

Kunle. My son. Just started vomiting! *(sounds of sympathy all around, as they all find seats)*

Councillor. On his father's birthday? I hope he's not jealous!

Alhaji. My congratulations anyway, Kunle my son. Many many happy returns. This small piece is for you. And I'll tell you a secret. Chief, close your ears. The present was chosen specially by my daughter Abeke herself. I won't tell you what it is. And if I were you, I won't let Mama Segun know about it.

Kunle. Thank you Alhaji. I intend to follow your advice!

Councillor. I am sorry for you. They're luring you on to the dangerous road of polygamy already, as my tenth wife would say.

Honourable. Well, this is also for you. From my wife. Unfortunately, she's too old to be a candidate. And I should know!

Kunle. Good gracious. Chief the Honourable! You're all so kind. I am simply overwhelmed. *(The Major stands up abruptly, heading for the door.)*

Alhaji. Major, hope nothing? What is this *fiun* like that, like you are gear one of *agbegilodo!** Or are we the ones giving you away?

Major. I'll wait downstairs.

Honourable. Why? Let's all go together.

Chief. But in fact, is it necessary anymore? Since we are all here. This place is comfortable enough. Why don't we just go on and have the meeting now? Unless of course Kunle objects.

Kunle. No, not at all, sir. If it is okay by you.

Honourable. No objections at all from me, my boy. As long as you push that thing *(indicating drinks trolley)* close to me!

Alhaji. I think we are all agreed. *(Kunle suddenly clutches his head.)* What's the matter?

Kunle. Nothing. *(shakes his head painfully)* Just a little headache.

Chief. You still haven't seen a doctor?

Councillor. It will pass. Must be the excitement and all that. Today's an important day for you, my son. You'll be better tomorrow. After the party. Ah, when I was thirty! *(sings, stentorously, joined by Honourable and Alhaji)*

> Happy days are here again!
> Happy days are here again
> The clouds above are clear again
> Let's sing the song of cheer again,
> Happy days are here again!

Major. *(breaking in)* You fools! You blustering idiots! *(shouting*

---

* Tipper lorry specializing in timber haulage, known for its grinding noise when climbing uphill, because it is invariably overused and badly maintained.

in parade-ground fashion) Atte-n-n-tion! As you were! Shut up your mouths! Silence! *(They cringe from him, frightened.)*

Councillor. *(stunned)* But . . . what's the matter with you?

Alhaji. Did we miss our way to an Army barracks? My friends . . . Or is the man mad?

Major. Why don't you listen to what he's going to say first.

Honourable. He's going to sell, so what's spectacular about that? He's incompetent, and he himself knows it. Does that mean we can't sing him a song?

Major. You see what I mean, Ox-head!

Honourable. No! Surely you don't mean—

Chief. *(to Kunle)* Open the meeting. Let us start.

Kunle. Gentlemen, let me formally welcome you to the first Board meeting of the Company since the unfortunate death of my father. It is the first one also that I will have the honor to preside over. You all know the reason why I find myself in this rather uneasy position, and I think I can guess what your feelings will be. Excuse me—*(He hastily swallows some tablets.)* There is going to be a necessary change of attitude, of course. Up till now most of you have known me only as the little inconspicuous son of Chief Gbadegesin Aremo. You have all, I must confess, treated me always with considerable affection and have even been like second parents to me in the past few months. I assure you, I appreciate all that and shall continue to do so. All I pray is that God will continue to preserve you all for us, your children, and that sweetness will be the harvest of your last years—*(murmurings of "Ase! Amen!")*

Alhaji. That's all right, but where is all this leading to?

Honourable. Patience, let him finish!

Kunle. Please bear with me. I am trying to get to a point that is somewhat painful to me. I knew you would all turn up for my birthday party today. That was the reason I thought we should kill two birds with the same stone, and so, slotted in this Board meeting, before the feasting. Well, you are all familiar with the details of my father's will. His stated wish was that I should succeed him as President of the Company on my thirtieth birthday. I am thirty today. And I have since taken steps not only to fulfill my father's desire, but also reconstitute this Board. In order to put it on a firmer footing. *(general exclamations all around)*

Honourable. But this is rubbish! What nonsense! The old man—well, I didn't know what he was up to. But damn it, you aren't taking him seriously?

Kunle. Honourable, I respect you very much, and I grant that you are entirely free to express your opinion. But I'd appreciate it very much if in the course of it, you'll extend to me the little but important courtesies expected of a Board member to his Chairman. Certain indecent expressions are not—

Honourable. I'll be damned! Is it you, born yesterday, who'll teach me how to speak! Your father made a stupid blunder by willing his position to a dumbclot like you; the least damage you could do is let us buy off those shares from you! Christ, what rubbish! What rubbish!

Kunle. Honourable, I am warning you—

Alhaji. That's enough, by Allah! Are we all going to sit down here and watch while you stick your finger in his nose! Al-aq-bar! Where the cockroach dare not walk, his son struts and says he's going to dance! Do you know what the consequences will be!

Major. What impudence! I've never seen the like before! Someone hardly big enough to wipe his own anus. Now daring to . . . to . . . !

Kunle. So I was dead right! I guessed none of you would want me as Chairman here. Especially after I went through all the books.

Alhaji. I wouldn't even employ you as an ordinary clerk, my boy, no hard feelings! You've read books, but what do you know about business? Your father was illiterate, but he was a giant of a man. He knew the business world inside out. But you, all you have in common is the name. But is it because the snail also has two horns that it will take on the role of a bullock?

Kunle. I am very glad. My conscience is free now to take the decisions needed. *(takes file from table)* I'll announce them—

Honourable. Let others stay, but I am going. I won't take being talked to in those tones—

Kunle. Let me start with you then, since you're in a hurry, Honourable. For a week now I've been studying the company accounts. The accountant, and the lawyer, I must say, have been most helpful. They helped me discover quite a number of things. As you know, my father was illiterate. He let a number of things pass; he never did bother with statistics. But I do. And I have found out how you, Honourable, have made it out so cleverly, that the soap company, which is our subsidiary, pays you alone a sum of five thousand naira every week. Not directly, of course. We pay it to one Odedare Enterprises. And Odedare Enterprises is registered in the name of one person I assume I don't have to disclose?

Councillor. It's not true, Honourable? You're not defrauding us?

Honourable. Fraud! Fraud! What is fraud, tell me! Is it what everybody does or not? Every bloody rich man in this country got his wealth by what you call fraud! And you know it! So what have I done wrong?

Chief. I don't believe it? Not you, Honourable!

Kunle. I've dismissed you from the Board. The lawyer will start judicial processes tomorrow to recover our money. You may go now if you wish *(Honourable rises.)* See you at the party. *(He goes out.)*

Alhaji. But surely we don't need to go to court. He's being punished enough!

Kunle. That's your opinion, Alhaji. I didn't understand it all at first, I confess. I didn't know what it was that drove my father to his early death. I didn't know he'd found out that his best friends, his trusted friends, had betrayed him and he couldn't talk. He was always a loyal man. And inside, the pain slowly burned him out. You're not hungry men. You're not in want. It's just that you stole your way up, all the way, and cannot stop stealing. You, Alhaji—

Alhaji. *(jumps)* Yes, me! What about me!

Kunle. Tomorrow, you'll see your face. In the hands of all the newspaper vendors. And later, on television. Your face, staring out as you're staring now.

Alhaji. *(frightened)* My face!

Kunle. In the papers. On TV! With a disclaimer by the Company. Anyone who does business with you does so at his or her own risk. You're no longer with us. You've been DISMISSED. *(exclamations!)*

Alhaji. *(horrified)* My face! My face on the street! Me, Alhaji Nassir Kofoworola! Dismissed!

Kunle. A rogue! A completely heartless rogue, who could plunder a friend without compunction. I won't even bother to take you to court. I'll just disgrace you before the whole country, and dare you to go to court.

Alhaji. My picture! *(turning around piteously)* Dismissed! Please save me. I have a family. I have friends. I have children—

Major. You can't do this, you know. We built this company with your father. We employed all kinds of means. It is the age we live in; we can't change the rules. Everyone plunders, whether from friends or strangers or the government! It's all in the game. The winner takes the loot; the loser goes to the gutter, or into the asylum. *We* played the game, and we won. Your father was no different. He had his teeth out just like any other—

Kunle. I don't want to hear anything about it. You're rotten, all of you, and you wish to spread it. I am saying no, no way!

Major. We'll get you, you rat. We'll get you sooner than you think! *(Kunle laughs.)*

Alhaji. *(fondling the ring on his finger conspicuously)* Yes, my face will appear! But so will yours, my boy! In the obituary column! Or my name is not Nassir Kofoworola! See?—*(hits Kunle in the chest, with the ring hand)*

Kunle. *(laughs)* You think you can frighten me! But your age is ended, my dear fathers. *(They turn to go, angrily. He calls after them.)* Stay for the party anyway. *(They go. Councillor rises.)*

Chief. Sorry, Councillor, but I wish to go next. *(Councillor sits back.)* I know you're sacking all of us, my boy. I have no wish to stay. But I am curious. What's my own offense? I've never stolen from your father.

Councillor. *(attuned)* You're not doing it, Kunle? You're not going to dismiss your own father-in-law too?

Chief. This is war, Councillor, don't you know? There'll be no favorites when the bullets are flying. Let him talk.

Kunle. Councillor, no one can live forever with shame and humiliation. Tonight, I am freeing myself of all burden. Tomorrow the lawyer is having a busy day. One of his assignments will be to file a divorce application on my behalf.

Councillor. What! How—

Kunle. The Chief understands. Two years ago he had an interesting discussion with my father, in this very room. That discussion eventually led to a wedding. He couldn't have forgotten the details.

Chief. I can't recognize you! No, not anymore, Kunle! You've grown, grown into a terrible young man! A monster! Ah, I'm glad my daughter's leaving you.

Kunle. Yes, you're glad now. But two years ago, two old men came here and decided that their business was more important than someone else's honor. My manhood was at stake, all my friends were anxious, but those two men met and put their feet down. And it didn't matter if I lived the rest of my life as a fugitive, running from those who would meet me and quickly hide their grin behind their handkerchief.

Chief. What are you saying, Kunle? She loved you. She was carrying your baby. Those were the important considerations. What did you expect us to do?

Kunle. It was not my baby! You knew that! You were only thinking of your profits!

Chief. It's not—Well what's the use? You won't believe me. *(sighs)* But that's your own personal grievance. What's the official story?

Kunle. Associating openly with a political party. In gross contravention of Company regulations. Every official is strictly forbidden to take part in open, partisan politics, or the penalty is instant dismissal. You've been seen times without number with politicians. At fund-raising rallies. On the rostrum. You've been photographed—

Councillor. But those regulations are a mere formality. They don't—

Chief. No, I have no defense. When feathers are mentioned, even the tiny *opere* bird owns up. So how can the *okin,* king of all the birds in the world, hide himself? I am guilty of partisan politics. Yes! I believe in our party's policies. And I shall always do my best to promote them, anywhere! I, Chief Samuel Seminiyi, with the ringing praise-name! Yes, the One-Whose-Chest-Beats-Like-A-Drum! I'll send in my resignation tomorrow—

Kunle. It's here, sir. Just your signature's needed.

Chief. *(stopped)* You're audacious, aren't you? I could still fight you, you know—

Kunle. You won't, father. Your finances are in a mess at the moment. I know that. And there's that castle you're building in Lagos, purely to boost your ego.

Chief. It's not that important. I could stop it.

Kunle. I know you, father. I know your pride. Besides, there's something else I know.

Chief. What?

Kunle. Madam Feyisope, the Manageress of Ireti Stores, was trapped in the fire which gutted her stores last month. She's been sent to a very expensive hospital in Switzerland.

Chief. And then?

Kunle. You still want me to go on? Madam Feyisope is your mistress. You set up the stores for her five years ago. And our Company has been paying her expenses in Switzerland. Father, I could decide to stop paying.

Chief. *(resigned, bitter)* You're a real bastard, aren't you? You'll end up very badly.

Kunle. Sign the letter, sir. *(The chief signs and turns to go.)* I hope you'll be staying for the party.

Chief. *(pausing at the door)* I'll have Bosede's old room cleaned up. Tell her she'll have a home to receive her back. She and her child. *(goes)*

Councillor. Last, and as they say, not the least. It's execution day today, I see. So where do I get mine? On the neck or in the guts?

Kunle. *(Pouring himself a drink. His head is clearly bothering him.)* From you, my dear Councillor, I have a special request to make.

Councillor. Not granted, sorry. I can't go and hang myself.

Kunle. That's not the request I was going to make.

Councillor. Or that I should swallow poison? Or something equally horrible! Thank you, my son, thank you!

Kunle. I want to know, Councillor. How would you like coming in as my partner?

Councillor. What! What did you say?

Kunle. A full-fledged partnership. Fifty-fifty. At absolutely no cost to yourself. We just take all the shares and split them up.

Councillor. *(laughing)* As easy as that!

Kunle. Don't laugh.

Councillor. But it's got to be a joke!

Kunle. *(giving him the papers)* Look at these. Do they look funny?

Councillor. *(reading them)* But . . . but this is crazy!

Kunle. *(gives him a pen)* All you have to do is sign, over there.

Councillor. *(not taking the pen)* Why? Why me?

Kunle. I told you, Councillor, that I went through the papers. It was like going through a street of latrines. Big men, filthy practices. How money degrades people! But they don't mind, as long as it covers them in lace and damask. They can stink all you care underneath. But you alone, Councillor, your hands are clean. We combed through all the records. Not a single blemish against your name, in all of your fifteen years in the place. It's quite a record! I believe you have a lot to teach me, sir.

Councillor. And so, you believe you can buy me?

Kunle. *(taken aback)* No sir! That's not what I mean! I mean—

Councillor. How far are you willing to go, if I refuse fifty percent?

Kunle. Sixty, sir. I'm kidding, seventy! Seventy percent.

Councillor. That's quite a lot.

Kunle. I don't want my father's business to die. And I can't handle it by myself, as you know.

Councillor. Then I am sorry for you, my son. You should have thought of that much earlier. Before you started whipping old men right and left like cattle in Sango.*

---

* Sango is a popular cattle market.

Kunle. They're worse than murderers, Councillor! They killed my father! They deserved it all.

Councillor. Why do you keep thinking your father could not protect himself? What makes you think he could not have acted if he wanted? *(seeing his state)* Sit down. Let me tell you, I am frightened of you, my boy. Of what kind of beast you have become. What! How, without compassion, how can we remain human beings? Or does decency mean nothing to you?

Kunle. They were guilty. They had to be punished.

Councillor. By you? You! You're just a kid with a new toy. A misguided kid padding up your chest like a *gareta* masquerade. And see, this is what I'll do with your papers! *(He tears them up, to Kunle's utter disbelief.)* I could have stayed with you if I thought I could still help. After all I am your godfather. But it's too late. See? The farce has got into your head, your fickle paper crown has turned real in your warped imagination, and see! See you galloping madly on your paper horse. You'll crash my friend! See? You will smash your skull soon or break your spine! For you think you have power, and it has turned your head. See? You see old men, and you rub mud in their mouth. Ah! If you were my son, see, my own son, I would seize you during all that time you were foaming and showering saliva on your father's age-mates! I would seize you in my hands, see? Seize you like dry stick, and break you into pieces.

Kunle. If only you would let me put in a word—

Councillor. No! You've said enough tonight! See? You took advantage of people coming here in all innocence to rejoice with you: You didn't think of their age or status, see? You just abused them and humiliated them, and dismissed them so ignominously from a Company to which many of them have given much of their life—

Kunle. Councillor—oh my head—Councillor, I understand now, you're just no better than them. Your hands are clean, you don't steal money yourself, but you'll do nothing to stop those who dip their fingers in the wallet behind everybody's back. You're an accomplice, sir, as guilty as the rest. With people like you, nothing will ever change. You're born to fold your arms behind your back and close your eyes and connive

at crime. And that's how you'll die, conniving and pretending to be blind!

Councillor. Good! I brought you a gift, you courageous man!
Let's test the strength of your galloping mouth. Take! *(He
brings out his present, rips off the wrappings, and thrusts it
violently at Kunle. His back is to the audience—so that we
don't see what it is. Note, it is important that the audience
does NOT see. Kunle is seen to leap backward with a
scream, his eyes filled with terror.)*

Kunle. *(as he collapses on the arm of the chair, clutching his
head and moaning)* No . . . no . . . please!

Councillor. *(advancing on him)* Face to face with terror,
death's image, would you be able to stand upright? Or you
don't know that that's what it is, each time you fill your
mouth with abuse, that you're standing on tip-toe? At the
door to which others who arrived before you hold the key?
(thrusting his hand forward again) Take!

Kunle. *(shouting)* No! *(The door opens at that moment, as
Bosede walks in, evidently on the edge of collapse herself.
Councillor hastily hides what he's holding in his pocket.)*

Bose. *(clearly in a state of shock)* Kunle . . . Kunle-o! . . . I'm
dead!

Kunle. *(still collapsing, not looking up at her)* Quick, pour me
a drink, Bose! A drink!

Councillor. *(to Bosede)* My daughter, what's the—

Bose. Kunle! Listen, your son, Segun! He's—

Kunle. Damn it, I don't want to hear! I'm dying! Get me a
drink, quickly!

Bose. *(grimly)* All right then, if you don't want to hear. You'll
have your drink! *(She goes to the trolley to pour a drink.)*

Councillor. What happened?

Bose. He wants a drink! *(She pours a drink, looks around
briefly, and takes another bottle. Hiding it from the others,
but clearly visible to the audience, she pours from this
second bottle into the glass. Then she brings it to Kunle,
handing it to him.)* Here! Here's your drink. *(He empties it
at a gulp, then shouts, clutching his belly. She runs out
sobbing. Kunle does a dance, in agony, and collapses on the
floor, moaning.)*

Councillor. *(retreating from him slowly)* Pain, you'll know what it is! *(But just as he reaches the door, it opens, and the Major enters.)*

Councillor. *(surprised)* I thought . . . I thought you were gone.

Major. No, I couldn't leave after what happened. I see he's taking it badly. *(pointing to Kunle)*

Councillor. What happened?

Major. Were you not here when his wife came?

Councillor. Yes. But she said nothing.

Major. Is that true? You mean she didn't tell him?

Councillor. What? Talk, or you'll make me burst a nerve!

Major. He died.

Councillor. Who? *(shouting)* Who died, Major?

Major. His son, Segun. He died on the way to the hospital. They drove in just as I was leaving. *(He stands abruptly to attention and salutes.)*

Councillor. Oh God!

Major. And you say she didn't tell him?

Councillor. No.

Major. So what's he doing there, with his head in his hands?

Councillor. Ask him. Poor Bose. I'll go and see her. *(hastens out)*

Major. *(approaching Kunle)* You know, I could kill you now. I have nothing to lose. Already my life is ruined. You bastard! *(He leans over to strangle him, back to audience. With a shock, he straightens up, exclaiming. Then he looks up fast over his shoulders. Quickly he runs out. Mother comes in, sobbing.)*

Mother. Kunle! My poor son. I said it, didn't I? I warned you. I said they'd get you, and now they've started. With your son. You see? They've killed him! *(She cries.)* Poor you, what will you do now? Reconcile with them? *(silence)* Kunle, I am talking to you! At least you can say something! *(She goes to hold him, to shake him. As soon as she touches him, however, his body topples over and the glass falls from his hand. He is dead. The mother screams. Everybody comes running in.)*

Mother. *(straightening up, facing them)* He's dead. My son is dead: Which of you killed him?

(Blackout)

MOROUNTODUN

[I have found a sweet thing]
A play based on the legend of Moremi of Ile-Ife

This play was first performed in a slightly different version, at the Arts Theatre, Ibadan, in 1979. The version published here was performed later the same year with a cast comprising the following members of the Kakaun Sela Kompany:

CHARACTERS

The Director	Segun Ojewuyi
Townspeople	
Titubi	Didi Unu Odigie
Titubi's followers	Foluke Areola
	Amatu Braide
	Bimbo Williams
	Dayo Ogundipe
	Tayo Omoniyi
	Esohe Omoregie
Drummers	The Cast
Deputy Superintendent of Police	Emmanuel Oga
Police Corporal	Kunle Adeyemo
Alhaja Kabirat	Amatu Braide
Alhaji Buraimoh	Segun Taiwo
Lawyer Isaac	Jide Adebamowo
Lati	Jonathan Amuno
Warder	Willie Igbinedion

Village People
Baba   Ayo Akinwale
Marshal   Sam Loco Efe
Bogunde   Tunde Laniyan
Kokondi   Jonathan Amuno
Mama Kayode   Bimbo Williams
Mosun   Esohe Omoregie

ONE

Stage opens on the dressing area, marked out by mats and wooden frames, etc., of an evidently ambulant and somewhat amateurish theatre company. A bench. Tables and stools, and possibly a table with a long mirror. Lockers.

A flurry of activity: actors making up, trying costumes, reading script, rehearsing gestures, miming some of the later actions in the play.

Enter the Director, rubbing his hands.

Director. Hurry up. Hurry up. Play opens in five minutes.
An Actor. Fair house today?
Director. Fair. Better than in the last town where we stopped.
Another Actor. And no signs of trouble?
Director. No signs yet. But don't worry.
Another Actor. That's what you said yesterday. Yet we were almost lynched.
Director. This time I've sent for the police.
Another Actor. The police! Is that a joke?
Director. Please hurry up. We're doing nothing illegal. We can seek police protection as much as anybody.
Another Actor. I hope you're right. Yesterday was hell.
Director. There'll be no disturbance tonight. *(He watches them for a while, then "steps out" of place and approaches the*

audience.) Good evening, ladies and gentlemen. We will soon be starting. But while the actors prepare, I'll try and give you a rapid summary of our play tonight. The play, as you will soon see, starts in the year 1969, the month of September. That year, if you remember, the civil war was raging in the east of our country, but this play has nothing to do with that. It deals with another war, the one that was later to be popularly known as the Agbekoya uprising, in which ordinary farmers, in the west of the country, rose up and confronted the state. Maybe you remember? Illiterate farmers, whom we had all along thought to be docile, peace-loving, if not even stupid, suddenly took to arms and began to fight against the government! Two, three, four . . . seven months! And the war was still hot and bitter. Farmers dying, policemen falling, soldiers going and not returning. Were they not all our kinsmen? If we could not speak about the war in the east, because of still decrees, would we also be silent about the one in the west? And suppose another should start in the north? Well, we decided not to be silent. We decided to go and rouse people up by doing a play on the subject. *(Noises begin, from the entrances. He looks up briefly, then continues.)* We decided to do a play about it, and take it around to all open places. And that was when our troubles began. *(Noises rise again, but subside as attendants are heard talking to crowd. Director takes out a handkerchief and wipes his brow.)* We thought we were contributing toward the process of finding a solution. But before we knew it, we had become part of the problem . . . *(Noises grow. The actors freeze, anxious. The Director fights to continue.)* As I was saying . . . the night of . . . *(The noise drowns his voice now.)* Please excuse me . . . I'll go and see . . . *(He walks quickly toward the main entrance but is soon violently pushed back by a shouting, near-hysterical mob, consisting mainly of women bearing placards and some handbills, which they begin to distribute around the auditorium. They are attended by a couple of drummers who are apparently trying to make money out of the occasion.)*

(Full lights return, flooding the entire theatre. Most of the actors on stage have quickly sneaked out. Now we can read some of the placards carried by the agitators: DOWN WITH AGITATORS! WIPE OUT THE INSANE LOVERS OF POVERTY! AWAY WITH HYPOCRITES! CRUSH THE PEASANT REVOLT! CLEAN THE CITY OF LOUTS! DEATH TO THE JOBLESS! NO FOREIGN IDEOLOGIES! TO EARN IS HUMAN! WHO DOES NOT WANT MONEY? etc. The intruders are also chanting.)

> Stand! Stand!
> Fight to be rich
> For happiness:
> Oh fight for your right
> To rise in life!
>
> With good luck and stubbornness
> With sweat, sweat, and cleverness
> De—ter—mi—na—tion!
> Ma—ni—pu—la—tion!
> Oh fight for your share
> And do not care!

(A little group, superbly dressed, with lots of jewelry and make-up, and wearing conspicuously the "Moremi necklace" then in vogue—a little gold dagger, surrounded with golden nuggets—takes over the stage. Leading them is Titubi, a pretty, sensual, and obviously self-conscious woman.)

Titubi. *(addressing the audience)* Look at me. Go on, feast your eyes. Am I not good to look at? Ehn? So what is wrong with being rich? *(Her speech throughout will be punctuated by rousing calls, ovation, etc., from her followers.)* So there's a peasant rebellion. And then? What have we got to do with it? Is it a sin to be rich? Ahn'ahn! It's disgusting! Night after night! Day after day! Lies! Insults! In the newspapers! On the radio. On the television, *nko*? And then here they come with a play! But it's got to stop! This is our country too, and we shall not run away! I, Titubi, daughter of Alhaja Kabirat, I am stopping this play tonight! And if you're wise, you'll go and return your tickets now and collect your money back. *(hisses)*

Director. *(struggling vainly)* Madam . . . please . . . excuse m— . . .

Titubi. Shut your mouth! Who are you?

Director. Please, madam . . . I . . . I am the director of this play, and—

Titubi. Oh so it's you! We've been looking for you. *(The mob seizes him roughly. A couple of slaps.)* No. No. Beat him . . . gently. Don't make the useless man into a hero. Where are your actors?

Director. *(shouting)* Gone for the police! The police!

Titubi. Very good. We'll soon have all of you in prison.

Director. We shall see. We shall see. We are respectable people. And all the men there, who have bought their tickets—

Titubi. Nobody will watch any show tonight. Either we stop it all, or we burn the place down. But nobody's going to watch anything here tonight. We'll all wait for the police.

Director. But why? Who are you? What have we done to you?

Titubi. It's now that you will ask. You go around the place, shelling us with abuse. Slanders! Yet—*(derisively)*—"Who are you? What have we done to you?"

Director. I assure you there must be a mistake. We've never abused anybody.

Titubi. No? Help him revive his memory. *(a couple of slaps again)* Gently, gently, don't leave any mark on the wretched man. We have respect for the law, even though the law is a donkey. These beggars have been riding it with glee down our spine all these days. And it is enough. We've been bruised enough. And enough of pretending not to notice! We didn't ask anybody's father not to be rich, did we?

Crowd. No-oooh!

Titubi. Did we see anybody's grandmother trading and overturn her wares?

Crowd. No-oooh!

Titubi. Did we send locusts to anybody's farm?

Crowd. No-oooh!

Titubi. Don't we pay our own tax?

Crowd. Yesssss!

Titubi. So, in what way are we responsible for the farmer's uprising? Ehn? What does our being rich have to do with it? Or is it only when we wear rags that we qualify to breathe the air? Tell me, Mr. Director! (slaps him) You mount these stupid plays, calling everybody a thief, simply because we work and sweat and use our brain. You want to say you don't like money, abi? If I offer you cash now, hard, glowing cash, you won't dance for me? Ehn? Look at it! *(An assistant opens out her handbag. She dips into it and brings out a handful of currency notes, which she begins to paste disdainfully on the forehead of the Director, who is now covered in sweat.)* Money! See, you're shivering already at the touch of it. It's given you a hard-on. Dance, *ijimere!* Dance for me! *(She starts the rousing song again, and her followers join. Again and again, clearly intoxicated now, she dips into the bag and flings out more money with increasing frenzy. There begins a furious scramble for the money, in which the Director finally joins. The drummers too are very active.)* Yeeesss! I have money and I can enslave you with it! I can buy all of your ringworm-infested actors if I choose . . . aaahhhhh.

(The piercing sound of a police siren, outside. Sounds of car doors banging. Noise of boots. Then a loud blast on the whistle. Steps approaching. Enter a Police Officer—actually a Deputy Superintendent—in mufti, accompanied by a Corporal in full riot gear: shield, tear gas gun and canisters, etc. Among the crowd, a moment of frozen indecision, and then—panic. Everybody runs out, through various exits, in disarray, leaving Titubi and the Director, who is still on his haunches collecting the scattered money. The Corporal quickly holds him.)

Superintendent. Is this the leader, ma'am?
Titubi. Yes.
Corporal. Got him! With stolen money too! You didn't think it wise to run, abi? You heard the law approaching, and you dared to wait.
Director. But . . . but . . .
Corporal. Silence! I gave you your chance to beat it. I shouted from a good distance. The others took the cue, and ran, but

you, all you could do was offer your yansh. Well, the law's going to kick it!

Superintendent. Take him away and lock him up. We'll take his statement tomorrow. And the name of his comrades. Madam, sorry for all this palaver. I was on a routine visit to the station when your actors came. My name is Deputy Superintendent Salami.

Titubi. *(taking his hand)* Pleased to meet you.

Superintendent. Thugs are all over the place nowadays. We try our best, but we cannot always predict where or in what shape they'll show up. But don't worry, I promise you there won't be any more disturbance tonight. Please continue your play.

Director. But, officer . . . Superintendent . . . I am the director of the play!

Superintendent. I beg your pardon?

Titubi. Don't listen to him.

Director. I sent for you. This woman led the rioters here.

Corporal. Shut up your mouth. You think we can't recognize a rioter when we see one, eh? Slandering a decent woman. Look, come quietly with me now or—

Director. But I swear to you that . . . oh God, where are these actors? Listen—*(Casting about desperately, his eyes light on the audience.)*—Ask them! They'll tell you.

Superintendent. *(after a moment's thought)* Madam, is it true what he says?

Titubi. *(arrogantly)* What does he say?

Superintendent. That you are the intruder here? That you brought the mob?

Titubi. Do I look like someone who would lead a mob?

Director. She's lying! She—

Corporal. Shut up and come with me now, or I'll lose my patience.

Superintendent. Madam, I want the truth.

Titubi. Well, I did. I led them here.

Corporal. What!

Titubi. But they're not rioters. They're ordinary decent citizens. Some even more decent than you.

Superintendent. You came to disrupt the play?

Titubi. We came to stop it.

Superintendent. May I ask why?

Corporal. *(looking at the Director malevolently)* He probably caused it.

Titubi. Exactly, Corporal.

Superintendent. Explain.

Titubi. Ask him.

Superintendent. I'm asking you. *(to Corporal)* And you, release the man.

Titubi. Please don't use that tone with me, Superintendent. If you'd been doing your work properly—the work you're paid for out of our taxes, remember?—I wouldn't be here.

Superintendent. Not bloody likely.

Titubi. And watch your language with me, Salami or whatever your name is! *(The Corporal, indignant, visibly changes sides.)* I wasn't bred in the gutter.

Superintendent. I'm still waiting for your explanation.

Titubi. And I said, ask him. He put up this show. They come here night after night and throw bricks at us—

Director. But that's—

Superintendent. I think this is enough. Madam, I appeal to you, please leave the stage now.

Titubi. And will the show go on or not?

Superintendent. Madam, don't force me to put you under arrest.

Titubi. What? Let me hear that again.

Superintendent. At least until the play's over.

Titubi. *(laughs)* Here are my wrists. Bring out your handcuffs. *(The Corporal hesitates, looking at the officer.)*

Titubi. Go on, what are you waiting for? Snap them on. *(laughs, strutting)* How many markets do you know in this town, you who call yourself Salami. Ehn, or are you too busy salaaming to look around you? This town is one long chain of markets, a roaring world of tough, fearless women. And do you know whose name, all alone, rules over all these women? Do you know or shall I tell you? If I open my mouth, and utter one single cry of pain, one call for help, now, the entire city will be in cinders this time tomorrow. You hear? You understand, salamund mouth? Hurry up and snap on your handcuffs.

Corporal. Woman, if—

Superintendent. Ah yes, that's what I was trying to recollect all along. Your face. Of course I recognize it. You're Titubi, the spoiled daughter of Alhaja Kabirat, head of the market women.

Titubi. Whether I am spoiled or not, you'll see tomorrow when you get to the office. You hear? Your superiors crawl to my dog-kennel. Not even ten of you can arrest me.

Superintendent. All right, if that's the way you want it. Take her in!

(The Corporal steps forward with handcuffs.)

Titubi. Dare it, you smelling pig. You offspring of some teak-laden litter at the back of a latrine! Dare to put your filthy hand on me and all of your wretched family will never finish paying for it.

Superintendent. Wait. *(sniggers)* Words are cheap, eh?

Titubi. Words can break the likes of you.

Superintendent. I congratulate you. Gestures are large, when the wind alone is the obstacle.

Titubi. Don't think you're clever. Every cobra is poisonous, whatever its gloss.

Superintendent. The hunter brings home a grass-cutter and beats his chest. What will happen to the elephant-killer?

Titubi. The shoulder is not smaller is it, simply because it has chosen to wear a low-necked blouse?

Superintendent. Oh the cat has claws. The tiger has claws. But what feat of courage is it when the tiger goes up to the cat and says, Hm, your anus is smelling?

Titubi. Enough. I can see you have some wit. You missed your calling. You should be making money selling cloth in one of my mother's stores at Gbagi.

Superintendent. I am going to arrest you, my young lady. Go on, Corple! *(The Corporal, with determined struggle, and aided by the Director, finally snaps the handcuffs on.)* But I'd like to tell you something. I'd like to say how terribly impressed I am by this show you've put up here. So you are Titubi, the Amazon going to war! You're wealthy, your mother owns the town, and you're going to defend with you very life all that possession. But tell me, if you're really serious, if you really want to save your fat-arsed class, why haven't you offered your services to crush this peasant revolt? You know there is a battle going on now, don't you? That the farmers and villagers around us have risen in open rebellion and are marching down upon the city? When they arrive, who do you think will be the first target? But you don't volunteer to help in fighting them. No. This mere wooden platform is your battlefield. Shit! This is where you come to put up a gallant fight, wasting my time! (spits) Go on. Titu-Titu, the magnificent Moremi of the sixties! Make your show, let them clap for you! Destroy the theatre! Burn it down! They'll put your name in the national archives! *Shi-oooh!* Corple, remove the handcuffs! Go on, free her! Give free rein to her prowess. *(The Corporal does so.)* Let's go, man. I'm going to sleep . . .

(He begins to march off, the Corporal following. The actors have gathered, jeering. Titubi seems about to collapse, sobbing. Then suddenly she looks up and calls:)

Titubi. Salami! *(Superintendent stops, without turning around.)* Salami, suppose I do volunteer?

Superintendent. *(turns now)* What?

Titubi. I said, suppose I offer to fight the peasants?

Superintendent. You're not finished with your pranks for tonight?

Titubi. It's their leader you've not been able to capture, isn't it? That's why the war drags on?

Superintendent. Well—

Titubi. *(hard)* Yes or no?

Superintendent. Well, yes . . . and no. Their leader proves elusive, but—

Titubi. But?

Superintendent. He may not really exist.

Titubi. He may not exist! A phantom leader!

Superintendent. I mean . . . there may not be just one leader, maybe a group of leaders . . .

Titubi. But someone leads that group?

Superintendent. Actually—

Titubi. You're a liar, Salami. You know he exists. And you know his name. You admitted it in your interview with the press last week.

Superintendent. Okay, so I admitted it. They call him Marshal.

Titubi. I can bring him to you.

Superintendent. You? *(laughs)* Corple!

Titubi. Don't laugh, Salami.

Superintendent. *(looks at her, stops laughing)* My word, I do believe you are serious.

Titubi. Two weeks. Give me only two weeks.

Superintendent. This is a dream? *(rubbing his eyes)*

Titubi. Two weeks. And I'll bring him here, on his knees.

Superintendent. What the entire Police Force failed to—

Titubi. Is that why you're afraid? That I might succeed?

Superintendent. *(after a pause)* What do you want?

Titubi. Can you arrange for me to be captured?

Superintendent. What!

Titubi. That's all the help I'll require from you.

Superintendent. You're not . . . crazy?

Titubi. Two weeks, I said. We've wasted five minutes of it.

Superintendent. *(after a pause)* All right, girl. I'm going to call your bluff. An idea has just struck me. Follow me . . . to prison.

Titubi. Prison?

Superintendent. Yes. That's where it's all going to begin. Come, I'll explain it all to you . . .

(They draw aside, and the Superintendent beings to talk. The Corporal goes out and returns with a prison gown. Titubi steps aside and changes into the gown. The Corporal collects her old clothes, including her jewelry. But she refuses to remove the necklace. The Corporal looks at the officer, who replies with a shrug. The Corporal goes out with her old clothes and reappears, in Warder's uniform.

Meanwhile, on stage, the actors rearrange the furniture of their dressing area, singing a prison work song.[1] The set now approximates a prison cell. They salute the officer with the mock song of prisoners and go out.

---

* All notes are at the end of the play text.

The Superintendent leads Titubi into the cell followed by the Warder.)

Superintendent. You understand?
Titubi. Yes. I'll wait.

(as the officer leaves—Blackout, except for a single spotlight from which the Director now speaks)

TWO

Director. And so that's it, ladies and gentlemen. We came here to do a play, a simple play. But History—or what some of you call Chance or Fortune—has taken over the stage. And it will play itself out, whether we like it or not. All we can do is either quicken it or slow down its progress. And let this be a lesson to you, my friends. In the affairs of men, History is often like . . . like a . . .

(Bogunde appears, walking stealthily, and calls out:)

Bogunde. Sh!
Director. Yes?
Bogunde. May we come in now? It's our cue.
Director. Yes, I think it's safe. Put on your costumes and make-up. Disguise yourselves well. For when you come in, no one must recognize your real identity. In this scene, remember, you'll be playing, not your real roles, but as . . .
Bogunde. Enough! Get out of the way!
Director. *(going, stops to talk to audience)* See what I mean? I'll see you later.

(Bogunde ushers in his men into strategic positions around the cell for the following scene.)

THREE

(Lights come on upon a scene overlooking Titubi's prison cell. A number of petty traders form a ramshackle street market, with fruit baskets and trays, portable clothes racks, tinsel jewelry and wristwatches, and other items common to the ambulant street traders of the West African cities.

Among the traders, in various disguises, are Bogunde and Kokondi. They keep a careful, but not too noticeable, watch on the prison, even while pretending to trade and converse.

Then Marshal walks in, under a wide straw hat, carrying some marketable items, including a bundle of what looks like firewood, but are in fact local rifles and matchets camouflaged. He goes to Bogunde, who is selling oranges—or any other fruit available. During their conversation, the other traders will also be calling Marshal to come and buy their own goods, as is common is any such market.)

Marshal. How much?

Bogunde. All clear over there now, Marshal. One shilling.[2]

Marshal. Pardon? You know me too I be seller like you.

Bogunde. Still the regular guards about the place. No reinforcements.

Marshal. Make I pay nine pence now, I beg. Any visitors inside?

Bogunde. Ah Oga! Na the price meself buy am! No one has come in or gone out of the place in the past hour.

Marshal. They haven't noticed your presence?

Bogunde. No.

Marshal. Good. I pay eight pence and take three. God bless.

Bogunde. I think we can attack the prison now.

Marshal. No. You wait as planned. You fit peel them for me?

Bogunde. Our warder is on duty. He'll open the gate as soon as he hears the signal.

Marshal. Thank you.

Bogunde. Alao's on the other side.

Marshal. Why not? I fit sell am to you. How many you want?

Bogunde. I'll take the whole bundle.

Marshal. I know say I meet good man today. Come look. *(Some of the other traders draw near.)* This na good man. Listen carefully, all of you. In exactly fifteen minutes the warders will go into the canteen for their lunch. The signal will be given. Be ready. Thank you. *(They all laugh as if at a joke.)* You know wetin? I get song wey I dey sing when I lucky like this. Make I teach you? You go sing with me?

Traders. Ye-e-e-s.

Marshal. Good. I go sing am. Make una join me. As you sing,

you go put hand forward. Like this. Then draw back. Forward—draw back. Ready?

*(He sings.[3] Lights fade on hands reaching out toward his bun-
dle, which, now partly undone, is seen to contain weapons.
Slow Fade-out.)*

FOUR

*(Titubi, in a prison cell, humming a song, in good spirits. The
traders' song of the last scene remains in the background,
occasionally breaking in strongly. Enter Alhaja Kabirat, richly
dressed and holding a handkerchief to her nose.)*

Titubi. *(running to her mother)* Mama!

Alhaja. *(coldly)* So this is where they put you, Titu!

Titubi. *(excitedly)* Yes, but only for a while. Did you get my
note?

Alhaja. That's why I am here.

Titubi. Isn't it fantastic! I'm so— . . . but how did you get in? I
was told this place is on top security, no visitors and all that.
Or . . . ah mama, you bribed the warders!

Alhaja. *(looking around)* No bed. No window. No fan or air-
conditioner. The walls damp and clammy. A terrible stench
that followed me all the way here from the gates. *(breaks
down finally)* Ah Allah! What have I done to deserve this?

Titubi. But it's all part of the plan. After that night in the
theatre, I agreed to it. I stay here. I pretend to be a prisoner.
Then when the peasants break in and find me—

Alhaja. Quiet! You want to ruin me, isn't it? That's your latest
insanity, abi? To destroy me completely before my custom-
ers. Ehn? Just supposed I wasn't in the shop, and someone
else had read the note before it came into my hands? What?
Everybody would have known by now that my own daughter
is in this . . . this latrine. *(She breaks down.)* Ah Allah, what
on earth could she have done? What unpardonable crime to
merit this kind of humiliation?

Titubi. But, mama, it isn't a punishment! I wasn't arrested for
anything. I came on my own free will.

Alhaja. I thank you. Let's go now anyway. And the policemen who brought you here, they will wish they'd never been born!

Titubi. Aren't you listening to me? I—

Alhaja. Enough, I say! I've swallowed enough of this foul air into my lungs. Let's go!

Titubi. You will spoil the whole plan. Maybe you've even spoiled it already.

Alhaja. Are you coming or not?

Titubi. Mama—

Alhaja. Titu! Or isn't it my daughter I am talking to?

Titubi. The peasant revolt, mama! You talk about it every day with your friends. I see all of you tremble. The peasants are upon us. They will eat everything up, all your wealth, the entire meaning of your life, unless someone acts.

Alhaja. And that someone is my daughter, abi?

Titubi. They're coming, mama, and the only way left is to infiltrate their ranks quickly, discover their real leader, and the source of their ammunition. I volunteered. *(more excited)* You see, mama, they are coming to this prison this week. The police have got the advance information that the peasants plan to raid this place to release their captured colleagues. So it's perfectly simple. The police will let them come and free the prisoners, including me.

Alhaja. And then?

Titubi. And then I go with them to their camp.

Alhaja. Are you still in your senses, Titu? You will go with who, to where?

Titubi. Look at this, mama.

Alhaja. What?

Titubi. This necklace, with its pretty dagger.

Alhaja. What about it?

Titubi. The latest fashion. Which we girls call "Moremi."

Alhaja. Are you teaching me! I sell it, by the hundreds.

Titubi. You taught me her story, mama. When I was still too young to understand. But I've never forgotten: Moremi, the brave woman of Ile-Ife, who saved the race. Now, when I wear this necklace, I feel a passion deeper than any passing vogue. It is as if I have become history itself.

Alhaja. Give me. Let me see. *(Titubi hands over the necklace.*

Alhaja flings it down and stamps on it.) There! There goes your passion. I'll tame you yet, before you run naked into the streets.

Titubi. I am going to do it, mama. You won't stop me.

Alhaja. We shall see. *(calling)* Lati! Lati! I had suspected something like this. Lati! *(Lati appears.)* Carry her!

Titubi. Wait! Mama, I—

Alhaja. Are you coming or not? *(An idea strikes her.)* Lati, when is the last plane leaving for Mecca?

Lati. Tomorrow afternoon, Alhaja.

Alhaja. Good, there's still time.

Titubi. *(reading her thoughts)* I'm not going anywhere!

Alhaja. You'll go on this year's pilgrimage, Titu. I was thinking of sending you next year, when you'll be more grown-up, but now, with this—Nothing like Mecca to help restore your mind.

Titubi. But I tell you—

(The Warder comes running in.)

Warder. Alhaja . . . Alhaja! Oga dey come! Quick, quick!

Alhaja. *(unmoved)* Yes?

Warder. Please, I beg, come. Come . . . he go ruin me, I beg . . .

Alhaja. Who?

Warder. Oga . . . Oga papatata. He head for this place . . .

Alhaja. Let him come. I have a few words for him.

Warder. But—

Alhaja. Shut up, idiot! I say let him come. He won't be in a position to even touch your hair by the time I—

(Enter the Deputy Superintendent who stops short, on seeing them.)

Superintendent. Well, well!

Alhaja. I've been waiting for you.

Superintendent. *(sarcastic tone)* I hope you made yourself comfortable.

Alhaja. This is my daughter!

Superintendent. Really? My name is Salami, Deputy Su—

Alhaja. My own daughter!

Superintendent. I'm willing to believe you, Alhaja Kabirat.

Alhaja. What is she doing here?

Superintendent. I'm more interested in what you are doing here, madam.

Alhaja. You're going to pay for this, Salami. You're going to pay so much that you'll regret the day you joined the Force.

Superintendent. I regret it already, Alhaja, if that will bring any comfort to you. In fact I've been regretting it ever since the day I signed up.

Alhaja. Let's go, Titu. *(shouting to Lati)* Carry her! Carry the insane harlot for me!

Superintendent. *(calm)* Warder! Take the gentleman to Room Six. Room Six. And then come back here. *(to Lati)* I'd advise you to go now, quietly, in your own interest.

Titubi. *(as Lati hesitates)* Go, Lati. Follow him.

(Lati and the Warder go out.)

Superintendent. He's your driver, isn't he?

Titubi. Yes.

Superintendent. And bodyguard? Maybe he'll get a light sentence.

Alhaja. What do you mean?

(The Corporal returns.)

Superintendent. Alhaja, your turn. A room in the B suite. Please follow Corple, or shall I lead you myself?

Alhaja. You're full of jokes, I can see. Go on, amuse me.

Superintendent. It's in the blood, madam. I can't help it. My father was the official clown at the State House for many years before he retired. He couldn't stand Independence, he'd said. Reality was so absurd that jokes were getting hard to invent. *(in a sudden sharp tone)* Take her away.

Titubi. *(as the Corporal steps forward)* Mr. Salami, that's my mother, you know.

Superintendent. So what! You think that should make me fall on my face?

Titubi. Your superiors do more.

Superintendent. You amuse me. I come in and what do I see? An infiltration into a maximum security prison. At a moment like this! Madam, I don't care how you got here, but I am certainly going to keep you, at least till the operation has taken off. After that we may talk.

Alhaja. You don't mean it, young man. Even if you're a dozen Salamis together, you wouldn't thrust your fingers in fire.

Titubi. Listen, the deal is off. Talking to my mother like that, you . . . you . . . toad! I'm going home!

Superintendent. *(laughs)* You're going home! As easy as that, eh? You think we're playing children's games here?

Titubi. Dare me, you hear! I'll see how you'll force me to go on your mission.

Superintendent. My mission! Is that what you believed when you volunteered?

Alhaja. Does he . . . does he know who I am at all?

Superintendent. Listen to me. The peasants out there are not more than a thousand strong. Let's say, even two thousand. Two thousand men, armed mostly with crude dane guns, matchets, bows and arrows. What's all that before the awesome apparatus of the State? Before our well-trained and well-equipped fighting squads? A wall of vegetable! So why have we not been able to crush them?

Alhaja. Are you asking me?

Superintendent. You should know, Alhaja. After all, these rebels are of your own creation, you who are used to feeding on others.

Alhaja. Look here—

Superintendent. I'll tell you. The peasants are strong, and seemingly invincible, because they are solidly united by the greatest force in the world: hunger. They are hungry, their children die of kwashiorkor, and they have risen to say no, no more!

Alhaja. It's a lie! No one has ever died of hunger in this country! I am surprised at you, a police officer, carrying this kind of baseless propaganda . . .

Superintendent. They claim that you and your politicians have been taking off the profits of their farms to feed your cities, to feed your own throats, and to buy more jewels and frippery. And so, at last, they are coming for the reckoning.

Alhaja. And that's why you are paid, isn't it? To stop them. Not to stay here gloating on their imagined grievances.

Superintendent. We will stop them, Alhaja, only when every-body concerned decides to cooperate. When those who are threatened are brave enough to offer their services. Other-wise—finish! For we are no miracle workers. And one of these fine days you'll wake to the noise of shooting in your kitchen. Your markets will be on fire, your pretty houses, your banks and insurance houses, the entire street will be burning. And there'll be nowhere for you to hide. No! There'll only be screams and blood everywhere, and you'll be made to watch as six, seven men mount your daughter and ride her to death—

Alhaja. Stop!

Superintendent. It could be tomorrow . . . it could be tonight . . .

Alhaja. Stop him, I say! In the name of Allah!

Superintendent. Allah, madam, is always on the side of those who do more than just fold their arms and watch. We needed a brave woman. Your daughter volunteered. She is to be commended.

Alhaja. (cowed now) You think that if she . . . if Titu follows this crazy plan . . . ?

Superintendent. Your daughter has the best credentials for this kind of job. She's willing to do it, and she's richly endowed. Pretty, sensual, daring, and with quite a reputation with men, if my information is correct?

Titubi. Thank you . . .

Superintendent. Above all, she's not known to be even re-motely connected with the police.

Alhaja. And you think you can do it, Titu?

Titubi. I will do it, mama. One woman did it before.

Alhaja. A woman?

Titubi. Moremi. Have you forgotten?

Alhaja. Oh!

Titubi. You think she was better than me?

Alhaja. (clinging to her) My poor poor doll!

Titubi. Wipe your tears, mama. I'll come back safe, you'll see. And the war will be over.

Superintendent. Good. If you've made up your mind—

Titubi. Nothing can stop me now.

Superintendent. In that case, there's no time to waste. Alhaja,

I'm afraid I'll have to cut short the leave-taking. You can cry in your own house as hard as you'll cry here. Please—Corple! Please follow him, Alhaja.

Alhaja. Goodbye, Titu. I'll not sleep till you come back. *(exit)*

Superintendent. She'll not sleep till you return. She'll be counting her profits in the market.

Titubi. You're just a dog, Salami. A loathsome dog.

Superintendent. Hired by cannibals, to do your hunting. Anyway, let's stop arguing, and I'll give you your final instructions. For it's going to be this evening.

Titubi. What?

Superintendent. The attack. We've got news at last. The peasants will be storming this prison today, in a couple of hours. You've got to be ready.

Titubi. I . . . I didn't know it would be so soon.

Superintendent. The important things in life are always like that: they come too soon or too late, but never at the time we expect. Anyway you know the instructions. Let them release you from here, with the other prisoners. Then follow them to their camp. They'll question you, but we've already rehearsed that part. Maybe we'll go through it once more before I leave you. When you get there, find out as much as you can. But don't take any risks. That's an order too. You're not to take any undue risks. *(She has turned her back.)* Are you listening to me?

Titubi. I heard you—

Superintendent. Then—

Titubi. *(turning sharply)* Tell me, Salami. You don't really believe it, do you? You don't believe she existed.

Superintendent. Who?

Titubi. Moremi.

Superintendent. Oh!

Titubi. But she did exist, didn't she?

Superintendent. A myth. We're dealing with reality here. And reality is a far more cruel thing.

Titubi. Yet it is the same reality that softens with time, isn't it, that turns into myth?

Superintendent. Well . . . What's that got to do with it? *(worried)* You're sure you can go on this mission after all?

Titubi. *(laughs)* My mother always complains that I dream too much. Do you think so?

Superintendent. *(after a pause)* We'll go through that interrogation scene we've rehearsed again. Then maybe I'll know. Get ready. I am the peasants' leader, and you have been brought before me. Are we set? *(Titubi nods, falls on her knees.)* Here we go. *(takes a different voice)* Hey, treat her gently! You'll never lose your manners of an alaaru. You think she's one of those bags of salt you used to carry at Agbeni, ehn? A woman is delicate. *(Titubi bursts out laughing. He stops.)* Look, do you know they are already outside? And you're laughing! *(Titubi composes herself again. He starts again.)* Treat her gently. Gently. A woman is delicate. Sorry, my daughter. You'll forgive his rough manners. What's your name?

Titubi. Titu . . . you still don't think I should use some other name?

Superintendent. No, not necessary. As I told you, none of the farmers has ever moved in the circles in which you are known. Your name won't mean anything to them. So you keep it, and you'll have no problems with remembering your identity. Shall we go on?

Titubi. Yes.

Superintendent. Rise, Titu. Sit down. *(offers "chair")* Now, can you tell us what you're doing here? My men say you insisted on coming.

Titubi. I was locked up there in the prison, sir, awaiting my trial. I didn't ask to be released, but your men came and set me free. They forced all of us out of the cells.

Superintendent. Well?

Titubi. Of course I'm grateful, but where do I go now? If I return there, it'll be much worse for me. They'll think I had a hand in planning it all.

Superintendent. You mean you want to return to prison?

Titubi. I have nowhere else to go.

Superintendent. You can't go home?

Titubi. No. Not any more.

Superintendent. Strange! . . . What about . . . your people?

Titubi. I have no people now. They've all renounced me.

Superintendent. Was your crime that terrible?

Titubi. Abominable.

Superintendent. You don't mind telling us about it?

Titubi. Well . . . do you really insist?

Superintendent. I'm afraid we'll have to know.

Titubi. What will you do to me?

Superintendent. Depends.

Titubi. On what? On my crime?

Superintendent. Did you kill someone?

Titubi. *(after a silence)* Yes.

Superintendent. Who?

Titubi. I killed my own children.

Superintendent. No!

Titubi. So you see!

Superintendent. Your own children!

Titubi. I wasn't myself. I swear I didn't know what I was doing. Suddenly I wanted to end it all, but in such a way that no part of me would be left in his hands. I mean, my husband. How I hated him! How I hated myself! I hated the fact that he'd ever touched me and loved me. I wanted to scrape all my skin off, cut my tongue, my lips, all the parts of me that had ever come into contact with him. I swear I wasn't myself! At last I said I'd kill myself and the children I had for him. I prepared the poison with a lot of sleeping drugs, locked myself in with the children . . . and we all drank it, one by one. The youngest, Ranti, just four months old, was the first to succumb. He dropped into sleep. Then the second, my daughter, Yetunde. She too dropped her head on the pillow by my side . . . It was then that terror struck me. I rose up to scream for help, but my feet gave way, and I fell in a crash to the floor . . . and that was the last thing I knew for a long long time . . .

Superintendent. So you're the woman! The story came to us on Rediffusion. It was on every lip! . . .

Titubi. They wouldn't let me die. They kept me for months in the hospital and spent lots of money, just to make sure I survived to face the punishment. They will kill me in the end, but only after I have lived through the prolonged hell of agony and remorse.

Superintendent. Yes, yes, I remember . . . I think you were a nurse at the General Hospital?

Titubi. *(breaking off)* You're just adding that on?

Superintendent. Yes. It just occurred to me. The woman was in fact a nurse. They might know.

Titubi. So I answer yes.

Superintendent. You went through the Nursing School, didn't you?

Titubi. I didn't finish the course. I got bored.

Superintendent. How much did you learn?

Titubi. Enough, don't worry. I was in fact quite good.

Superintendent. If we use it, it means the farmers will be needing your help. And that way, you'll win their trust even more rapidly.

Titubi. Then let's use it. If they don't ask, I'll tell them.

Superintendent. Right, where were we?

Titubi. Almost the end of the interrogation. I was telling them about my children.

Superintendent. Continue. Finish up.

Titubi. *(going into the role again)* Three lovely children. My sons, so handsome and troublesome, thinking they owned the world . . . and my daughter, so gentle . . . ah, children are beautiful! Their voices echo in my head. I cannot sleep. I know I shall not know peace again till they put my neck in the noose that is waiting for me. Because I have lost the courage to take my life myself. I begged the warders, but they all shrank from me . . . and that is why I followed your men. Please, I beg you, if compassion is one of the things that keep you together, please, help me. Help me end my life now. Kill me . . . *(She begins to sob.)*

Superintendent. Take her away!

Titubi. *(near hysterical)* You won't help me? You won't end my suffering for me?

Superintendent. *(applauding)* You'll live, woman. Very very good. Even I was impressed. If you can remember all that, you'll make it.

Titubi. *(unmoved)* Thank you.

Superintendent. Well, all that remains is for me to wish you good luck. *(He offers his hand. She does not take it.)*

Titubi. Goodbye. *(He looks at her for some time, in silence, and then goes out. Titubi walks slowly around the cell.)*

They are already outside, he said. They'll soon be here! I . . .
I am afraid, suddenly . . . *(pause)* No! Moremi was not afraid!
(snaps her fingers backward over her head) Fear go away!
Doubt and trembling, retreat from me! . . . *(She retrieves the
Moremi necklace from the floor and looks at it.)* She was a
woman, like me. And she waited all alone, for the Igbo
warriors. All her people went into hiding, but she alone
stood and waited. I can feel her heart beating, like mine . . .
But how lucky you were, Moremi! How I envy you! Look, I
have only the dampness of these walls around me, to wish
me goodbye. But you, you had the scent of the market
around you. The smell of fish, the redolence of spices, sweet
decay of wood, smell of rain-washed thatches, the tang of
mud at your feet . . . ah Moremi! What were your thoughts at
that lonely moment? Can I read your mind . . . ? Maybe it
would strengthen me . . .

*(She puts on the necklace and seems to go into a reverie. Light
changes occur, slowly, dimming gradually on the cell and
brightening simultaneously on a small market square. The
Moremi praise-song[4] wells up and then sinks into a faint background. Titubi, still in her reverie, joins in the singing. She
remains visible throughout the following scene.)*

FIVE

*The market square. Moremi herself, sitting on a bamboo bench
or stool, is only faintly defined yet. The scene is several decades
ago, nearer the dawn of the Yoruba civilization at Ile-Ife. The
manner of dressing and make-up should suggest this historical
context. A voice calls, from offstage.*

Voice. Moremi! Moremi! Are you not afraid?

*(Startled, Titubi turns to see, and then freezes, in a half-light,
watching the scene. In the market, the lights grow into the
brilliance of sunlight. Moremi raises her head.)*

Voice. Are you not scared, Moremi?

(The speaker appears. It is Moremi's friend, Niniola.)

Moremi. Niniola!

Niniola. Moremi! The Yeye-Oba group are coming, to pay our
last respects, before the Igbo warriors arrive. I took a short
cut to reach you first.

Moremi. Thank you, Niniola. I am glad to see you.

Niniola. I asked, are you not afraid?

Moremi. Well . . . up till this moment, I never thought of it.
Fear was . . . a faraway land. When I went to Esinmirin to
make my pledge, my heart was as stout as the iroko tree.
Right up till the last moment of my departure, when I held
my son Oluorogbo to my breast and bade him farewell. The
priests led me darkly into the grove for the appropriate ceremonies, and then slowly, we danced past the shrine of my
husband's grandfather, Oduduwa. You know, going from god
to god, looking into their impressive eyes, then walking
through the streets, past the throngs of silent forms, the
people watching, immobile, I felt like one drunk on wine. I
felt strong and light, the noon breeze was in my veins . . . but
then we arrived here, in the market, and the priests left. And
I was alone, alone with these empty spaces . . . and . . .

Niniola. And?

Moremi. You say our comrades, the Yeye-Oba, will soon be
here?

Niniola. Yes. If you listen hard, you can just catch their singing.

Moremi. It's as if . . . as if it's suddenly grown cold. *(sighs)* Let
them come quick. Perhaps, surrounded by their voices and
the whirl of their feet . . . perhaps if we dance together again,
like before, for a little while, perhaps Moremi will recover
her courage.

Niniola. Listen, if you're afraid—

Moremi. No! Please, Nini, don't mention that word again.
Please, or you will see me weaken and run.

Niniola. But that's why I've come, Moremi. It is not too late.
You can still change your mind.

Moremi. What? Moremi should change her mind at the last
minute?

Niniola. Why not? Listen, I admire your courage, and I love
you, but this is clearly the path of death. The Igbos are cruel
and wanton. If they capture you—

Moremi. I cannot turn back. If we never risked our life, how shall we come to value it?

Niniola. I've heard you say this before, even in our much younger days when we understood nothing. The lure of death seems to have fastened to you unrelentingly like a leech. Your hunger for fame is limitless. You'll never have enough. Now you must step in even where the gods have failed. You must be godhead itself!

Moremi. Are you angry, Nini?

Niniola. Come with me. Step back from this mad adventure.

Moremi. My friend . . . perhaps you are right. I am too ambitious. When I see the stars, I long desperately to touch them. Yes, Niniola, I am jealous of the gods!

Niniola. What!

Moremi. We fall on our knees, we multiply our supplications, we pile up the sacrifices. But suppose, Niniola, just suppose the gods are indifferent to us?

Niniola. *Eewo!* What are you saying? May such evil words never come from your mouth again. May the air dissolve them and scatter them into nothingness. Please, Moremi, if you must go, go. Follow the restless spirit that drives you. But don't add the burden of blasphemy . . .

Moremi. You talk of beauty and success and glamour! But what is all that to me when, one fine day, in the midst of the most splendid rejoicing, with the choicest meat in my teeth, without warning at all, the Igbos can arrive suddenly, locusts in the air, and eat everything up? That is the life our gods have provided for us after all our rituals and sacrifices. No, no! Nini, it is time for us to rise, to stand and square up our shoulders by our own courage, and stop leaning on the gods.

Niniola. The gods are with us—

Moremi. With their backs turned to us—

Niniola. The gods will never turn their back! May the afternoon never suddenly take on the shroud of night in our life!

Moremi. Futile prayers! How many times already we've watched our festivals change into periods of mourning when the Igbos set on us. Yet we have made sacrifices upon sacrifices till the earth is glutted with blood. Our priests have scraped their throats hoarse on incantations, and their latest ploy is to try and make us accept defeat as fate. Tell me, my friend, what more shall we do to learn that the gods will not help us? I have decided. Moremi shall be the clay that the race requires to remold itself.

Niniola. You frighten me, Moremi. You repudiate the gods! So what of your pledge to Esinmirin? Who will give you protection on your journey? Suppose you never come back now?

Moremi. *(amused)* Come, Nini. Embrace me. I am glad you came and talked to me. Now Moremi is no longer afraid. Let the women come and we shall dance together, like the procession on a bridal night. Your doubt and your fear have strengthened me. I shall go, and I shall return.

(Enter the women who make up the Yeye-Oba Group, singing a solemn dirge.[4] They fan about Moremi, Niniola joining them, and kneel, their hands extended in homage.)

Moremi. Oh stand, stand up my friends! What's all this song of mourning? Abeke, Bisi, Jumoke, Rama, ah-ha, am I gone already to the land of our ancestors that you accompany my corpse with such lament? This is a day of joy, my friends! The land is going to be reborn, by the daring of a woman! Adunni, come, you've always been my keenest rival. Let me have the joy of competing with you again, and of beating you as usual! Come. *(She calls out a song,[5] which they pick up, and a dancing competition begins, first between Moremi and Adunni, and then with other partners. At the height of it, a piercing cry, bringing them back to reality. A warrior runs by, calling "The Igbos! The Igbos! Run!" The women scatter at once in great panic, with Niniola, the last to go, making an unsuccessful attempt to drag Moremi along with her. Moremi, now alone, begins to preen herself. From behind her, Oronmiyon, dressed as another warrior, enters and calls her.)*

SIX

Oronmiyon. Don't be afraid. It's me.
Moremi. My husband!
Oronmiyon. Sh!

Moremi. What are you—

Oronmiyon. Hush, I said.

Moremi. *(agitated)* At a moment like this, outside the palace and unprotected! And in this uniform!

Oronmiyon. Listen—

Moremi. You frighten me. It is taboo for the king—*(Recollecting herself, she curtsies.)*—Kabiyesi.

Oronmiyon. Oh, forget that now.

Moremi. It is taboo for the king to walk the afternoon like this, alone and unshaded, with your face naked. What is the matter?

Oronmiyon. I slipped out through one of the hidden doors in the palace walls. Yes, the tasks of a king, who is also a husband, will sometimes require the tactics of a slave. (laughs) It won't be the first time.

Moremi. But why now? The Igbos are—

Oronmiyon. Listen to me, Moremi. I know the Igbos will soon be here. They have crossed the moat already on the east side. That is why I have come. For you. It is not too late to change your mind. I'll lead you back through the hidden passage into the palace.

Moremi. What, my lord?

Oronmiyon. I know you are a woman of tremendous courage. Right from the day of your arrival, you became the real favorite of the royal chambers. Your beauty and your special grace, Moremi, were the principal ornaments of the palace—

Moremi. *(teasing)* And yet, my lord, only two moons ago, took another wife?

Oronmiyon. Of course you understand. Kings are like Mother Bee. They must clothe themselves in people. The palace must fill its hives with the nectar of female voices. That is how our fathers made it. But your place of eminence was never in dispute, for your courage is strong, like our ancient rafters. Your name alone holds up with esteem the tottering roof of our beseiged kingdom. And I suppose now that that was why I consented to this plan of yours, almost without reflection. I said to myself, echoing your words, that Moremi is the only person in this land who can succeed, if we are ever to discover the great secret of the Igbos, if we are ever to

find a counter to this mysterious power of theirs that turns
   my bravest warriors into helpless *(omolangidi)* each time
   the marauders come upon us . . .
Moremi. And now you have changed your mind, isn't it? You
   have found the great secret that can defeat the Igbos who
   even now are bearing down upon us?
Oronmiyon. The secret I have found is you, Moremi.
Moremi. When time presses, my lord, we discard the horse of
   enigmas.
Oronmiyon. Well, I shall explain later. For now, just come with
   me.
Moremi. And what will your subjects say afterward of Moremi,
   the ambitious woman of Ile-Ife? Will they not laugh and say,
   look at the brave brave hero who lost her nerve at the crucial
   moment and fled with her tail between her spindly feet?
Oronmiyon. This is no time to worry about that. Come
   quickly!
Moremi. My husband!
Oronmiyon. I say, do not worry. I, Oronmiyon, I am the public
   opinion. Subjects only echo the ruler's caprices.
Moremi. So what about the mothers who will crowd to your
   palace tomorrow, as before, their hands empty again, those
   hands that only this morning hold laughing children to their
   breasts? Ah, the thought that Oluorogbo, a prince born, can
   be stolen like that, stripped of his inheritance, and turned
   into a slave before nightfall . . . !
Oronmiyon. That will never happen, I assure you.

(Terrifying shrieks are heard, still rather far off.)

Moremi. Do you hear them, my lord? The Igbos are drawing
   near, combing the streets and alleys, scaling our walls with
   ease. And you know what is happening, as our story repeats
   itself. Already our men tremble by their household shrines,
   their prayers stuck in their teeth. Our warriors are beginning
   to babble like Obatala's misfits. The women are pissing
   shamelessly in front of their screaming children. Your
   priests are again going to pieces in helpless rage, their
   vaunted charms now impotent like *Osanyin* left in the rain.
   (shrieks again) They are near, they approach, Kabiyesi, you

can do nothing other than gnash your teeth. Once again we are encircled, and the mysterious paralysis is beginning to spread in our veins like the stupor of *majele*. Nothing in Ife has been discovered to counter it: no leaf or bark, no grass, no ritual amulet, we are lost, lost . . . And yet Moremi is prepared to stake her life, to take the risk of captivity in order to be able at last to penetrate into the enemy camp and learn their magic. What do you say, husband? Shall I stay behind and forsake all this so that this evening you can come and tickle my tender parts?

Oronmiyon. *(shouting)* Stay! I command it!

Moremi. And I say, no! Go back quickly to the palace. For at this spot and in this moment, I am already beyond the lashing whips of your command!

Oronmiyon. You . . . you dare to defy me?

Moremi. Face to face we stand together, in the onrushing waters of danger. In my own hands I hold the paddle of my destiny.

Oronmiyon. Can I believe my ears, that this is Moremi talking to me!

Moremi. My husband, be yourself. Be the hero you've always been. Like in those days when you hurried back from Ijebuland to claim your throne from usurpers. Your exploits refurbish the throne of your ancestors. But when muscles slacken suddenly in the midst of dispute, they say it is time to use other tactics. I must go.

Oronmiyon. And which husband, be he king and all, will dare walk proud again, who has openly sacrificed his wife to ward off his own death?

Moremi. No! Nobody sacrifices Moremi. Nobody! I have chosen, all by myself. Neither by the gods' cajoling, nor by your designing. Moremi chose, and carries the burden upon herself. Please go now.

Oronmiyon. I shall carry you, you stubborn woman! Come—

Moremi. *(after struggling vainly with him and about to weaken)* My husband! *(bursts into tears)* I see now that you really love me!

Oronmiyon. But of course! What do you—

Moremi. Ah alas! Why do you come to show me now that it's too late?

Oronmiyon. What do you mean, too late? There's still time to slip back into the palace if you come quickly.

Moremi. I . . . I didn't know you loved me so much. And now . . . I am no longer worth saving.

Oronmiyon. Look, let's just go and—

Moremi. I thought you no longer wanted me. When you took your last wife—

Oronmiyon. Asake, yes?

Moremi. I became so jealous that . . . that . . .

Oronmiyon. Ehn-hen?

Moremi. Forgive me! It . . . I . . . it was Arogundade.

Oronmiyon. Arogundade? Ah, I see, the trader from Ijesaland. What about him?

Moremi. He . . . he . . . please forgive me. I've been unfaithful to you. I . . . I slept with him.

Oronmiyon. Abomination! You . . . you . . . *(He knocks her down brutally. Shrieks much closer now.)* Well, your fate is sealed. By your own hands. No unfaithful woman may again enter the king's chambers, as you know. It would be instant death . . . *(He bends down and raises her up.)* As you said, Moremi, you have chosen the manner of your own exit. You have chosen well. And it's much better like this . . . But I forgive you. I promise, this town will remember you. And if you can, by this act of daring, cleanse yourself, we shall be here to receive you. Farewell, my love. *(He runs off. Moremi laughs, and begins again to preen herself. Then suddenly she freezes, to become her legendary statue, watching the following scene.)*

SEVEN

Lights come up bright on the prison cell as, simultaneously, a war song[6] fills the air in a sudden violent upwelling. Armed peasants, led by Bogunde, break into the cell, frightening Titubi into a corner.

Bogunde. Free the woman! You see how these animals behave, to keep a woman in this hideous place! I am sorry for our brothers who have been languishing here all these days. Woman, you are free. We farmers from the village release you. Go home and tell your friends. Goodbye. Men, let's go.

(They go. Titubi, somewhat dazed, runs after them.)

Titubi. Wait for me! Please, wait for me!

(Blackout)

EIGHT

Caught in silhouette only, the peasants sing and dance to a clamorous song of harvest.[7] As the celebration begins to die down, the Director appears in a spotlight and speaks above the song:

Director. There she goes then, my friends, bravely walking into danger. Stepping carelessly into the unknown. Ah, women! My friends, the world is strange and women reign over it. Let us salute their courage. Their capacity for love. Moremi, I remember you and I celebrate you . . .

(He goes off into the Moremi praise-chant, as lights gradually fade, leaving us with the farmers:)

Moremi o!	Hail Moremi!
Ebo dede tii beku	The huge sacrifice that
Ese dede tii barun	wards off death
Ikoyi rogun rile tori bogun.	The big offering that prevents diseases
A gbon bi asarun	Like the Ikoyi, you fearlessly
A laya bi iko	faced battle.
Moremi a fori laku	Moremi
Kaye o la roju	You dared death
O faya raigun	To bring peace to the world
Kile Ife o le toro.	You braved war
	That Ile-Ife might be peaceful

Ohun rere o nii gbe o	No kind deed is ever forgotten
Moremi doro, o dorisa.	Moremi has become a deity (worshiped yearly)
Moremi doorun,	Moremi, like the sun,
O mu yan-yan!	You shine so brightly!

NINE

The set now represents a room: Baba's parlor, in the village. Modest furnishings. Bric-a-brac. Screams begin as the Director's voice fades and before the lights come on. Lights: we see a small wood fire, in a clay pot. By the fire, a small group of peasants. Two or three of them hold down a woman, only barely identifiable as Titubi, on the mat. Her condition is as appalling as the others: only half covered, her cloth wrapper shredded and mud-besplattered. She is covered in sweat, groaning in evident pain. Mosun holds a bowl of water. Marshal, on knees or crouching, takes out a knife from the fire.

Marshal. Hold her again. Tight now. (*They do so. He applies the knife to Titubi's shoulder. She screams. He leans forward and sucks at the incision.*) That's it! I've got it out at last. (*shows it; various reactions, of relief, etc.*)

Bogunde. It's a splinter!

Wura. Not the real bullet? (*looking*)

Kokondi. How lucky!

Mosun. Look, she's fainted. Poor girl.

Marshal. She'll be all right. Bring the water. And the herbs.

Wura. Leave the rest to us.

Kokondi. I'll dress it properly. At least she taught us how to do that.

Marshal. (*washing his hands*) Right. Go ahead with it.

(*Baba comes in, tired. Marshal goes to him. As the dialogue progresses, the men wash the wound, apply the herbs, and then tear off a strip of cloth to make a rough, but conspicu-*

ous, bandage, with which they bind the wound. Titubi sleeps through it all. Bogunde carries out the fire, and returns.)

Marshal. How many?
Baba. *(gravely)* Ten of theirs. Three of ours.
Marshal. A heavy day.
Baba. One of the reasons I called this meeting.
Wura. Marshal's plan was good. With those trees we felled across the road, they could not bring their lorries and big guns close enough. They had to come on foot. And we were waiting for them.
Koko. Otherwise the casualties would have been higher.
Marshal. They've been buried?
Baba. *(nodding)* Hm-hm. How is she? *(indicating Titubi)*
Marshal. A flesh wound. She'll survive.
Baba. I'm relieved. She's been useful to us.
Marshal. So you all say.
Baba. We needed a nurse badly, and—
Marshal. *(ironically)* And she served the purpose.
Baba. More than. She surpassed even my expectations. *(They both draw slightly aside.)* There were nights she didn't sleep at all, nursing the wounded.
Marshal. The bitterest poisons, they say, come in the most tasty mushrooms.
Baba. You've never really liked her, have you?
Marshal. Let's just say I don't believe she is what she claims.
Baba. She nursed you, once—
Marshal. *(impatiently)* I know. I am trying to repay it.
Baba. Look here, she came here, badly battered. An abandoned woman, suffering from the burden of her past. We promised to help her, to give her a second lease on life . . .
Marshal. You promised, you mean. Always too soft.
Baba. Yes. I promised. And she's more than earned it.
Marshal. You promised. You always promise. Words are cheap.
Baba. I'll let that pass, Marshal.
Marshal. You give your word. And we give our life.
Baba. *(angry)* Everybody in this camp, Marshal. Whether we carry a gun or not. We all give our life.

Marshal. Yes. And a few manage to live longer than others.

Baba. *(pause)* Look, let's not quarrel, Marshal. You're a fine fighter, the best here. But the trouble with you—

Marshal. And if the woman is a spy—

Baba. I disagree. I've watched her work. It can't be all pretense.

Wura. *(calling)* Marshal!

Marshal. Yes?

Wura. You want to inspect it?

Marshal. You've finished?

Kokondi. *(proudly)* Come and look.

Marshal. No. Let her sleep.

Mosun. *(picking it up)* What do we do with this?

Marshal. What?

Mosun. Her fancy necklace.

Kokondi. Better put it on her. I hear it's their latest madness in the city.

Wura. Yes. They call it Moremi.

Kokondi. Indeed! Last year they were wearing a blade. Now it's a dagger. Soon it will be an ax.

Baba. City people!

Marshal. Put it back on her.

Mosun. Right, Marshal.

Marshal. And bring those two out, Bogunde.

(Bogunde leaves, with Kokondi.)

Baba. Prisoners?

Marshal. You'll see.

(Bogunde and Kokondi return with prisoners.)

Baba. What! Alhaji Buraimoh!

Marshal. And Lawyer Isaac.

Baba. What are they—

Marshal. They led the vultures here.

Baba. It's not possible. You mean they're still at this game?

Marshal. Tell them, Bogunde.

Bogunde. They were hiding in the police lorry at the rear. They didn't know we would spot them. But Alao and I were there, in the bush. We set the lorry on fire. They ran out like rabbits.

Marshal. Now we know how the police were able to find this place.

Kokondi. This used to be our last resort. The police had never been able to reach us here. But where shall we go now?

Baba. I see. I'm sorry, Mosun. This must be hard for you.

Mosun. Justice will have to be done, Baba.

Baba. *(to Marshal)* That means we have to move again?

Marshal. Yes, I'm afraid.

Bogunde. I've already given the orders.

Marshal. Somewhere temporary.

Baba. Good. We'll leave in the night.

Wura. Marshal suggests we evacuate the women and the children at once. Bogunde and I agree.

Baba. You think so?

Mosun. It would be the wisest thing.

Wura. Since our raid on the prison, we've had to move camp five times. Five times. Even at the beginning, before their so-called Commission of Inquiry, it was not so bad.

Kokondi. The Governor has obviously declared an all-out offensive against us. A total war.

Mosun. And we're running short of ammunition.

Bogunde. That is serious.

Baba. We may have to agree to negotiate.

Marshal. Over my dead body.

Baba. Without ammunition—

Marshal. We'll fight with our bare hands. Till death.

Wura. With our teeth and fingernails.

Baba. So you support him on that.

Bogunde. We've gone through all this before—

Marshal. City people have no compassion. The well-fed dog has no thought for those who are hungry.

Wura. That is the truth. We cannot run away.

Marshal. The rulers in the city will not rest till they've wiped us out completely, or brought us down, cringing on our knees. We'll not negotiate.

Baba. Right. Back to present business. Alhaji Burai—

Wura. Wait. Should Mosun sit on this?

Mosun. Listen, we have a law, and we shall make no exceptions.

Wura. But—

Mosun. My father sent my mother out of his house when I was three. But even if I loved him passionately, I would still do my duty, as one of the chosen representatives of our people.

Baba. That is true. Still, you don't have to stay—

Mosun. Why? Because I wasn't there, an open target like the others, when the police brought their guns? Could my father tell the bullets to bypass his daughter? When the tax men marched through our farmlands, trampling our precious crops and our hardworn harvests, did they spare those of my father's daughter? And the sanitary inspectors who dipped their dirty fingers at will in my cooking pot? Ehn? Did my buttocks not burn too on that hot tin roof they sat us on at the barracks when we went up to protest? Where was my father? And when they finally rounded us up and flung us in prison, and the warders stripped us naked, and began to poke their fingers in us to humiliate us, did they remember my father, the big Alhaji who wines and dines with the Governor?

Marshal. *(quietly)* He's still your father, Mosun.

Mosun. Thank you for reminding me. Baba, I think we were talking about evacuating the children?

Kokondi. Mosun—

Mosun. For God's sake! What's wrong with all of you today? Marshal, even you! Didn't you say oppression and injustice know no frontier of blood or decency? That treachery is a poison that must be burned out wherever found? A viper! So why are you all trying to make exceptions for me?

Marshal. *(after a silence)* The women and children will be evacuated, to stay with relatives and friends or in-laws in the city. That will save them from the continuous panic of our movements each time the government forces attack.

Bogunde. And it will be better for our resistance. Mosun, won't you say goodbye to your mother before they leave?

Mosun. *(going)* Yes, I'll go and—*(stopping)* Ah, I see. You're with them too, Bogunde. You also wish to create privilege in our ranks.

Kokondi. I think we'd better just leave her.

Wura. She's right. We must share everything. Both the good and the bad.

Marshal. They'll need an escort. Wura, you'll lead them?

Wura. Are you coming along?

Kokondi. Why?

Wura. You know I can't handle them all alone.

Baba. Sorry, but we all have our hands full with other things.

Wura. Still it'll be too much for me.

Marshal. Okay, I'll come along. At least as far as the edge of the forest.

Bogunde. You and I were going to look at the defense lines—

Titubi. Could I . . . could I go instead?

(They are startled; they've forgotten her presence.)

Baba. You?

Titubi. *(still in pain)* They . . . may need a nurse on the way too.

Kokondi. But you are in no shape to—

Titubi. I'm still alive.

Mosun. You need to rest, Titu. Already you've done more than enough for us.

Titubi. If I go, then Marshal can stay.

Marshal. Out of the question. You'll stay. I'll go with the children.

Baba. Thank you, Titu, but we can't let you exert yourself again until you're healed. I mean, you, a stranger among us, you have—

Titubi. A stranger! That's all I keep hearing. How much must one do to qualify to be one of you? *(embarrassed silence)*

Baba. You're right, my daughter. Forgive us. The outsider who shares our salt and our suffering is already a kinsman.

Marshal. She stays behind, whatever the case. Let's get on to the trial of these two.

Baba. Now?

Mosun. Now! I want it over with.

Baba. In that case, let's—

(A sudden upwelling of noise, offstage. Onstage, the men and women go into swift movements of self-defense, with Marshal and Bogunde leaping in a crouch toward the door. Bogunde caterwauls out, with Marshal covering him. All these in a few seconds. There is a frozen moment. Then Bogunde returns, calling urgently.)

Bogunde. *(to Titubi)* Sisi! Can you walk? They need you urgently.

Marshal. What is it?

Bogunde. Fresh tragedies, Marshal. The vultures had poisoned our stream before they retreated.

All. What!

Marshal. How many people?

Bogunde. Only two yet, fortunately. Ligali and his daughter.

Baba. You think Titu can still help?

Titubi. *(going painfully)* I'll see what I can do.

Baba. Wura, you'll go with her?

Mosun. I'll come too.

Wura. Marshal?

Marshal. All right, I'll come along.

(Exeunt Bogunde, Marshal, Titubi, Wura, and Mosun.)

Baba. *(after some silence)* Bring them forward and remove the cloth from their mouth. *(Kokondi does so.)* Alhaji! And you, Lawyer Isaac! How will you explain all this?

Isaac. *(all shaken)* Baba . . . please . . . help me. It wasn't my fault, I swear! It was Buraimoh, ask him. He misled me.

Buraimoh. You'll always be a worm, lawyer. Go on, abase yourself before these pigs.

Baba. We trusted both of you. When all this started, it was you we first approached. We met, all the villages in this Council area, and decided to send a delegation to meet you. Bogunde, Wura, poor Akande who is now dead, with a ball in his head, Kokondi and I, we were the people chosen. We took Saka's lorry, and then from the motor-park, we walked to your office, Isaac. I remember it was raining, and we were all soaked when you opened the door. So you wouldn't let us into your office, but spoke to us on the balcony. After that you drove us to Alhaji's mansion on the hill. Both of you, we knew well. You were born here in our midst. Your father's farms, lawyer, lie next to my family land. And Marshal had his first employment as a boy, working on Alhaji Buraimoh's fields. So when the government announced its threats to raid us, and then flooded our villages with fierce-looking men with their guns and whips, it was you we immediately thought of. We said, they live in the city where these vandals come from. Both of them are big men, they can talk to government and make it listen. And you gave us your word . . .

Isaac. Please . . . let me defend myself. Let me—

(Marshal and Bogunde return.)

Baba. Yes?

Bogunde. It was too late. Sisi could not help anymore.

Marshal. Terrible, the way they writhed to death.

Baba. May their souls rest with our ancestors.

Marshall and Bogunde. *Ase!*

Baba. Poison! What is the land turning into?

Bogunde. All because we refuse to pay money we haven't got. Because we refuse to let men with two balls like us march upon our heads.

Baba. Not even in the worst days of our history. Not even Gaha put *majele* in water for children to drink.

Marshal. They will pay for this. The war will never end.

Baba. You hear all this, Buraimoh and Isaac? What your friends did?

Marshal. Baba, the women and children leave immediately.

Bogunde. Titu is accompanying you, I hope you know.

Marshal. You didn't—

Bogunde. I agreed. She was very insistent.

Baba. But I thought we had—

Bogunde. You won't stop her now. Ligali's daughter died in her arms.

Baba. I see . . .

Bogunde. I've never seen a woman look so shaken . . . and then so determined. She will come with you.

Marshal. And if her concern is all an act.

Baba. Then you will find out, won't you?

Marshal. Right, let her come along. I can take care of serpents. But before we leave—the trial?

Baba. Yes, call Wura.

Marshal. And Mosun. We can't leave her out now. *(Exit Kokondi.)*

Baba. This will have to be quick.

Bogunde. Yes. Soon it'll be nightfall.

Buraimoh. *(suddenly laughing)* A trial! Ha ha. This one here, this common thug, his father came here almost in the nude. We took the wretched man in from the open roads to save him from starvation. We even married a wife for him. And now their son dares, dares to look me in the face.

Marshal. It is true that my father and others slaves themselves to death, to make you rich and prosperous. Yes, I know, slave-owning becomes such a habit that you are enraged when the slave stands up to claim his rights as a human being. That is why you are doomed, Alhaji.

Baba. Here they come. *(Enter Kokondi, Mosun, Wura.)* Let's begin.

Buraimoh. Welcome, welcome. Lawyer, you see them? Stop shivering man! That's what inspires these ants to—Listen, what is our crime? I demand to know.

Baba. Your betrayal of the cause.

Buraimoh. Hear that! Allah-akbar! Where do you think you are? China? Cuba? Mozambique? Or some lunatic asylum? Who's been teaching you these funny words?

Baba. Are you ready to defend yourselves?

Buraimoh. Look at them, Isaac! By Allah, stop it I say! Aren't you a man? You took your share after all. Just look at who's going to try you. Kokondi, who drives your mammy wagon—

Kokondi. Drove, you mean. I quit long ago.

Buraimoh. You were sacked, idiot! After the accident at the bridge. You ran here to avoid the police.

Kokondi. Yes? Ask Lawyer who took my money and yet gave me forged particulars.

Buraimoh. I see. The day of reckoning, ehn? Each one with his little grievance. Mosun here was abandoned. I threw her mother out of my house. And Wura, welcome. Your child died. I refused to claim it on my return from Mecca. Go on, start your own accusation.

Wura. Your life is filled with uncountable sordid actions, Alhaji. But you are merely wasting time. We are not here for private squabbles. Tell us why you turned traitor. Defend yourself.

Isaac. I was never a traitor, I swear to you! I'd like you to consider my case separately—

Buraimoh. Shut up, you professional liar! Let me think.

Marshal. Think quick. Before the blood dries.

Bogunde. We wanted your help, but you used us. You sucked our veins.

Isaac. I did not use you. I defended you all as best I could at the Inquiry. The papers said so—

Wura. And what came of it? After all the eloquence, what did you get for us?

Isaac. It wasn't my fault. The government took the decisions.

Mosun. Which merely happened to benefit you, isn't it?

Baba. We said we couldn't pay the tax, that harvests were poor, that we could hardly feed our children. And what happened? The government said, all right, we'll change the tax collectors—

Bogunde. And you, Isaac, our own lawyer, you became the new *akoda*—

Isaac. We had to find a compromise. All I did was in your interest.

Wura. And you hired your own men to go on tax raids—

Isaac. Farmers! They were farmers like you.

Kokondi. With whips and guns?

Buraimoh. Why don't you just kill us, since you're so determined—?

Baba. We said we didn't want the Council anymore. That its agents fleeced us, that inspectors smashed into our homes to remove whatever they wanted. That's what we told you to help us expose at the Inquiry. We said you should demand that all the officials be probed and made to declare their assets. And what happened? They merely reshuffled the Council, and made you, Alhaji Buraimoh, its new chairman. You came here, demanding our cooperation, and when we refused, you brought the police back—

Buraimoh. I had a plan. If you had listened, instead of following this cannibal. Marshal indeed! Wallahi, I was going to get your sons scholarships into the big schools in the city. I was going to start a pipe-borne water scheme. Your roads would have been tarred, your homes lit—

Marshal. And you would have accomplished all that, wouldn't you, the day fowls begin to grow teeth?

Buraimoh. You see what I mean?

Wura. Alhaji, the next time you have a nightmare, try and sell it to someone else . . .

Buraimoh. But listen, can one achieve everything in a single day?

Marshal. A day was enough, Alhaji, to destroy Wasimi.

Buraimoh. *(cowed now)* What . . . What do you mean?

Marshal. It was you that led the police there, wasn't it?

Buraimoh. No . . . no . . . I swear by Allah . . .

Marshal. In the night, when the people were asleep. We were not even armed then. All we said was that we would not work with your Council. So you led the policemen from house to house, identifying the so-called agitators. You had a mask on, but your voice, Alhaji . . . we recognized your voice . . .

Isaac. I wasn't there. You know that. I refused to follow them.

Baba. And today? Why did you come today?

Isaac. The devil! I was misled!

Marshal. They looted our homes and set them ablaze, while we loafed there in their city, signing worthless papers.

Mosun. I think we've said enough. Let's have the verdict.

Baba. Marshal?

Marshal. *(turning up his clenched fist)* Guilty.

Bogunde. *(same gesture)* Guilty.

Wura. *(the same)* Guilty.

Kokondi. *(the same)* Guilty.

Mosun. *(the same)* Guilty.

Baba. Take them away.

Isaac. *(whining)* No . . . no . . . I plead for mercy . . . please . . .

(Kokondi and Bogunde lead them away and then return.)

Marshal. The sentence?

Mosun. Death.

Wura. Mosun, I—

Mosun. Stop it. There will be no exceptions.

Marshal. Death then. Do we all agree?

Baba. No. *(They look at him.)* They say that when we scratch the body, we do not think of the itch alone. The skin also is delicate.

Wura. So what do we do?

Baba. Buraimoh is Mosun's father; we cannot erase that. And as long as there's blood between our fingernails, they say, there will be lice in the hair. Lawyer's father also sat with me on the same pew in church, at that time when we could afford the luxury of Sundays. The verdict cannot be death.

Mosun. Go on, break me. Let my life lose all meaning.

Baba. This will only enrich it, my daughter. It is legitimate to kill in war. We're jackals then. But executions are a different thing. Especially when the victims are our own kinsmen, even when they've gone astray. We don't want our people to lose all respect for human life.

Kokondi. It is a strong point you have there, Baba. But what punishment then will be adequate?

Baba. I propose they lose all the harvest from their farms. And they'll be retained here as hostages till the war is over.

Wura. Well, I agree to that. In spite of all they've done.

Bogunde. In view of the special circumstances.

Kokondi. Marshal?

Marshal. What do you want me to say? You've all decided. Just keep them out of my sight, that's all.

Baba. I'll take full responsibility for their life.

Marshal. Wura, can we leave now?

Wura. I am ready. *(They start to go.)*

Baba. *(calling)*Marshal?

Marshal. *(stops)* Yes?

Baba. Good luck.

Marshal. I won't need it.

(Blackout.)

TEN

To a brisk rhythm,[8] *reinforced by the blasts of a police whistle and the barkings of a dog, the actors rearrange the set. It is now the office of the Deputy Superintendent. Furniture merely sym-*

bolic: *a desk, a file cabinet, governor's portrait, a table, chairs,
etc. The Corporal stands behind the chair of the Deputy Superintendent, who is half leaning back listening to Alhaja Kabirat
shouting across the table.*

Alhaja. I say I want news of my daughter!
Superintendent. I heard you, Alhaja.
Alhaja. What has happened to her?
Superintendent. I assure you we're trying our best to find out.
Alhaja. That is not enough! Two weeks you said. Only two
   weeks. And now it's five weeks since she left.
Superintendent. I know.
Alhaja. And I've been rotting away in that hotel.
Superintendent. What? Corple, I ordered the best hotel.
Alhaja. You know that's not what I mean.
Superintendent. You're not resting enough?
Alhaja. I don't need rest!
Superintendent. You're sure you've not seen her since?
Alhaja. Where would I have seen her?
Superintendent. *(conciliating)* Calm yourself, Alhaja. You
   agreed to all this. You offered to cooperate.
Alhaja. Yes, I—
Superintendent. We put out the news that you had gone away
   to Mecca with your daughter. We even had photos of your
   departure faked and printed in the papers.
Alhaja. All so you can win another pip!
Superintendent. We'll not go into our motives again, Alhaja. You
   know very well you're doing this as much for yourself as for us.
Alhaja. Well, I want my daughter.
Superintendent. And your shops are doing fine; you can't com-
   plain. I myself bring you the reports every night from your
   chief accountant.
Alhaja. That rogue? You think I trust him behind my back?
Superintendent. Well, it's all for the protection of your daugh-
   ter.
Alhaja. I ask you again, how is she?
Superintendent. And I tell you again, we're awaiting reports. I
   know for certain that up to a few hours ago, she was fine.
Alhaja. A few hours ago!

Superintendent. Unless of course you've seen her since?

Alhaja. You're not mad, Salami? Where would I—

Superintendent. You're right. Corple here saw her with his own eyes.

Alhaja. *(to Corporal)* You saw her! Where? Where? Tell me?

Superintendent. She was apparently helping the farmers to evacuate their children to the city. My men recognized her in time fortunately.

Alhaja. Ehn? What do you mean "fortunately"?

Superintendent. There was a blunder. A stupid blunder. But perhaps you know the details already.

Alhaja. By Allah, will you talk sensibly! What happened?

Superintendent. You've seen her?

Alhaja. What are you hiding from me?

Superintendent. But you've seen her?

Alhaja. Is my daughter hurt?

Superintendent. *(pauses, looking at her)* I believe Titu is all right. *(stands)* The sergeant who led the party is an ox. As dumb as a gun butt. I've had him detained. He ordered an attack on the people. And there were only women and children, unarmed.

Alhaja. No! Allah!

Superintendent. An accident of war. When people are stubborn, these things are bound to happen. Fighters can't always be gentlemen. Now see the cost. And the incident seems certain to toughen the farmer's resistance. I doubt if anyone can break them now.

Alhaja. Titu was not one of the casualties?

Superintendent. Do you know?

Alhaja. Listen, I—

Superintendent. The lawyer. He was a casualty.

Alhaja. Which lawyer?

Superintendent. You haven't heard? Lawyer Isaac, who was helping us track these ruffians down. They were once with the peasants, he and Alhaji Buraimoh, till we found their price.

Alhaja. How do they come into this?

Superintendent. We bought them. But the peasants captured them and almost put them to death. During the evacuation, they seized the chance to escape. And then got shot by mistake, by my boys. You see the irony. That's war for you.

Alhaja. And my daughter?

Superintendent. This recurring question. "My daughter! My daughter!" It's like a scene in a play. Do you like the theatre, Alhaja? Me, I'm simply crazy about it. Ask Corple, he's our Secretary in the Police Drama Club. I'm President.

Alhaja. Look here, Salami—

Superintendent. And it's funny too, when you think that I first met your daughter in a theatre, where, permit me to say, she was making a fool of herself. But she gave us an idea: our next play at the Club's going to be based on the legend of Moremi, and . . . you know, a scene like this, me and you, this could be a scene from the play! I can just picture it! Note this, Corple, Alhaja is Moremi's mother, the Yeye Oba. It's, er, let's say three years. Yes, three years since your daughter left. I am Oronmiyon. You come furious to the royal chamber to confront me. Your eyes are on fire. Like an Amazon's. You stamp your foot and you scream—

Alhaja. (beside herself, hitting the table) WHERE IS MY DAUGHTER, YOU MADMAN?

Superintendent. Corple your cue. You're Kabiyesi's bodyguard, and see, his royal person is being assaulted.

Corporal. (stepping forward into the game) Stand back, my Queen Mother. Stand back. The King's person is sacred. No one must foul it.

Alhaja. Ah, Titu! Titu!

Superintendent. Titu? Did I hear someone call Moremi? (To Corporal) Leave her Majesty, Aresa. (going to her) Calm yourself, dear mother. This fury becomes common slaves, not the Queen Mother. We understand your distress. Your daughter Moremi was our favorite, and her absence hurts us. (The Corporal controls his laughter with difficulty.) But we always remember she took the pledge by Esinmirin, our river goddess, and we are reassured. She will return.

Alhaja. Take me back to the hotel, please. I accept my fate.

Superintendent. You lament your daughter. We lament the land. We weep for the lack of peace, for the violence in the air. We weep that rebels beyond our power fall upon us at

will and make mockery of our manhood. Our towns are
unsafe. Food no longer reaches the markets, taxes are unpaid.
All over—

Alhaja. WILL YOU STOP THE FOOLISHNESS! *(long silence)*

Superintendent. Suppose she returns?

Alhaja. What?

Superintendent. Suppose she has already returned?

Alhaja. Titu? When?

Superintendent. The game is ended, Alhaja. Now I'm asking
questions. Suppose your daughter returns, and for some reason she does not want to see us. Whom is she likely to go to
first?

Alhaja. I don't know what you mean.

Superintendent. Where are you hiding your daughter, Alhaja
Kabirat?

Alhaja. Me, hiding her?

Superintendent. I told you the game's over. Where is she?

Alhaja. But that's what I want to know.

Superintendent. Don't play tricks with me.

Alhaja. I should be saying that!

Superintendent. A complete ambush. Carefully laid at the ex-
act spot. No one could have escaped. But my men recognized
your daughter and naturally spared her life, thinking she was
coming to us. And then, what do you think happened?

Alhaja. Yes?

Superintendent. When the shooting was over, and prisoners
were being taken, zero! Your daughter was not to be found
anywhere. Now Alhaja, there may be such talismen, able to
make men vanish into the air, but I don't believe in them.

Alhaja. So you think . . . I . . . I am hiding her somewhere?

Superintendent. With the collusion of my men, yes. Not all of
them are above the temptation your money can offer.

Alhaja. But why would I want to do such a thing?

Superintendent. Tell me.

Alhaja. I know nothing about it, I swear.

Superintendent. Think again. I am a patient man. *(holding it
up)* See? This is the file on your activities since this thing
started. This is your protest letter to the Governor. Of course
he hasn't even seen it. So. And these? Both Isaac and Burai-

moh were in your pay. These are copies of your checks to
them in the past few weeks. What were you paying them for,
Alhaja?

Alhaja. It is legitimate to try to save one's daughter from ruin.

Superintendent. That's not what you said, that day it began.
Why didn't you let me know you had changed your mind?

Alhaja. You're an officer of the state.

Superintendent. Protecting your wealth, or mine?

Alhaja. Well, where is my daughter?

Superintendent. Things will begin to turn pretty rough soon,
madam, if you don't tell me.

Alhaja. But I don't know. I'm telling the truth.

Superintendent. Where is Titu?

Titubi. (appearing) Here, Superintendent.

(They whirl around in surprise. Titubi has Marshal covered
with a gun, his hands in the air. The bandage is still on her.)

Superintendent. Titu! And—

Alhaja. (her arms open, but not daring to approach) My . . .
my . . .

Titubi. I said I would do it, didn't I?

Alhaja. My daughter! (She bursts out crying.)

Superintendent. You did it! By God! You're Moremi!

Titubi. (to Marshal) Sit down. But don't try anything.

Superintendent. So this is the Marshal!

Titubi. I went, and I returned, triumphant. Like a legend. You
didn't believe me, did you? But mother, I did it!

Alhaja. My daughter! (still sobbing)

Titubi. But I am not the same as I went away. A lot has happened. And I have a long story to tell you.

Superintendent. I am dying to hear it.

Titubi. Then sit down. For it will be long. I lived among the
farmers, just as you sent me. And this is what happened . . .

ELEVEN

Lights come up abruptly on another scene, by a streamside.
Some peasant women, very shabbily dressed, but quite gay, are
washing clothes, rinsing some, etc. The sense of their high

spirits must be immediate with the lighting of the scene. Titubi walks forward and picks up a bucket.

Titubi. I'll go down again to the stream.
Mosun. What for? Better don't kill yourself woman. You've been climbing up and down those slippery steps all morning.
Titubi. It doesn't matter. My legs can take it.
Molade. Take a rest. We've almost finished anyway. We don't need more water.
Mama Kayode. Yes, it's true, Titu. You work too hard. All night you're up, nursing the wounded. And then you have to come down with us again to wash their clothes in the morning. Don't you get tired at all?
Wura. She's trying to pay us for her upkeep, as they do in their hotels there in the town. If you haven't the cash, you wash the plates . . . *(laughter)*
Titubi. But really, I'm not tired.
Mosun. Okay, but put down your bucket. We've said we don't need more water. Abi, Mama Kayode?
Mama Kayode. I have finished. If I dare to rinse these pants just once more, Ba Kayode won't have a pair of knickers anymore, he'll have a fishing net!
Molade. But are they clean enough to satisfy our husband, the sanitary inspector? *(laughter)*
Wura. Ah, the sanitary inspector, with his one leg. How I miss him!
Molade. He's a lucky man. He had advance warning before the men put fire to the Health Office that day. He fled to the city. Otherwise, what your husband would have done to him!
Mosun. Remember the episode of the umbrella?
Mama Kayode. That day he stopped Titus in the rain! *(She turns to Molade, and they begin to play-act.)* Come here!
Molade. Sah?
Mama Kayode. I say come here, and you are saying sah, sah!
Molade. Sorry, sah.
Mama Kayode. Sorry, sah. Where are you going?
Molade. To Mama Laide, sah.
Mama Kayode. In this rain?

Molade. It's my wife. She's in labor. She needs help.

Mama Kayode. And you wait till it's raining before you remember the way to Mama Laide's place, you cunning man!

Molade. Sah? Can I go now, sah?

Mama Kayode. Nonsense and sorbodination! I am talking to you and you tell me can I go?

Molade. Sorry, sah. But my wife—

Mama Kayode. Shorrop! Concobility! My wife my wife! Do you ever hear government mention his wife? I mean, if the governor were to talk of his wives, private, personal, official and confidential, do you think they will have time to run government? But you, bush man with your only wife, it's always my wife my wife!

Molade. Please sah . . .

Mama Kayode. Open your mouth. You see? Black gums. Wider! Hen-hen. *Yooro.* Beriberi. Yellow comatose. Is this a mouth or an outpatient's clinic? My dear bush man, I am hereby issuing your mouth with warrant. Eight o'clock T sharp on Tuesday, you are ordered to present it for prosecution . . .

Molade. But . . . sah . . . sah.

Mama Kayode. Case dismissed, God's case no appeal! I advise you not to open that mouth again. It's an offense under the bye-law to foul a public place, section dee chapter six, bracket roman letter two . . . hey, what's that in your hand self?

Molade. You mean this umbrella, sah?

Mama Kayode. Hen-hen that's what you call it, this dirty, smoky, cob-infested jagbajantis! I bet it's got lice in it too.

Molade. But it's brand new! Alabi just sent it to me from the city last week—

Mama Kayode. Well, it's under arrest. You're lucky. I can't ask you to detach your mouth, which is exhibit one, Queen versus Baba Alabi, alias Titus, nineteen gbongbonrongbon. But I will certainly not allow this umbrella to go on soiling the rain, which is a public property under the bye-law. So hand it over at . . . yeee-pah! *Ori mi o! (For Titus has whacked him on the head with the umbrella. He hobbles after him, and then tumbles.)* . . you will see! *(picking* *himself up)* You will see! Are you laughing? Titus spent the next two weeks in jail.

Titubi. What! Because he wouldn't give up his property?

Mosun. All our properties were public property while the inspector was here. If you argued, you went to work free of charge for the government in the white college.

Titubi. And you didn't protest?

Molade. What are we doing now? Our men are killing them man for man.

Titubi. I mean before. Before the bloodshed.

Wura. We hired a letter-writer. Everyone contributed to pay him. First petition: nothing. Second petition, nothing again.

Mosun. A third. A fourth. Another one.

Wura. Grievances upon grievances. The letters multiplied, the letter-writer grew pregnant.

Molade. But not even a note of acknowledgment.

Titubi. Nothing at all?

Mosun. Oh yes! The Council Officials grew more daring and more ruthless.

Mama Kayode. To punish us for all those petitions. Bribery rates went up.

Wura. Kickback and kickforward hit inflation.

Molade. Tax assessments began to gallop like antelopes.

Mosun. One day we went and burned down the Council Office. That was the first time in months I slept soundly.

Wura. Eh the Governor! Don't forget the visit of the Governor!

Molade. Yes! First they sent policemen to kill us, but we ran away.

Mama Kayode. They sent soldiers, and we ambushed them.

Mosun. Then one day, one man called Governor came down from a giant iron hawk, from the sky.

Mama Kayode. He stood there. His cheeks were shining. My God, I remember, he was so handsome I was afraid to look.

Molade. It was Baba who replied him. After the Governor had spoken, Baba stepped forward. I was hiding behind my husband.

Mama Kayode. The Governor's voice was sweet, you could almost drink it. And at first it was difficult to follow his words. They seemed to come from a church organ. *(mimicking)*

"Ladies and gentlemen, I know you have some grievances. But I have come to speak to you as the father of all the people in this state. This killing must stop. It is senseless for anybody to shoot guns against the government. That person will be crushed. So I am appealing to you. Think of your wives and children. Lay down your arms now and let us talk. All the people who have been misleading you till now, you must hand them over to the government, for they are your enemies, who don't want you to have peace and progress. We shall deal with them. And above all, you must pay your tax, it's the only way we can help you . . . Pay your tax! Pay your tax!"

Wura. *(laughing)* Ah you remember everything, everything.

Mama Kayode. And then Baba stepped forward. He bowed. Like this, very low. He said: "Your Excellency, my son, we have listened carefully to your fatherly appeal. Our roads have been so bad for years now that we can no longer reach the markets to sell our crops. Even your Excellency had to make your trip here by helicopter. Your council officials and the *akodas* harass us minute to minute and collect bribes from us. Then they go and build mansions in the city. Sanitary inspectors like Mister Bamsun are bloodsuckers. Your Marketing Board seizes our cocoa, and pays us only one third of what it sells it to the *oyinbo*. We have no electric, and we still drink *tanwiji* from the stream. Many of our children are in jail for what your people call smuggling. We protested and your police mounted expeditions to maim us and reduce our houses to ashes. But all these do not matter any more. Now that we have listened to your kind and fatherly appeal, we shall forget all our sufferings and pay our taxes. I promise we shall now send in the money promptly, through the same route your appeal has come to us—by helicopter!" *(general laughter)* Oh, you should have seen the Governor's face!

Titubi. So what did he do?

Wura. What else, do you still ask? You nurse the casualties every night.

Titubi. You know . . . before this . . . I could never have believed that life was so unkind to anybody.

Molade. It's unkind only till you begin to fight back. After that—

Titubi. Yes? Tell me. Teach me.

Molade. You should teach us, good woman. Where you find your strength.

Titubi. Me? What strength—

Wura. Remember the song she taught us yesterday?

Mama Kayode. Let's sing it. Enough of the talking.

Mosun. I agree. Start it, you're Olohun-iyo. *(They sing the song "Iyawo nfo'so."[9] As they pick up the song again, singing softly, lights go up on the Deputy Superintendent's office. The characters still in the same postures. Titubi walks back into the office with the gun to address them.)*

TWELVE

Titubi. That was when I began to ask questions. Questions. I saw myself growing up, knowing no such sufferings as these. With always so much to eat, even servants feed their dogs . . . Yet here, farmers cannot eat their own products, for they need the money from the market. They tend the yams but dare not taste. They raise chickens, but must be content with wind in their stomach. And then, when they return weary from the market, the tax man is waiting with his bill . . . It could not be just . . . In our house, mama, we wake to the chorus of jingling coins. And when we sleep, coiled springs, soft foam and felt receive our bodies gently. But I have lived in the forest among simple folk, sharing their pain and anguish . . . and I chose . . .

Alhaja. What do you mean?

Titubi. Wait! I have not finished. Listen to the rest. For without knowing it, the shame of my past had come flooding into my eyes. *(Tears are falling freely from her eyes. Lights transfer back to the streamside.)*

THIRTEEN

(Mama Kayode goes to Titubi.)

Mama Kayode. My dear, do not cry. Or don't you understand? We're fighting to live.

Mosun. Our men fall, but we do not mourn.

Wura. Water fertilizes the earth, blood the spirit of the race.
Molade. We struggle, our dirges wash us clean.
Mama Kayode. We're older than pain and betrayal.
Wura. Older than your politicians and your rulers.
Mama Kayode. We own the earth; we are the earth itself.
Molade. And the future is ours. Is for our children.
Mama Kayode. So come, my daughter, wipe your tears.
Wura. Tell us about your wedding song.
Titubi. What? What wedding song?
Molade. Will it be as sweet as the song you taught us?
Titubi. But . . . what do you mean? *(The women laugh.)*
Wura. Ehn-ehn! Is it because I've not broken your head for stealing him from me?
Molade. She thinks we haven't noticed.
Titubi. Noticed what?
Wura. Nothing, nothing-o! But if I were to talk!
Mosun. Don't mind her. The way her eyes devour him.
Titubi. Who? Whom are you talking about?
Mama Kayode. A riddle! Shall I tell it?
Women. Yes! Tell it!
Mama Kayode. Listen:
  Oruku tindi tindi
  Oruku tindi tindi—

Women.
  Oruku gba gbo!

Mama Kayode. I say
  Oruku is in my hands:
  Catch it!
  I launch a riddle-o!

Mosun.
  Oruku bi gba omo:
  A thousand kernels
  Nestle in a thousand nuts:
  We await your riddle-o!

Mama Kayode.
  Oruku tindi tindi
  I launch a riddle-o!

Molade.
>May your riddle ripen well
>As it falls! May oruku
>Swell our mouths with succulence!

Wura.
>I catch your riddle-o!

Mama Kayode.
>*Oruku tindi tindi . . . (pause)*

Molade. Hen-hen you see now? Titu is silent!

Mosun. Titu, the riddle hangs in the air. Won't you speak?

Wura. Or is she afraid of something about to be disclosed?

Titubi. Okay, I catch it! I have nothing to hide. May your riddle ripen well—

Mama Kayode.
>Oruku is growing:
>A thousand baby seeds
>In your fingers—

Titubi.
>Seek me:
>I turn your words
>To costly beads . . .

Women.
>We adorn ourselves
>In their jungle:
>And grown is the riddle.

Mama Kayode. Listen:
>The he-goat wears a beard
>The she-goat also wears a beard:
>Oba Lailo!

Mosun. I know that one!

Molade. Me too, but I won't say! Not yet.

Wura. Titu, do you care to enlighten us?

Titubi. Why me? This is a trap, isn't it? I withdraw from the game . . .

Wura. All right, I'll solve the riddle. Love! Someone's in love!
>Tinrin tintin!

Mosun. What an understatement! When the she-goat also grows a beard, that means—

Molade. An inferno! The love all-consuming!

Titubi. So who is in love now?

Wura. Why the panic? Has anyone mentioned your name?

Mama Kayode. Listen:

Ruku ruku yekete:
The carrier of the corpse is bow-legged,
The corpse itself is also bow-legged,
Oba Lailo!

Wura. Now we're getting nearer to target. Who knows that one?

Mosun. There is a horse, and there is a rider, both keeping the same secret. That's all I'm going to say.

Molade. But who are they? I am sure Titu wouldn't know anything about this either?

Titubi. I've told you, I'm out of it.

Mama Kayode. Listen:

Oruku is going home to roost:
Firewood is gathered
In a hundred places,
But the bundle is tied up
In a single spot,
Oba Lailo!

Mosun. I know the man!

Molade. I too can guess. Titu, can you tell us?

Titubi. I am not in love with any man!

Molade. She denies it again!

Mosun. She thinks we've not been seeing them together!

Mama Kayode. Anyway I must congratulate you. I didn't know anybody could ever bring him back again to what he was before the war began.

Mosun. She's a good nurse.

Titubi. Am I? You know, he still frightens me—

Molade. Who? I thought you swore there is no man?

Titubi. Stop teasing me . . .

Mama Kayode. Lucky Marshal . . . and look! See who is coming!

Mosun. My friends, pack your things, our presence is needed at home! *(Laughing, they begin to gather their things together.)*

(Lights die out on the streamside scene as Titubi walks back to the Deputy Superintendent's office.)

FOURTEEN

Titubi. And that was it. I knew at last that I had won. I knew I had to kill the ghost of Moremi in my belly. I am not Moremi! Moremi served the State, *was* the State, was the spirit of the ruling class. But it is not true that the State is always right . . .

Superintendent. *(who has been watching her with increasing alarm, leaps up)* By God, you bitch, you—! *(But she is alert and keeps him covered.)*

Titubi. Keep still, Salami. My hands are jittery on the trigger, and I won't like to kill you in error.

Superintendent. *(raising his hands quickly)* All right, all right, girl, just keep calm.

Alhaja. *(trembling with shock)* Titu! Titu! Please don't do it. You're my only daughter. They'll kill you.

Titubi. *(Laughs, but shrilly: she's overstretched.)* Mama, our life itself is not important. Nor all these glittering tinsels we use to decorate it . . . Ask your friend Salami. He knows the truth now. In another week, he'll be asking to negotiate. He won't be in such a hurry to order the massacre of children . . . for there's no way you can win a war against a people whose cause is just. As long . . . *(She's beginning to falter now.)* . . . as . . . long as the law remains . . . the privilege of a handful of powerful men . . . ah, I am tired . . . Marshal! . . . you didn't believe me, did you? You never believed I was sincere?

Marshal. Titu, I—

Titubi. Take the gun. *(She hands it over to him.)* Let a new life begin.

(Blackout.)

FIFTEEN

As at the beginning of Act Eight, dancing silhouettes celebrate harvest and gradually disappear. Lights now come up. It is a fortnight later. The peasant women again, by the streamside. They have finished their washing, the clothes piled up in the calabashes. Now they are relaxing, singing, washing their feet in the stream, etc. Someone is putting finishing touches to the plaiting of Titubi's hair.

Mosun. So tomorrow we negotiate.

Molade. Yes. And the war will be ended.

Wura. Titu! I don't know how you found the courage to do it.

Titubi. Don't ask me.

Mama Kayode. God will reward you my daughter.

Wura. What's that song of hers again? (Molade starts to sing.)

Molade.

> Be always like this day
> Beside me. Wear hope like a jewel:
> It never fades.

(The others join the song.)

Wura. *(looking up suddenly)* Didn't I say it? Now look who is coming!

Woman. What! What are we seeing! Eeeh-oh, Titu-Titu!

Titubi. Tell me, what should I do?

Molade. See how she's trembling!

Titubi. He warned me yesterday that he would be telling me something important this morning. Something important!

Mama Kayode. All right, let me handle this. Form a circle round her and leave all the talking to me.

(They do so, arranging themselves in a circle, with Titubi in the middle. They pretend to be very busy as Marshal enters, accompanied by Bogunde and Kokondi.)

Marshal. Good morning to our mothers. I am happy to find you here, all together. *(Silence. Marshal looks at his companions in amazement.)*

Bogunde. Dear women, we salute you. *(silence)*

Kokondi. We come with a great joy. And we wish you to be witnesses of a memorable event.*(silence)*

Bogunde. Mama Kayode! Toun! Mama Iyabo! All of you, Marshal is greeting you!

Marshal. Bogunde, can it be that the war has done something to the ears of our women?

Kokondi. Titu, Marshal is here. *(pause)* Strange disease. It must have come in the night.

Bogunde. It's the Monster Majẹngbọrọn! It has an appetite for female ears.

Marshal. Women, have we done something to wrong you? *(silence)* Bogunde, there's a cure for this. I learned it from my great grandfather, that indomitable hunter of spirits. *(He takes his gun from Kokondi.)* Bogunde, I want you to go among them. Start with Mama Kayode in particular. This is what you'll do. *(whispers in his ear)* Good. Go on. And the first person who utters even the faintest sound will have her head blown off.

(Bogunde steps forward. The women look up, watching apprehensively. He goes to Mama Kayode, walks round her, and then suddenly bends to tickle her. She stiffens, tries to resist, but finally collapses in laughter.)

Mama Kayode. Please . . . please, I beg you.

Marshal. What is that I hear? Give way, let me shoot at her!

(She flees behind another woman, who also runs, till finally they form a circle by linking hands and dancing around Titubi, so that she's still inaccessible to Bogunde. They improvise a short song.)[10]

Marshal. *(dropping his gun)* We surrender, sweet women. Tell us now. Why may I not speak with her?

(The circle comes to a stop, but does not break up.)

Mama Kayode. Shall we pity them?

Women. Yes. Answer him.

Mama Kayode. She does not want to speak to you.

Marshal. Me? But why?

Mosun. You're too brutal, she says.

Marshal. I'm a commander of war—

Molade. And you are too cruel.

Marshal. Not to friends. Never to friends.

Wura. But can you tell friend from foe?

Marshal. I confess, sometimes it's hard—

Mama Kayode. Your face often fills her with fright.

Marshal. A mask only. A commander's make-up. Plead for me. Tell her, my face shall soften in the breeze of her caresses.

Mosun. Hear that! He's talking of caresses already.

Molade. Without winning her first.

Marshal. Tell her, I bring her a priceless gift.

Mama Kayode. Show us.

Marshal. I want her to hold it herself, in her fingers.

Mama Kayode. Give it to me.

Marshal. No. Into her fingers only.

Mama Kayode. All right, go away. She won't take it.

Marshal. No?

Mama Kayode. No.

Bogunde. Let's go, Marshal.

Marshal. *(retrieving his gun)* Right, let's go. *(They make to go.)*

Titubi. *(running through the circle)* I'll take it!

Women. Traitor!

Mama Kayode. Now he'll have you for cheap!

Marshal. Don't be so sure. Let her open this packet.

(Takes it from Kokondi and gives her. She opens it to general exclamations of surprise. There are two coral necklaces, which Titubi holds up in surprise.)

Marshal. You see? They are from my mother's long-forgotten casket. Wear them.

Titubi. But . . . but I . . . I can't. I c— . . .

(The women snatch them from her, force her to kneel and wear the beads round her neck. Marshal takes his gun, touches her forehead, the ground, then his forehead. The crowd hails.)

Marshal. This is a moment of delight, and I have chosen it to be among you all, in this place, where the journey of our ancestors ended. Titubi, I am going to dress you in a new name, so that, from this moment, the whole world knows how precious you are to me.

Mama Kayode. May the name last her—

Women. *Ase.*

Mama Kayode. As long as the long length of a ripe life.

Marshal. We have met your parent. We have been to the house from which your manners were furnished. We know the stream of blood along whose banks your family spreads its seeds. We have seen you in our midst, different from how you came. And we have grown to cherish you, and that is enough. Now, I call on this earth I am standing on. *(Takes gourd from Kokondi and pours libation. Bogunde softly chants an incantation, beating a rhythm on his weapon.)* I call on you trees and animals that people our forests and are our kinsmen. I summon the seeing eyes our ancestors. And you, my very dear friends, standing in this charged embrace of sunlight and wind, bear witness. I give her, not a gun, nor a matchet, but costly beads of *iyun.* For her war is not to kill, but to heal. Her battlefield among the wounded and stricken. Therefore I pluck her name like this, all ripe and golden, not from the laden shelf of our violent heroes, but from the storehouse of beauty and tenderness. I name her—MOROUN-TODUN!

(Ovation! The women begin to sing the praise-song: "Morountodun ęja ǫsǫn!" They beat out the rhythm on their hands and feet. Marshal drinks from the gourd, and hands it to Titubi who also drinks. She rises and embraces him. Kokondi sings a love song.[11] The dance and merriment are at a peak when Baba enters. Everything freezes.)

Baba. I heard the sound of singing . . .
Molade. Yes! We were dancing.
Wura. Marshal has just finished a naming ceremony.
Baba. A new child, and not to my knowledge? *(The crowd laughs.)*
Titubi. Baba, look at my beads!
Baba. Ah I see.
Mama Kayode. He named her Morountodun!
Baba. *Eja oson!* A beautiful name!
Marshal. She's the goddess of beauty herself.
Baba. I am happy to hear such words from your lips again, Marshal.
Bogunde. Baba, women are cunning.
Kokondi. And dangerous.

Baba. And sweet. Morountodun! I should have been invited. We have all gained from her sweetness. My daughter, I give you my blessings. May the name last you—

Women. *Ase!*

Baba. As long as the long eye of the sky.

Titubi. *(at Baba's feet)* I'm so happy, Baba! If only I could open my heart, like a book—

Baba. I couldn't read it, my daughter. But I know you are happy. Alas.

Titubi. Alas?

Baba. These sounds should lead to a wedding, but—

Women. Yes, Baba? Go on.

Baba. When is it that we have carried weapons to a wedding? Marshal, is it true what I hear?

Marshal. What do you hear?

Baba. That you have summoned all the commanders to the grove?

Marshal. Yes. *(Women exclaim in alarm.)*

Baba. Why?

Marshal. What other reason? To continue the struggle.

Baba. Even when there's no longer need for armed confrontation?

Marshal. It is you who say so.

Baba. And the Committee? Tomorrow—

Marshal. The other side merely wishes to buy time, to rebuild their spent forces. And to divide us.

Baba. How shall we know their intentions if we don't give the truce a chance?

Marshal. Are we to argue this out in front of the women?

Women. We want to hear this too, Marshal.

Marshal. Of what use is knowledge gained in the grave?

Baba. Tomorrow, Marshal. Only a day. Why not give tomorrow a chance?

Marshal. Tomorrow is too important for me to gamble with.

Baba. And so, behind my back, you're preparing for an attack?

Marshal. Can we do so in front of you?

Baba. We declared a truce with the police. On our honor. Tomorrow we're supposed to hang our weapons.

Marshal. Words! I am tired of words!

Baba. I'm still the leader here.

Marshal. Here, in the village. Not at the battlefront.

Baba. So you're disobeying me!

Marshal. We cannot follow you into a pit.

Baba. And Bogunde, Kokondi? You're with him on this? *(They look away.)*

Titubi. Marshal! Marshal . . . you're not going away? You're not going to fight again? *(She's heartbroken.)*

Marshal. I have been given no other choice . . . Morountodun. I was born poor . . . You understand? Look, it is well calculated. Tomorrow, when they think we are idling here, washing our wounds and hanging out our shredded hopes to dry, we are going to appear there, suddenly out of the air, and hit them. Now that we have the ammunition. Bang! Right where their heart is. The very building that houses their Commander and his odious officers. There can be no better time than this!

Baba. Tell me again: you mean you're going to attack the Central Police Station?

Marshal. We'll destroy the place. Reduce it to rubble, forever. Let all prisons fall!

Bogunde and Kokundi. Let all prisons fall!

Baba. You're insane all of you! That place is almost a fortress! You'll never get in!

Marshal. You said the same thing when we were going to raid the prison. But we did it.

Baba. I know. But that was just lucky. The Central Police Station is extremely fortified. You'll all be killed.

Marshal. How do you know?

Baba. How do I know? Haven't I slept there before?

Marshal. Nobody will sleep there again, after tomorrow. All the filthy cells and dungeons in which our people groan their life out. And fine young men are broken, beyond recognition, into blabbering idiots. The torture chambers and solitary confinements where men are changed to rat and roach. Everything will go down in one huge conflagration. And then true freedom can begin at last . . .

Baba. He named you Morountodun. Speak to him.

Titubi. Marshal . . . what about me?

Marshal. *(as if unaware of the interruption)* ... And who knows, maybe it will be time then to rest our weapons and let them grow to rust ... at least until the next cry of desperation. And maybe afterward our own children will have a decent chance to grow up like human beings, not like animals having to scrounge for left-overs in the sewer of history ... I am dreaming, and so much still to do! Bogunde! Kokondi! Kick me awake! Let me hear a song of fire to rouse my spirit! *(Kokondi starts a war song,*[12] *which they all pick up.)* That's better! Now I am a man again ... Morountodun, I have clothed you in a name of honor. My fists to a superb woman! I shall not see you again before the men and I depart early in the dawn tomorrow. But when we return ... let's go quickly, men. *(They salute Baba, and go out, chanting their song. There is a short pause, while Baba and his people look in the direction of the men's departure.)*
Baba. *(sighing)* They will not come back.

(All action freezes. A long pause. Short Blackout.)

SIXTEEN

The actors begin to reemerge to change their costumes. We are back in their changing room. The Director, walking quickly from the audience, is going toward his actors, when he seems to check himself, and turns to the audience.

Director. Oh, you're still there? I suppose you'd like to know how the story ended? *(He walks back a bit. The actors go on about their business, unconcerned.)* Well, the old man was right. Marshal and his men did not come back. It was, you'll admit, a suicidal mission? ... In the end, peace came, but from the negotiating table, after each side had burned itself out. Yes, that's History for you ... But still, you must not imagine that what we presented here tonight was the truth. This is a theatre, don't forget, a house of dream and phantom struggles. The *real* struggle, the real truth, is out there, among you, on the street, in your homes; in your daily living and dying ... We are actors, and whatever we present here is mere artifice, assembled for your entertainment. Tomorrow the play may even be different. It depends. Some of the scenes for instance seemed to be . . .

(A shout of irritation from the actors interrupts him. Then two or three of them overpower him, clamp their hands over his mouth. Mama Kayode begins the song in which they all join, clapping:)

Be always like this day
Beside me. Wear hope like a jewel:

It never fades
It never fades
It never—

(The song cuts off in a general freeze. Lights come on in the auditorium. Onstage, on opposing platforms, Moremi and Titubi are caught in harsh spotlights, looking at each other. Blackout.)

NOTES

Playwright's note: The songs that follow were those used in my 1979 productions at the Arts Theatre, Ibadan. Most of them were composed by Tunji Oyelana as is usual with my productions. Directors need not feel bound to use the same songs, especially where the linguistic circumstances call for other substitutions, although it should be remembered that songs in Yoruba help to preserve the Yoruba locale of the action.

1. Warder yi warder yi o
   Inọmba tere, ku ntere, inọmba.
   Ta lo n pe warder yi o?
   Inọmba etc. . . .
   Emi fẹwọn se yanga
   Inọmba etc. . . .
   Ki lo wa şe nile yi o?
   Inọmba etc. . . .
   Oko ni mo wa şun
   Inọmba etc. . . .
   Aya mi le ju okuta

2. Pounds, shillings and pence, as in the former British system, were the currency in use in Nigeria at the time of the Agbekoya uprising in 1968.

3. Pabambari!

Ko sohun toju o ri ri
Ehn-ehn!
Ko sohun toju o ri ri
Ehn-ehn!
Yanmu yanmu loun agbe dide!
Pabambari!

4. Mọrẹmi o e-e-e
O ku iya abiyamọ
Igbanu o, ko daya
Oja gboro, ko dele o
Oson imu kii deru koju
Atẹlẹsẹ kii jẹbi bata
Iya tori ọmọ faya rogun
Mọrẹmi o e-e-e
O ku iya abiyamọ

5. Gaga roro!—Eewo!
Owo ale ana—Eewo!
Emule emule—Eewo!

6. Any war song will do.

7. Esuru n ta wukẹ
Agbado yọ kondo
Ẹgẹ see gunyan
Ẹgusi so kiji
At'ẹfọ oni'ru
Awa o le gbagbe koko nitori işu
Ẹn ẹn ẹn-ẹn
A o le gbagbe koko tori işu.

8. Kondo ọlọ paa
Jaguda lo n gba
Kondo ọlọpaa
Ipata lo n gba
Ye-ye-ye!
Owo ikokoro
—Obinrin lo n gba
Owo ipalẹmo, obinrin etc. . . .
Owo jokojẹ obinrin etc. . . .
Owo ibale obinrin etc. . . .
Owo ibase obinrin etc. . . .
Owo işilọkun obinrin etc. . . .
Owo ọkọ o si ni'le obinrin etc. . . .
Anabi ba ni şele d'ero
Ka le ri un fẹ!

9. Iyawo n fọ'sọ
Ilşkẹ nsasọ
Iyawo n fọso o
Ilẹkẹ n sasọ

Ilẹkẹ ma sasọ mọ
Je ki iyawo fọsọ o
Bere bomi jubu
O di'le Gomina
Sẹkẹrẹ atibọn
Ko le dun papọ o
Ni'le oloyin
Sun kẹrẹrẹ
Gba kẹrẹrẹ . . .

10. Ẹ bun mi lọnọ lọ
    Ọno o si!

11. Ọkọ mi ọkọ mi ọgagun ija
    Tere ja
    O gba mi lọgbagbara
    Tere ja
    O fa mi ni ifa gombo
    Tere ja
    Of fa gombo oju ogun
    Tere ja
    Oju ogun a ke ruru
    Tere ja
    Ojola nla o furagbọn
    Tere ja
    O furagbọn o fu yẹyẹ
    Tere ja
    O ni yẹyẹ yẹuke. . . .

12. Ohun oju ma ri lode o
    Wi ki n gbọ
    Ohun oju ma ri lode o
    Wi ki n gbọ
    Oyinbo n dako
    Gbẹgẹdẹ gbina, oyinbo n dako
    Okun n ru oyinbo n dako
    Odo n gbe'ja oyinbo n dako
    Obinrin ṣoja oyinbo n dako
    Okunrin n kibọn oyinbo n dako
    Kibọn kibọn ki! oyinbo n dako